Leadership in a Post-COVID Pandemic World

Leadership in a Post-COVID Pandemic World

Edited by
David McGuire and Marie-Line Germain

DE GRUYTER

ISBN 978-3-11-079853-1
e-ISBN (PDF) 978-3-11-079910-1
e-ISBN (EPUB) 978-3-11-079919-4

Library of Congress Control Number: 2023942180

Bibliographic information published by the Deutsche Nationalbibliothek
The Deutsche Nationalbibliothek lists this publication in the Deutsche Nationalbibliografie; detailed bibliographic data are available on the internet at http://dnb.dnb.de.

Cover image: mbbirdy/E+
Typesetting: Integra Software Services Pvt. Ltd.
Printing and binding: CPI books GmbH, Leck

www.degruyter.com

Contents

Authors' Biographies

Dr. Barbara A.W. Eversole is a Professor of Human Resource Development at Indiana State University, in Terre Haute, Indiana, USA. She teaches courses in work-life integration, HRD strategy, organization development, and managerial coaching. Dr. Eversole's primary research interest is studying how to make workplaces more accommodating of the non-work lives of employees, both in the for-profit sector and higher education. She also studies managerial effectiveness, women leaders, and mother-scholars' careers in academia. Dr. Eversole has published in a variety of scholarly journals and presented at national and international conferences. She also serves on a number of editorial boards.

Dr. Thomas N. Garavan is Professor of Leadership Practice at University College Cork and is a leading researcher worldwide in learning and development, HRD, leadership development and workplace learning. He has published over 200 articles, book chapters and books and has over 15,000 citations. He is Editor of the European Journal of Training and Development and Associate Editor of Personnel Review. He is a member of the Editorial Board of Human Resource Management Journal, Human Resource Development Quarterly, Human Resource Development Review, Advances in Developing Human Resources and Human Resource Development International. He is the recipient of the Academy of Human Resource Development, Outstanding HRD Scholar Award 2013 and the Hall of Fame Award in 2021. He has won numerous awards for best papers in HRDI, HRDR, and HRDQ.

Dr. Marie-Line Germain is an internationally recognized scholar who holds a tenured position as a full Professor of Human Resources and Leadership. She holds a Ph.D. in Leadership with a specialization in HRD. Professor Germain founded the HR Consulting Initiative, which provides pro bono HR support to organizations nationwide and abroad. She is also the founder of the podcast show, Dear Human Resources. Dr. Germain has been a visiting professor-scholar in China, Finland, France, Japan, South Korea and was selected as a Fulbright Specialist (U.S. Department of State) in Ghana, Africa. She is the author of 4 books and has published numerous peer-reviewed research articles, book chapters, and editorials. In addition to her scholarship, Dr. Germain is an experienced consultant specializing in psychosocial risks, mental health in the workplace, and personality disorders of corporate leaders. Dr. Germain holds several leadership positions, including Senior Director of the Eastern Academy of Management International Conference, the V.P. of International Affairs at the Eastern Academy of Management, the Editorial Board member of the journal Career Development International, and the Book Review Editor of the European Journal of Training and Development. She has made numerous media appearances, and has lived, studied, and worked in France, Scotland, and England.

Dr. Siham Lekchiri is an Associate Professor in the M.S. program of Human Resources at Western Carolina University, in Cullowhee, North Carolina. She earned a B.S. in Business Administration with a major in Management and a minor in Human Resource Development (HRD) from Al Akhawayn University in Ifrane, Morocco, and she has an M.S. in Human Resource Development from Indiana State University, in Terre Haute, Indiana. She also completed her dissertation to earn her Ph.D. from Indiana State University Consortium in Technology Management with an emphasis on Human Resource Development and Industrial Training. Dr. Lekchiri's teaching background includes courses in strategic HRD, organizational development, consulting, research in HR, and talent acquisition and retention, among others. Her research interest is on the challenges that women face in the workforce in male-dominated environments and cultures. She is also co-Editor-in-Chief of the Industrial and Commercial Training Journal while also serving as a reviewer for a number of journals. Prior to starting in academia, Dr. Lekchiri was a Human Resources Consultant in Morocco.

https://doi.org/10.1515/9783110799101-203

Dr. Clíodhna MacKenzie is a lecturer in the department of Management & Marketing at Cork University Business School at University College Cork. Clíodhna holds a Ph.D. in business from the University of Limerick. She has previously worked for a number of technology firms in the private sector. Her academic research focuses on organizational and leadership failures, risk-taking, governance, ethics and critical management studies. Clíodhna's work has been published in a number of academic journals including: International Journal of Contemporary Hospitality Management, Human Resource Development Review, Human Resource Development International, Advances in Developing Human Resources as well authoring a number of book chapters in Smart Talent Management, 2nd Edition, The Emerald Handbook of Work, Workplaces and Disruptive Issues in HRM.

Dr. David McGuire is Professor in Human Resource Development at Edinburgh Napier University. To date, he has published two textbooks and over 40 journal articles in journals including European Journal of Training and Development, Advances in Developing Human Resources, Human Resource Development Review and Human Resource Development Quarterly. David serves as Editor of Industrial and Commercial Training and also sits on the Editorial Boards of three leading HRD journals (Human Resource Development Review, Human Resource Development Quarterly and New Horizons in Human Resource Development). He has been the recipient of a number of prestigious research awards including Scottish Crucible award, Fulbright Scholar award, Government of Ireland scholarship and a number of Emerald Literati awards. He has significant experience in teaching at undergraduate and postgraduate levels in the areas of HRD, managing diversity and leadership.

Dr. Aisling Tuite is a Lecturer in Management in the School of Business at South East Technological University (SETU) in Ireland. She has an interdisciplinary background in organization studies, sociology and technology which informs much of her research interests and methodologies. Aisling's research centers on the individual and their network of social relations within organizations and institutions in long-form studies that explore biographical experiences of organizational change and transformation. These studies focus on banking organizations and public employment services and explore broader areas of identity, professionalization, care, gender, digitalisation AI and algorithms, and ethics.

Dr. Jia Wang is a Professor of Human Resource Development at Texas A&M University, College Station, Texas, USA. As a scholar, Dr. Wang has been actively promoting individual, organizational, and national development through culture-sensitive and evidence-based research. She has examined critical and contemporary HRD issues in five interacting dimensions: international/national and cross-cultural HRD, workplace learning, organizational crisis management, workplace incivility, and career/family issues. Her research work has been disseminated through a variety of channels including academic journals, research conferences, blog posts, webinars, and a practitioner-oriented book. She is the past Editor-in-Chief of Human Resource Development Review, a member of four international journal editorial boards, and an award-winning researcher, teacher, and mentor. She received her Ph.D. in Human Resource and Organizational Development from the University of Georgia, USA and her M.B.A. from Aston University, UK.

Dr. Muhammad Zeeshan is a lecturer in Human Resource Management at Glasgow Caledonian University. His Ph.D. was titled "Comparative analysis of intercultural competency and interdisciplinary competency." Dr. Zeeshan won the first GCU London studentship award for his Ph.D. His current research focuses on responsible leadership, intercultural conflicts, and contemporary management challenges. Dr. Zeeshan has teaching experience in delivering management-related modules in the U.K. and in his home country of Pakistan.

Part I: **Introduction**

David McGuire and Marie-Line Germain

Chapter 1
Introduction: Leadership in a Post-COVID Pandemic World

Abstract: The chapter explores the key shifts in leadership brought about by the COVID-19 pandemic. It examines how the pandemic has relocated where and how work is done and the crisis leadership lessons learned from the COVID-19 pandemic.

Keywords: Pandemic, leadership skills, communication, support, technology, partnership, environment, organizational culture

The COVID-19 pandemic represents one of the deadliest virological outbreaks in human history. With over 6.5 million confirmed deaths to date (WHO, 2022), the pandemic, which arose in 2019, has wreaked havoc on families, communities and society as a whole. It has also placed extraordinary demands on business and political leaders, as they confronted the uncertainty brought about by a far-reaching, complex, global event threatening human life as well as business continuity and survival. As the outbreak spread from China across the world in spring 2020, high levels of infection and death rates led to significant pressures on public health systems worldwide. Consequently, in an attempt to slow down the spread of the disease, some national governments imposed an array of restrictions ranging from national lockdowns, stay-at-home orders, travel bans, to social distancing measures. In the midst of great instability, many turned to national leaders to offer direction, assuredness, comfort and help in making sense of the new reality. As Ahern and Loh (2020) point out, effective navigation through the pandemic required large-scale behavior change and the need to move quickly beyond "business as usual" to embracing a rapid, dynamic, adaptive response as well as instilling hope for the future. Yet, Maak and colleagues (2021) make clear that many national leaders not only failed to provide a sense of hope, and instead engaged in selfish, destructive and toxic behaviors to the detriment of the populace.

Organizational leaders globally were faced with the stark reality of months of disrupted business activity, characterized by raw material shortages, inadequate cross-border supply chains, high levels of staff absence, and an inability to meet customer needs. Forced through necessity to move their businesses quickly into the digital space, organizational leaders rapidly set about reorganizing operational priorities.

David McGuire, Edinburgh Napier University, Scotland
Marie-Line Germain, Western Carolina University, USA

https://doi.org/10.1515/9783110799101-001

New and reconfigured organizational systems and processes soon followed, with lean and agile businesses showing a capacity to pivot and implement adaptive solutions more quickly (Uhl-Bien, 2021). In the face of an existential threat, many businesses saw a cohesive group spirit emerge amongst staff.

As the longer-term economic and social impact of the pandemic begins to take shape, it is timely to consider the leadership lessons arising from the experience of the pandemic and explore how these are shaping organizational practice. In this introductory chapter, we examine some of the key features of the pandemic and the leadership skills that were necessary to deal effectively with the pandemic. We then provide an overview of the expert contributions that are included in this book. Finally, we offer some concluding remarks, highlighting the shifts and transitions that have taken place in leadership research and practice arising from the COVID-19 pandemic.

Leadership Skills Required to Deal with the COVID-19 Pandemic

The COVID-19 pandemic was unlike other crises organizational leaders faced. The first year of the pandemic (2020–2021) saw over 113 million individuals infected with the virus globally (WHO, 2021). Some studies report that 40% of survivors were affected by the symptoms of long-COVID (Crist, 2021). Not only was the pandemic a public health crisis, but it had far-reaching economic, social, cultural, educational and political consequences, which may have a sustained long-term impact on how we live and work for years to come. Giunipero et al. (2022) argue that the unanticipated scale and duration of the pandemic marked it out as different from other crises, with disruptions occurring in waves of two to three months. Nadler and Tushman (1995) consider pandemics as an example of discontinuous change, which they argue, are accompanied by unpredictable, mass scale disruption and disequilibrium. Within this context, Shufutinsky et al. (2021) argue that incremental attempts at change in a pandemic context are unrealistic and require leaders to take a broader, more comprehensive approach to redevelopment.

The pandemic has seen an acceleration in digital change and transformation in organizations (Bartsch et al., 2020; Krehl & Buttgen, 2022). Work-from-home mandates imposed during the pandemic led to the establishment and transformation of remote working methods, with technology companies introducing new software to allow workplace activities to be accomplished remotely. Leaders themselves had an important role to play in building acceptance for and creating a culture of empowerment in relation to technology (Kurt & Erdogan, 2021). In this context, Horná and Kmec (2020) asserts that leaders are expected to take an active role in online environments through coaching and supporting staff. As a result of the pandemic, much attention is now given to the concept of e-leadership – a concept that according to Avolio et al. (2014) is in a very early stage of development. Still, in this new digital age, leaders will be expected to use online platforms for much more than simply top-down messaging and use online communications to build engagement and the employer brand – which may be particularly important when employees are working remotely outside the physical environs of the organization.

The experience of the pandemic has led to the re-evaluation of leadership effectiveness. Prior to the pandemic, we saw the rise of populist leaders at a national level such as Donald Trump, Boris Johnson and Jair Bolsonaro (Grint & Holt, 2022). As Schneiker (2020) points out, populist leaders use defensive attribution tactics to deflect responsibility for a crisis and differentiate their own actions from those of perpetrators. Indeed, Taraktas and colleagues (2022) report that populist leaders often downplayed the severity of the Coronavirus pandemic and de-emphasised the risks associated with contracting the virus. For her part, Waylen (2021) highlights how the hypermasculine approach of these leaders contributed to the delaying, downplaying and undermining of public health messaging during the pandemic. In contrast, the measured, considered and compassionate response of some female leaders such as Jacinda Ardern during the pandemic has led to reconsideration of what leader characteristics are most needed in crisis situations (Johnson & Williams, 2020; Park 2022; Soares & Sidun, 2021). Delves (2022) argues that the COVID-19 pandemic has changed the leadership landscape, casting aside narrow, individualistic thinking towards embracing more collaborative, innovative and inclusive approaches. In short, the COVID-19 pandemic has helped identify eight key skills and attitudes required from leaders during times of extreme turbulence.

1. Proactive, Adaptive and Purposeful Action

The need for leaders to act quickly and decisively in the face of an existential threat is one of their primary duties. Haslam et al. (2020) assert that a core task of leaders is to mobilize people to act and to create a shared sense of unity and responsibility in crisis situations. Likewise, Seijts et al. (2022) maintain that leaders are expected to exercise good judgment and to act virtuously and with integrity. They consider judgment as the application of character or practical wisdom (phronesis) to a context-specific situation. Alongside good judgment, effective leaders need to show that they can lead proactively, adaptively and flexibly in response to changing situations. New work patterns demand that leaders figure out what are the immediate priorities, whilst rethinking how organizations can adapt and thrive in a new environment (Bagwell, 2020). Most importantly, however, in crisis situations, leaders need to act with purpose (By, 2021). By (2021) defines purpose as a clear and stable intention to pursue a worthy idea or activity that is meaningful and has consequences beyond the individual and organization. He introduces the Telos Leadership lens and argues that leadership purpose should be guided by internal goods and should be focused on achieving the best possible outcome for the greatest number of stakeholders.

2. Clear Communication

A strong set of communication skills is needed in order to lead effectively in crisis situations. Holtom et al. (2020) argue that leaders who communicate with urgency, transparency and empathy, can help individuals adjust and cope with uncertain and rapidly changing conditions. For leaders, the goal of communication in crisis situations is to direct action, inform decision-makers, set the overall tone, and counsel victims (Garnett & Kouzmin, 2009). Yet, leaders need also to have some appreciation of the scale and magnitude of the crisis. Shufutinsky et al. (2021) argue that when leaders are unprepared, untrained or inexperienced in crisis situations, they can often wrongly focus on appearances, media cycles, and reactive adjustments. Instead, they maintain that the focus of communication needs to be on an actual crisis response and on attending to actual organizational needs and priorities. Clear communication is also critical in order to engage, connect, and align team members with organizational strategy. Johansson et al. (2014) asserts that leaders need to "engage employees in dialogue, actively share and seek feedback, practice participative decision making, and be perceived as open and involved" (p. 155). They argue that leaders' communication behaviors are thus socially co-constructed, based upon, constituted in, and shaped by interactions with employees.

3. Consistent and Comforting Support

Leaders play an important role in shaping organizational climate and offering psychosocial support to employees. This duty is particularly important in crisis situations. Duckers et al. (2017) identify three key responsibilities of leaders in this regard: first, a consideration of the needs of employees and the problems they are experiencing; second, the provision of a supportive context and the social acknowledgement of an individual's experiences; and third, the evaluation and identification of lessons from a crisis response. The pandemic has elevated the discussions about employee health and well-being to center-stage, with increasing attention being focused on how leaders can provide support for employee physical and mental health (Collings & Sheeran, 2020). During the COVID-19 pandemic, positive reinforcement and appreciation of work was viewed as highly important as a way of acknowledging the contribution of employees to the business (Dirani et al., 2020). Indeed, research suggests that initial efforts to adapt to the COVID-19 pandemic led to the intensification of work with a concomitant lack of organizational healthcare opportunities (Gunther et al., 2022). When combined with inadequate work facilities at home and the blurring of work and life boundaries, there is an increasing realization that organizations need to provide employees with stronger care-centered leadership and greater resources to support their physical and mental health.

4. Embracing New Technologies

Undoubtedly, the long-lasting nature of the pandemic led to significant innovation and the deployment and use of new technologies. As Dwivedi et al. (2020) point out, the word "Zoom" and "Microsoft Teams" have been incorporated into everyday usage with these platforms now commonly adopted in a range of personal and workplace settings.

With large numbers of employees working from home and a preference for hybrid work in the post-pandemic environment, there has been a significant growth in the use of work-from-home tech platforms. The growth in technology has led to increased research into the notion of e-leadership or digital leadership and how leaders can forge meaningful connections with followers in remote settings. Blau and Presser (2013) refer to e-leadership as the ability of the individual to influence the behavior of others via technology to achieve a set of organizational goals. Research by Deloitte (2020) presents a range of challenges facing traditional leaders who transitioned to e-leadership during the pandemic, including the adoption of new e-leadership styles; the redefinition of roles and responsibilities; the recognition of different employee needs; and the need to manage work-life boundaries and ensure the well-being of employees. Indeed, Krehl and Buttgen (2022) call for a new genre of leadership scholarship dedicated to the study of digital tools in supporting virtual leadership practices.

5. Building Partnerships and Engaging with Stakeholders

The COVID-19 pandemic led to a recognition of the need to build strong partnerships in response to crisis situations. National governments partnered with universities, biotechnology companies, and a wide range of manufacturers and logistics companies for the development of a vaccine, the distribution of personal protective equipment, and to combat supply chain shortages. Collings et al. (2021) assert that the pandemic reinforced the need for leaders to adopt a stakeholder approach, recognizing the responsibilities that businesses have to employees, customers and community partners, and the need to involve such partners in the decision-making process. Moreover, in leadership terms, the pandemic led to a shift towards a partnership approach by leaders, whereby the interests of leaders and followers were coupled within a unitarist frame, with less emphasis on power differentials and paternalistic command-and-control structures (Haslam et al., 2021). This was communicated through a narrative of shared identity and collective goals with leaders appealing to the values of strength, endurance, and perseverance in mobilizing support.

6. A Focus on Evidence-Based Decision-Making

In the face of uncertainty in crisis situations, it is imperative that leaders adopt an evidence-based approach to decision-making, rather than prejudice, subjective opinion, ideology or narrow self-interest. Maak et al. (2021) argue that a commitment to an evidence-based approach using a variety of sources safeguards the decision-making process from political manipulation and misdirection and that leaders play an important role in fostering an evidence-based culture within organizations. In crisis situations marked with a high level of uncertainty, as it was the case with the COVID-19 pandemic, Yang (2020) posits that it can often be difficult and time-consuming to collect evidence and that issues such as reasonableness, appropriateness and trained intuition may arise, but that any evidence collected should be evaluated against hierarchies of scientific quality. Indeed, it is clear from the pandemic that there was a desire amongst the populace for scientific evidence as a way of achieving a measure of assurance in individual decision-making. For their part, Cooper and Nagel (2022) assert that despite some entrenched scientific skepticism, large portions of the population adopted expert-recommended directives in relation to social distancing, quarantining, and mask-wearing.

7. Developing Planetary Consciousness
The COVID-19 pandemic has reinforced the need for leaders to embrace a more holistic communitarian view of leadership. Caro (2022) emphasizes the importance for leaders of developing a planetary mindset that is rooted in a common human identity and that affirms the importance of positive, ethical values that transcends cultures and ideologies. According to Marques (2022), leaders need to be courageous in setting away from self-imposed barriers to thinking and responding constructively and innovatively to the challenges present in a post-pandemic environment. For his part, By (2021) maintains that the United Nations sustainable development goals (SDG) framework offers a valuable approach for building meaningful global partnerships that allow individuals, organizations, and societies to grow within a holistic, sustainable, communal frame of reference. He argues that a global mindset and greater planetary consciousness will move leadership approaches away from short-term and target-driven initiatives towards a more societal, collaborative and collective focus needed to solve real world problems.

8. Positively Reframing Organizational Culture
As we move into a post-pandemic world, many senior leaders are acknowledging the need to reframe organizational culture to recognize the centrality of resilience and learning from failure. Organizational leaders ought to routinely hold frank discussions about their mistakes and failures. They need to support innovation and experimentation, as well as remove consequences for failures due to situational complexity (Wilson & Dobni, 2020). In that way, Wilson and Dobni (2020) argue that a failure-learning orientation is directly correlated with a firm's innovative capacity, its ability to achieve milestones and raise capital, and its status as a leading organization within its sector of operation. Similarly, Madi Odeh and colleagues (2021) highlight the importance of building responsive and adaptive organizational cultures that are resilient to change and that have the capacity to build trust and reduce fear amongst employees. They further argue that adaptive cultures encourage timely decision-making during normal and crisis times and boost levels of flexibility and creativity within organizations.

Overview of Contributions to this Book

This book brings together a collection of thought-provoking and evidence-based contributions from leading international researchers who offer fresh insights into how leadership approaches and practices have evolved in light of the COVID-19 pandemic. It is divided into four main parts.

In **Part I**, **Chapter 1**, Drs. McGuire and Germain introduce the book, its main sections, and its goals.

Part II includes four chapters in which leading researchers examine and consider how different aspects of leadership have evolved in light of the COVID-19 pandemic, and propose some leadership lessons for a post-COVID world.

Dr. Muhammad Zeeshan's **Chapter 2**, "Leadership Lessons arising from the COVID-19 Pandemic", looks at leadership challenges during the COVID-19 pandemic in the business, politics, education, and healthcare sector. The author discusses the leadership oversights and mistakes that could have been avoided during the COVID-19 pandemic and the possible leadership lessons learned from the pandemic.

In **Chapter 3**, titled "Was Leadership Emergency Planning Adequate? How Has the Pandemic Reshaped Organizational Emergency Plans? Dr. Jia Wang reviews the effectiveness of emergency plans and looks at key learnings from the experience of operating through the COVID-19 pandemic. She proposes an action plan to help organizations optimize their future emergency planning.

Drs. McGuire and Tuite, the authors of **Chapter 4**, "Leadership in a Post-COVID World: Embracing an Ethics of Care Approach", examine how leaders can foster workplace environments built upon the pillars of compassion, support and care for others. They argue that the pandemic has increased the expectation that leaders must act responsibly and demonstrate an ethic of care. Such an approach upholds the value and integrity of all employees and shows a genuine concern for employee welfare.

In the final chapter of Part II, **Chapter 5**, "Narcissistic Leadership Through the COVID-19 Pandemic: The importance of empathy for leadership effectiveness", Dr. Germain examines the characteristics of dysfunctional leaders as they encounter crises such as pandemics. She focuses on highly narcissistic leaders who often flourish in emergency and tumultuous situations. Despite their apparent competence, their notorious lack of empathy can harm their colleagues and organization. Her chapter emphasizes the toxicity of narcissistic leaders in times of crisis and argues that leadership effectiveness is best achieved by cultivating empathetic leadership.

Part III of this book comprises three chapters, which take a sectoral look at how the COVID-19 pandemic has affected leadership in the domains of higher education, politics, business, technology, hospitality, and healthcare, and the subsequent lessons learned.

In Chapter 6, "An Overview of Leadership Changes in Retail, Technology, Hospitality, and Healthcare post-COVID-19", Drs. Germain and McGuire provide an overview of how the COVID-19 pandemic has profoundly changed the way leaders lead in four sectors: retail, technology, hospitality, and healthcare.

In **Chapter 7**, "Higher Education Leadership in a Post-Pandemic World: Dealing with and Adjusting to a New Normal", Drs. Siham Lekchiri and Barbara A. W. Eversole contend that leadership is a continuous learning journey that requires a shift in leadership decisions and behaviors. Since early 2020, higher education leaders have experienced some substantial changes, including the necessary move to remote versus in-person learning, vaccinations and mask mandates, and the shift to the Work From Anywhere movement, among others. These decisions have required swift and visionary leadership. The authors look into the reality of change in higher education leadership during the COVID-19 pandemic and they address the expectations for an effective change in leadership.

Chapter 8, "Political Leadership During the COVID-19 Pandemic: Paradox, Politics, Power and compassion", is authored by Drs. Thomas Garavan and Cliodhna McKenzie. They posit that the COVID-19 pandemic was a once-in-100 year event that presented significant leadership challenges for leaders across the world including effective crisis leadership. They critique crisis leadership utilizing a paradox theory lens, and unpack whether embracing paradoxical thinking provides clues to why some leaders were more successful than others in responding to the COVID-19 pandemic. They point out that female political leaders such as Angela Merkel and Jacinda Ardern were far more successful than many male political leaders such as Boris Johnson and Donald Trump in adapting to the challenges presented by the pandemic. The authors apply the concept of the paradox mindset to illustrate how female political leaders leaned into COVID-19 paradoxes and improvised solutions where many male political leaders faltered. They consider whether paradoxical leadership and a paradox mindset represents one small step, or one giant leap in understanding what it means to lead and be a leader, especially in times of crisis. Finally, they generate several general insights that are useful in the context of major crises and consider the potential for incorporating paradox mindset as instrumental to *not* solving paradox tensions but rather, leaning into paradoxes in order to successfully navigate *through* them.

Part IV comprises the conclusion (**Chapter 9**), which summarizes some of the key organizational and sectoral leadership lessons learned from the COVID-19 pandemic. Drs. McGuire and Germain also delve into how such lessons will shape leadership actions and activities beyond the COVID-19 pandemic.

References

Ahern, S., & Loh, E. (2021). Leadership during the COVID-19 pandemic: building and sustaining trust in times of uncertainty. *BMJ Leader*, *5*, 266–269.

Avolio, B. J., Sosik, J. J., Kahai, S. S., & Baker, B. (2014), E-leadership: Re-examining transformations in leadership source and transmission. *Leadership Quarterly*, *25*(1), 105–131.

Bagwell, J. (2020). Leading Through a Pandemic: Adaptive Leadership and Purposeful Action.*Journal of School Administration Research and Development*, *5*, 30–34.

Bartsch S., Weber E., Büttgen M., et al. (2020) Leadership matters in crisis-induced digital transformation: How to lead service employees effectively during the COVID-19 pandemic. *Journal of Service Management*, *32*(1), 71–85.

Blau, I,. & Presser, O. (2013). E-Leadership of school principals: Increasing school effectiveness by a school data management system. *British Journal of Educational Technology*, *44*(6), 1000–1011.

By, R. T. (2021). Leadership: In Pursuit of Purpose, *Journal of Change Management*, *21*(1), 30–44.

Caro, D. H. J. (2022). Towards Transformational Leadership Beyond the COVID-19 Pandemic. In K. Dhiman, S. F. & Marques, J. (eds) *Leadership after COVID-19. Future of Business and Finance*. Springer, 203–219.

Collings, D. G., McMackin, J., Nyberg, A. J., & Wright, P. M. (2021). Strategic Human Resource Management and COVID-19: Emerging Challenges and Research Opportunities. *Journal of Management Studies*, *58*(5), 1378–82.

Collings, D. G., & Sheeran, R. (2020). Research insights: Global mobility in a post-COVID world. *Irish Journal of Management*, *39*(2), 77–84.

Cooper, D. H., & Nagel, J. (2022). Lessons from the Pandemic, Climate Change and COVID-19. *International Journal of Sociology and Social Policy*, *42*(3/4), 332–34.

Crist, C. (2021, November). *More Than 100 Million People Worldwide Have or Had Long COVID: Study.* https://www.webmd.com/lung/news/20211118/millions-worldwide-long-COVID-study

Deloitte (2020). *Leading Virtual Teams: Eight Principles for Mastering Virtual Leadership of Teams.* https://www2.deloitte.com/global/en/pages/about-deloitte/articles/COVID-19/leading-virtual-teams.html

Delves, R. (2022). Leadership for an Unknowable Tomorrow. In K. Dhiman, S.F. & Marques, J. (eds), *Leadership after COVID-19. Future of Business and Finance*. Springer, 99–114.

Dirani, K. M., Abadi, M., Alizadeh, A., Barhate, B., Garza, R. C., Gunasekara, N., Ibrahim, G. & Majzun, Z. (2020) Leadership competencies and the essential role of human resource development in times of crisis: a response to COVID-19 pandemic. *Human Resource Development International*, *23*(4), 380–394.

Dückers, M. L., Yzermans, C. J., Jong, W., & Boin, A. (2017). Psychosocial crisis management: the unexplored intersection of crisis leadership and psychosocial support. *Risk, Hazards & Crisis in Public Policy*, *8*(2), 94–112.

Dwivedi, Y. K., Hughes, D. L., Coombs, C., Constantiou, I., Duan, Y., Edwards, J. S., . . . & Upadhyay, N. (2020). Impact of COVID-19 pandemic on information management research and practice: Transforming education, work and life. *International journal of information management*, *55*, 102211.

Garnett, J., & Kouzmin, A. (2009). Crisis Communication Post Katrina: What are We Learning? *Public Organizational Review*, *9*, 385–398.

Giunipero, L. C., Denslow, D., & Rynarzewska, A. I. (2022). Small business survival and COVID-19 – An exploratory analysis of carriers. *Research in Transportation Economics*, *93*, 101087

Grint, K., & Holt, C. (2022). The boy who cried Flow: Unicorns and fabulist leadership in times of COVID-19. In M. Witzel (ed), *Post-Pandemic Leadership* (pp. 38–48). Routledge.

Günther, N., Hauff, S., & Gubernator, P. (2022). The joint role of HRM and leadership for teleworker well-being: An analysis during the COVID-19 pandemic. *German Journal of Human Resource Management*, *36*(3) 353–379.

Haslam, S. A., Reicher, S. D., & Platow, M. J. (2020). The new psychology of leadership: Identity, influence and power. London: Routledge.

Haslam, S. A., Steffens, N. K., Reicher, S. D., & Bentley, S. V. (2021). Identity leadership in acrisis: A 5R framework for learning from responses to COVID-19. *Social Issues and Policy Review*, *15*(1), 35–83.

Holtom, B., Edmondson, A. C., & Niu, D. (2020). 5 Tips for Communicating with Employees During a Crisis. *Harvard Business Review*. https://hbr.org/2020/07/5-tips-for-communicating-with-employees-during-a-crisis#:~:text=Every%20leader%20knows%20that%20communication,quick%20decisions%20to%20mitigate%20harm

Horná, P. T., & Kmec, L. (2020). The Post-COVID-19 Challenges in ethical leadership. Journal of Global Science. forthcoming.

Johnson, C., & Williams, B. (2020). Gender and Political Leadership in a Time of COVID. *Politics & Gender, 16*, 943–950.

Johansson, C., Miller, V. D., & Hamrin, S. (2014). Conceptualizing Communicative Leadership. *Corporate Communications, 2*(2), 147–165.

Johnson, C., & Williams, B. (2020). Gender and Political Leadership in a Time of COVID. *Politics & Gender, 16*, 943–950.

Krehl, E. H., & Büttgen, M. (2022). Uncovering the complexities of remote leadership and the usage of digital tools during the COVID-19 pandemic: A qualitative diary study. *German Journal of Human Resource Management, 36*(3) 325–352.

Kurt, Y,. & Erdogan, D. (2021). Leadership in the Post COVID-19 Era: New Leaders of the New Normal. In E. Al-Aali & M. Masmoudi (eds.) *Global Perspectives on Change Management and Leadership in the Post-COVID-19 Era*. IGI Global, 199–207.

Maak, T., Pless, N. M., & Wohlgezogen, F. (2021). The Fault Lines of Leadership: Lessons from the Global COVID-19 Crisis. *Journal of Change Management, 21*(1), 66–86. DOI:10.1080/14697017.2021.1861724

Madi Odeh, R. B. S., Obeidat, B. Y., Jaradat, M. O., Masa'deh, R., & Alshurideh, M.T. (2021). The transformational leadership role in achieving organizational resilience through adaptive cultures: the case of Dubai service sector. *Journal of Productivity and Performance Management, 72*(2), 440–468.

Marques, J. F. (2022). Courage as a Roadmap Toward Sustainable Practices in a Post-COVID World. In K. Dhiman, S., F. Marques, J. (eds) *Leadership after COVID-19. Future of Business and Finance*. Springer, 187–202.

Nadler, D. A., & Tushman, M. L. (1995). Types of organizational change: From incremental improvement to discontinuous transformation (p. 15–34) In Nadler, D.A. & Tushman, M. L. (eds.) *Discontinuous Change: Leading Organizational Transformation*. Jossey-Bass.

Park, S. (2022). Gendered leadership during the COVID-19 pandemic: how democracy and representation moderate leadership effectiveness. *Public Management Review, 24*(11), 1802–1823.

Schneiker, A. (2020). Populist leadership: The superhero Donald Trump as savior in times of crisis. Political Studies, *68*(4), 857–874.

Seijts, G., de Clercy, C., & Miller, R. (2022). Character and Trust in Crisis Leadership: Probing the Relationships Among Character, Identification-Based Trust, and Perceptions of Effectiveness in Political Leadership During the COVID-19 Pandemic. *The Journal of Applied Behavioral Science*, 1–28.

Shufutinsky, A., Long, B., Sibel, J.R., & Burrell, D.N. (2021). Shock Leadership: Leading Amidst Pandemics and Other Chaotic Change. In E. Al-Aali & M. Masmoudi (eds.) *Global Perspectives on Change Management and Leadership in the Post-COVID-19 Era*. IGI Global, 136–159.

Soares, S. E., & Sidun, N. M. (2021). Women leaders during a global crisis: Challenges, characteristics, and strengths. *International Perspectives in Psychology: Research, Practice, Consultation, 10*(3), 130–137.

Taraktaş, B., Esen, B., & Uskudarli, S. (2022). Tweeting through a public health crisis: communication strategies of right-wing populist leaders during the COVID-19 pandemic. *Government and Opposition*, 1–22.

Uhl-Bien, M. (2021). Complexity and COVID-19: Leadership and Followership in a Complex World. *Journal of Management Studies, 58*(5), 1400–1404.

Waylen, G. (2021) Gendering political leadership: hypermasculine leadership and COVID-19, *Journal of European Public Policy, 28*(8), 1153–1173.

Wilson, G. A., & Dobni, C. B. (2020). Implementing a failure learning orientation. *The International Technology Management Review, 9*(1), 27–33.

World Health Organization (2021). *A year into the COVID-19 pandemic, a high speed journey. Where are we now? (Coronavirus Update 51)* https://www.who.int/docs/default-source/coronaviruse/risk-comms-updates/update51_pandemic_overview_where_are_we_now.pdf?sfvrsn=709278aa_5World Health Organization (2022). *WHO Coronavirus (COVID-19) Dashboard*. https://COVID19.who.int/

Yang, K. (2020). What can COVID-19 tell us about evidence-based management? *The American Review of Public Administration, 50*(6–7), 706–712.

Part II: **Leadership Lessons for a Post-COVID World**

Muhammad Zeeshan

Chapter 2
Leadership Lessons Arising from the COVID-19 Pandemic

Abstract: The chapter looks at leadership challenges during the COVID-19 pandemic in the business, politics, education, and healthcare sector. The author discusses the leadership oversights and mistakes that could have been avoided during the COVID-19 pandemic and the possible leadership lessons learned from the pandemic.

Keywords: Responsible leadership, empathy, communication, teamwork, strategic thinking, effective teamwork, flexibility

When the world faced the COVID-19 crisis, many conventional business sense, that had worked for decades, proved inadequate. Many small, medium, and large businesses that could not adapt to these market shifts had to close. Despite substantial financial grants from the United Kingdom government, numerous organizations were unable to overcome their challenges. COVID-19 did not just reveal the vulnerabilities in business operations but also exposed numerous leadership styles that proved unfit to handle crises of this magnitude. Business leaders gained valuable insights from the 2008 financial crisis, but these lessons proved insufficient in mitigating the impact of the COVID-19 pandemic on organizational operations. This is due to the multi-faceted nature of the effects of COVID-19 (Contini, et al., 2020). Market closures led to millions losing their jobs worldwide, forcing governments to intervene by pumping billions into the economy to prevent businesses from collapsing (CNBC, 2021). Furthermore, the lockdown aggravated these problems and caused a loss of revenue for organizations. In light of the challenges and vulnerabilities that were exposed during the pandemic, current leaders must learn the essential lessons that can prepare them for similar crises and equip them with the competencies to deal with a multitude of risks.

In this chapter, the author discusses the core competencies that can equip organizational leaders to make the right decisions in uncertain times. These core competencies are Communication, Empathy, Flexibility, Responsible leadership, Effective Teamwork, and Strategic Thinking. Scholars such as (Cockerell, 2009; Goleman, 1995; Doh & Quigley, 2014; Molloy, 2021; Luthra & Dahiya, 2015) have argued in favor of these competences by highlighting the positive role they play in making a leader successful. The following sections will explore these competences in greater detail and the role they can play in helping leaders navigate difficult times.

Muhammad Zeeshan, Glasgow Caledonian University, Scotland

https://doi.org/10.1515/9783110799101-002

Communication

Communication is one of the essential components for any organization, because it helps build relationships and makes the workings of any organization possible. In the organizational context, communication is a vital administrative function and a means for transmitting information (Adu-Oppong & Agyin-Birikoran, 2014) internally and externally between employees, departments, customers, and other stakeholders. From a theoretical standpoint, communication can be defined as "the process of transmitting information and common understanding from one person to another" (Keyton, 2011, p133). Scholars such as Arnet (2009) believe that effective communication helps promote harmonious, peaceful relations, which are key for any successful organization. Furthermore, effective communication is imperative in stimulating and enhancing the capability to transfer knowledge. The consequences of ineffective communication for any organization can be immense. It can create difficulties when information is not transferred clearly between stakeholders, resulting in a loss of productivity and efficiency.

Communication during the time of COVID-19 was critical as it helped maintain employee productivity and engagement during a time of uncertainty (Argenti, 2020). This is because COVID-19 created significant stress and anxiety for employees due to the unprecedented uncertainty in the world markets. During this time, effective and transparent communication was essential to ensure that employees were supported and had the means to carry out their tasks effectively.

The uncertainty increased manifolds as most workers were put on furlough or asked to work from home (Delegach, et al., 2021). This made it especially difficult for the employees to collaborate with their colleagues. The day-to-day tasks were affected as employees struggled to cope with this change (Ripp, et al., 2020). In addition, isolation had a negative effect on employee wellbeing, which consequently created further challenges for the organizations. As a solution, many organizations introduced digital tools such as Microsoft Teams, Zoom, and Slack as means to stay connected with each other (Karl, et al., 2020). These real-time communication technologies have proved to be hugely influential in improving agility and staying connected.

Even in the post-COVID world, the importance of communication is undisputed. The business world faces enormous challenges, such as high-interest rates, inflation, and recession in some countries, such as the U.K. (Rogoff, 2023). As a result of these challenges, many organizations have laid off thousands of employees (Wall Street Journal, 2023), whereas many others are unsure of their future. Therefore, effective and transparent communication is an ever-important competency that needs to be demonstrated by organizations and their leaders to build a sense of trust among their workforce. Scholars such as Erburu and colleagues (2013) believe that effective communication is essential even in the most normal of times, as it is required for a well-constructed strategy, which helps drive employee commitment. However, this becomes of even more significance in complicated times due to the high anxieties prevalent in the workforce (Poglianich & Antonek, 2009). In these situations, the role of leaders in ensuring effective communication becomes immense. They need to provide their employees with clarity as to what has happened and what its impact is on the organization. Furthermore, they must provide clear instructions on what is expected of them. For instance, the European Central Bank (ECB) has changed its communication policy to be more transparent and the ECB has categorized their transparency level into five categories. Figure 2.1 illustrates how it works in practice.

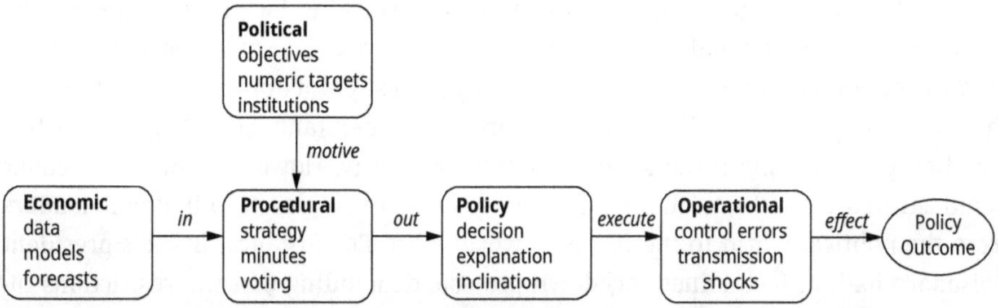

Figure 2.1: Categories of central bank transparency (Geraats, 2002).

Figure 2.1 demonstrates the initiatives ECB has taken to improve its communication. These initiatives are economic, procedural,policy and political in nature so that a holistic approach is adopted for promoting transparency. It also demonstrates how communication is central and vital in all walks of organizational workings. Reddy and Gupta (2020, p. 3794) highlight that effective communication is proactive, polite, imaginative, creative, constructive, professional, and progressive. These communication sub-competencies show that when it comes to communication, one has to understand what it actually means practically, and what characteristics an individual needs to demonstrate to be able to have effective communication.

Empathy

The beginnings of the word empathy go back to the 1800s, when a German psychologist named Theodore Lipps coined the term "einfuhlung", which means "in-feeling." It was used to describe the emotional appreciation of someone else's feelings (Ioannidou & Konstantikaki, 2008). Empathy is defined as "the capacity to share and understand another's state of mind or emotion" (Ioannidou & Konstantikaki, 2008, p. 118). It is associated with an individual's ability to "put oneself into another's shoes."

Empathy is of enormous importance in the organizational context. For employees to stay loyal to their organizations, it is essential that they can trust that their corporate leaders have the ability to see things from the employees' point of view and understand the struggles employees go through. This is necessary to build trust between an employee and an employer. Otherwise the relationship can be damaged, resulting in low morale and employee disengagement. Empathy allows leaders to create an effective environment where employees' voices are valued and heard. For Goleman (1995), empathy is a must-have virtue for leaders as "it can inspire, motivate, envision and lead others to great effectiveness." Cockerell (2009) highlights that empathy plays an essential role in leadership by connecting people so everyone feels included and heard.

Especially during the COVID-19 pandemic, where employees on all different hierarchical levels were concerned about their jobs, working locations, and even the health of the company and the general economy, there was a strong need for leadership to show empathy by understanding employees' points of view and providing them with some level of stability and support. This understanding of their perspective could only be possible if the leader possessed empathy. However, not every leader demonstrated empathy in these challenging times. Examples of empathetic leaders from the political world to the business world exist. For instance, Brazil's president Bolsonaro had, in fact, joined lockdown protests demanding that the restrictions introduced to control the spread of the virus be lifted (BBC, 2020). There are other instances of Bolsonaro trying to portray himself as a strongman by giving potentially harmful statements. For instance, he stated that he "would not feel a thing" if the coronavirus infected him, disparaging efforts to contain the illness (Guardian, 2020). This shows a severe lack of empathy and judgment toward the thousands of people who died due to the pandemic. There are also other organizational examples available that show an apparent lack of empathy toward their staff during the pandemic. For instance, not all organizations allowed their workforce to work from home, especially in some developing countries. This shows an apparent lack of understanding and empathy toward the wellbeing of employees. Even though there is clear evidence that demonstrates substantial benefits of working from home, some organizational leaders, even today, force their employees to work from corporate offices. It should also be noted that the risk of COVID-19 is still prevalent in 2023, as some people are still dying from the pandemic (ONS, 2023). So, forcing employees to work every day from an office can be seen as a clear sign of apathy toward the workforce. One such leadership example is the CEO of Tesla, Elon Musk. In 2022 Elon Musk emailed the staff, "Everyone at Tesla is required to spend a minimum of 40 hours in the office per week. If you do not show up, we will assume you have resigned" (Reuters, 2022). This shows apathy and a clear autocratic leadership style which arguably is linked with employee dissatisfaction and demotivation (Kahn, 1990).

Even in this current uncertain economic time, where interest rates have rocketed, inflation is at a 41 year high in the United Kingdom, and the cost of doing business has increased manifolds (Palmer, 2022). There is a need for empathetic leaders who can understand and relate to its workforce and can try to help them whenever possible because the current business uncertainty that exists all around the globe can create stress and anxiety for employees.

Another significant organizational issue is the announcement of mass layoffs in organizations worldwide (Wall street Journal, 2023). The following table provides a picture of the scale of layoffs by some of the big business giants.

Table 2.1: Large organizations and loss of jobs (Wall Street Journal, 2023).

Organizations	Loss of Jobs
Amazon	6,600
Disney	7,000
IBM	3,900
News Corp	1,250
Phillips	4,000
Zoom	1,300
Goldman Sachs	3,200
PayPal	2,000
FedEx	12,000

Table 2.1 reflects a number of companies that have announced mass layoffs. This is why empathetic leadership is required to create stability and comfort for the employees. It seems inevitable that many jobs will be lost. However, an empathetic leader can provide transparency and honesty that can be a source of comfort and stability for these employees who are still unsure of their futures. This will promote transparency within the organization and lead to better employee wellbeing and reduced stress levels (Dutton et al., 2014). This also leads to better decision making when the leadership is aligned with the needs and expectations of the employees, thereby making decisions that can not only help the employees but can lead to sustained growth for the organization.

Flexibility

Cambridge dictionary (2023) defines flexibility as "the ability to change or be changed easily according to the situation". Organizational flexibility is of immense importance for organizations to deal with market fluctuations and vulnerabilities, both internally and externally. These internal environmental factors include staff working conditions, wages, and the overall economic health of the organization (Ramendran et al., 2013). Analytical tools such as PESTLE (politics, economics, social, technical, legal, and environment) provide good analysis of these external factors (CIPD, 2021). In the organizational context, various flexibilities have been identified, such as structural, operational, functional, and wage stability (Ramendran et al., 2013). In the last few decades, the world has changed a lot, and this change has been multidimensional in nature.

From globalization to the mass migration of people, resulting in the need for organizations to be flexible and be able to work with people of different backgrounds (Engelsberger et al., 2021). The liberalization of markets worldwide have compelled organizations to be more flexible to compete with organizations from around the globe.

Aside from the market factors, other events, such as the COVID-19 pandemic, have changed how organizations work in many ways. COVID-19 brought a crisis of such immense proportion that significant organizational changes were required. Without said changes, organizations would face long-term negative implications (Savic & Dobrijevic, 2022). This was because the COVID-19 pandemic generated threats to all kinds of business operations and business models. The pandemic raised many questions for the organizations, such as where employees will work. What kinds of services and products would work during this time? Aside from these challenges, there were restrictions imposed by the governments that organizations had to abide by. All this unpredictability required flexibility and an organization to be agile and be taken as a fluid living organism that can mold itself to different changing conditions (Morgan, 2006). Agile organizations are intended to be fast, flexible, and resilient. Research conducted by McKinsey and Company (2020, cited in Savic & Dobrijevic, 2021) points out that the agile organizations before the pandemic, where adaptation to changes was deeply rooted in their DNA, were able to manage the impact of COVID-19 much more successfully. Savic and Dobrijevic (2021) have pointed out that agile operating models are still relatively new for several businesses, so it can be quite difficult to develop flexibility and agility quickly.

Nonetheless, it can be said with certainty that for the implementation of these agile models, flexible leadership is required that has the ability to adapt and implement new initiatives and programs required for organizational growth. There is also evidence that suggests that small businesses were more likely to permanently close during the pandemic due to their lack of flexibility (Fairlie et al., 2022). There is an obvious explanation, as smaller companies need more resources than bigger ones. However, it can also be argued that due to their small size, they might be better placed to make quick changes as the decisions do not have implications on thousands of employees scattered around the globe, as is the case with multinational organizations. Nevertheless, it can safely be said that this level of organizational flexibility can only be possible if the leadership is flexible and is able to make quick decisions that are important for the organization.

Good examples of promising flexible approaches were observed in various educational institutions during the pandemic. Many educational institutions were closed, preventing students from going to schools, colleges, and universities. Many institutions showed flexibility and introduced innovative online teaching methods that were able to replicate some level of class experience. However, it is also important to note that not all educational institutes could do that, especially in the developing world. Many institutes were closed, with pupils/students without access to education. This is also partly due to the initial costs associated with this medium of instruction but also potentially due to the potential lack of flexibility and adaptability in these organizations.

Responsible Leadership

Scholars have been studying organizational leadership for some time, from a leader's behavior and traits using situational and contingency theory to charismatic and transformational leadership (Angelo et al., 2004). One of the main reasons for this has been to understand the characteristics of effective leadership, which is integral to any organizational success.

An evolving theory stream has attempted to assimilate research in leadership, CSR and ethics to triangulate the concept of "Responsible Leadership" (Doh & Quigley, 2014). This is why various leadership theories and models have concentrated on the ethical dimensions of leadership, for example, servant, authentic, and transformational leadership, each of which stresses a leader's integrity, ethical decision making, and concern for others (Avolio & Gardner, 2005; Fry, 2003). The CIPD (2017, p. 1) defines leadership as "The capacity to influence people, by means of personal attributes and/or behaviors to achieve a common goal." Whereas, Maak and Pless (2008, p. 6) define responsible leadership as "A specific frame of mind promoting a shift from purely economist, positivist, and self-centered mind-set to a frame of thinking that has all constituents and thus the common good in mind too." Drawing from these definitions, it can be argued that responsible leadership is about accepting responsibility and looking for the benefits of all stakeholders instead of a few individuals.

Moreover, Maak and Pless (as cited in Pless, 2007) have also presented nine roles of a responsible leader, which are differentiated between values-based roles such as a steward, leader, citizen, and servant, and operational roles such as storyteller, networker, architect, change agent, and coach. The following Figure 2.2 illustrates these roles.

Responsible leadership is of enormous importance in the most normal times as it concentrates on ethics and morality. In the recent past, high-profile issues such as Enron, Theranos, and FTX have demonstrated the effect of unethical practices on organizations and the wider society. Some of these organizational leaders are in jail (McEvoy, 2022) for unfair/unethical practices, whereas some of these organizations lost vast sums of money, and employees lost their jobs. COVID-19 was another significant challenge for world markets and organizations that needed responsible leaders to steer their organizations from one of the most difficult of times. As discussed in earlier sections, many employees lost their jobs or were furloughed, creating uncertainty within the organizations. Here, responsible leadership was required to show care for the employees and not just the immediate share price or profitability. During these times, leadership needed to show one of the main facets of responsible leadership, i.e. stewardship (Pless, 2007). By demonstrating stewardship, leaders needed to

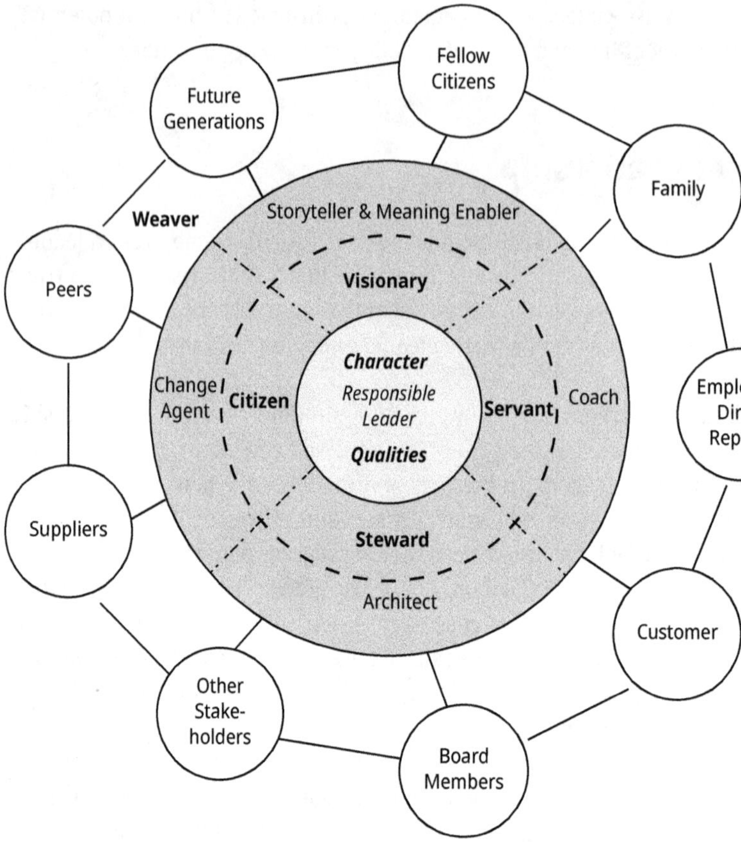

Figure 2.2: The roles model of responsible leadership (Maak & Pless, 2006, p. 107).

focus on the employees they work with and the wider community, not just the organization's self-preservation.

The CIPD (2023) published a report in regard to the lessons learned through the crisis. The report offers functional applications for leaders resulting from the challenges and opportunities created by the pandemic. These are as follows:

- *Rethink talent streams, leadership development and your own leadership practice: New ways of leading are essential to success, and leaders should maintain the humane and personal leadership that emerged during COVID-19.*
- *Understand the importance of work as a community, not just a workspace or a series of tasks: Invest in building cultures of trust and recognise that many in the workforce may require sustained and focused 're-engagement' after prolonged social isolation. Be alert to tensions inherent between individual needs or demands and the collective good of the organisation and community.*

- *Remain purpose- and principles-led through continued uncertainty: The pandemic has strengthened purpose for many, and it is a purpose that will allow organisations to thrive in a post-COVID-19 economy.*
- *Engage in a deep understanding of your ecosystem and orientate yourself externally: Leaders need to understand the needs of multiple stakeholders (whether or not they are able to meet all those needs is another matter). HR leaders must also look upwards and outwards, engaging with a broader range of stakeholders beyond the boundaries of the organisation.*
- *Be active in addressing inequalities and champion social justice within the workplace as issues for all to own: To avoid the emergence of a two-tier workforce, leaders must acknowledge divisions and tensions between parts of the workforce and address imbalances.*

It is also important to note here that there are other essential sub-competencies that a responsible leader needs to have to be able to operate in these turbulent times. For instance, an effective leader needs to possess emotional intelligence to be able to have the ability to understand and recognize the emotions and perspectives of others to help them during uncertain times. Scholars such as George (2000) have proposed a strong link between emotional intelligence and effective decision making. A responsible, emotionally intelligent leader will potentially have the ability to regulate their feelings so that rational decisions can be made in difficult times. Furthermore, they will be skilled enough to evaluate the implications of their decisions and actions on their workforce. This is especially important in turbulent times because solid evidence shows that a workforce that feels their leadership is caring will be more engaged and motivated to stay and perform at a higher level (Yan, et al., 2021). Resilience is another important sub-competency that responsible leadership should exhibit. Especially now, with the cost of doing business running incredibly high (Palmer, 2022), organizations and their leadership need to show resilience to lead in these challenging times. The research conducted by the Resilience Shift in 2020 has provided critical components of resilient leadership (Willis & Nadkarny, 2020). Figure 2.3 illustrates these components.

Figure 2.3 demonstrates that specific behavior characteristics are required along with technical capabilities, which are essential in navigating organizations through challenging and uncertain times. Along with resilience, leaders need to be agile as well. Denning -(2021) recommends that one of the ways to do this is to avoid conventional organizational hierarchies which are based on the traditional systems of decision making. It is important to decentralize decision making by giving more autonomy to the teams themselves, enabling rapid responses to ever-changing situations.

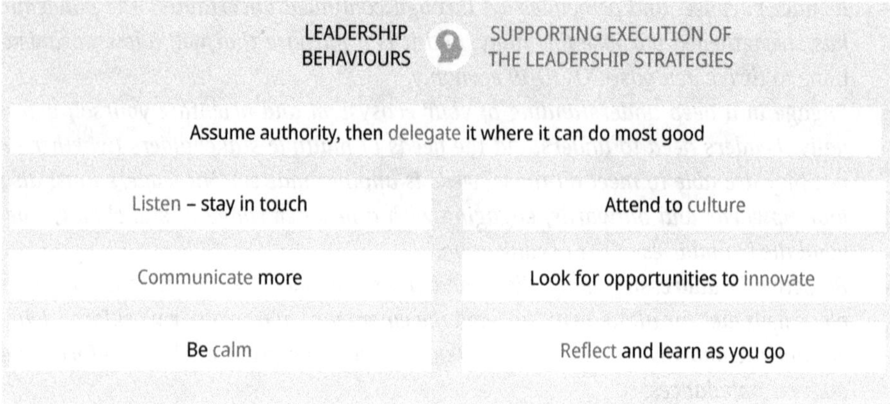

LEADERSHIP BEHAVIOURS
SUPPORTING EXECUTION OF THE LEADERSHIP STRATEGIES
Assume authority, then delegate it where it can do most good
Listen – stay in touch
Attend to culture
Communicate more
Look for opportunities to innovate
Be calm
Reflect and learn as you go

Figure 2.3: Leadership Behaviors (Willis & Nadkarny, 2020, p. 17).

Effective Teamwork

Effective teamwork is a critical competency for any successful individual and organization (Nancarrow et al., 2013). A substantial body of research suggests that effective teamwork is essential on an individual and an organizational level (Chawla & Jain, 2021; Birkinshaw & Gibson, 2020). For instance, the research conducted by Harvard Business Review suggests that organizations with effective teamwork performed, on average, 147% better than their competitors (Goleman & Boyatzis, 2017).

Teamwork refers to "The activity of working together in a group with other people, especially when this is successful" (Cambridge, 2023). Effective teamwork can potentially increase employee engagement, satisfaction and productivity, helping the organization reach its goal and objectives (Chawla & Jain, 2021).

Teamwork was particularly important during COVID-19, because the pandemic had compelled businesses to adapt to new working methods. For instance, employees had to adapt to remote working or partial shutdowns (Alvarez-Torres & Schiuma, 2022). In these situations, effective teamwork was required to be able to manage such drastic changes. Furthermore, effective teamwork was one of the seminal competencies that helped organizations to remain flexible and resilient during the pandemic (Lajcin & Porubcanova, 2021).

The McKinsey and Company study indicates that companies with an effective teamwork culture performed much better than their counterparts because of the collective capability to navigate these challenging times (Birkinshaw & Gibson, 2020). Moreover, a substantial body of evidence suggests that effective teamwork helps in innovation (Gonzalez-Roma, 2008). Although COVID-19 created many challenges, it also led to innovation in many areas, such as healthcare, education, and more. It was only through effective teamwork between different interdisciplinary teams that included epidemiologists, statisticians, and programming experts, who successfully pinpointed the pandemic's route causes. Thereafter, they were able to realistically forecast the trajectory and later develop vaccines that changed the course of the pandemic. All of this was only possible with effective teamwork.

Teamwork is equally vital in the post-pandemic world because the world of business is still uncertain. The economies of numerous countries are still very volatile and recovering from the effects of the pandemic (Jabeen, et al., 2022). This is also having an adverse effect on organizations because the geo-political and economic landscape of macro-economic factors have potentially strong relationships with organizations (As-Saber, et al., 2001). This is why a holistic teamwork approach is required in these uncertain times that can play a positive role in creating these challenges into potential opportunities.

Another significant opportunity and challenge is the increased movement of people between different countries. There is some evidence to suggest that migration has increased manifolds after the strict restrictions imposed during the lockdowns (Benton, et al., 2021). Scholars such as Alderwic and colleagues (2021) have highlighted that intercultural collaborations resulting from the increased migration have the ability to generate new ideas that lead to solving complex problems. However, that is only possible if these intercultural differences are managed well. Otherwise, they can create many conflicts between different teams, consequently affecting the everyday workings of an organization, which is why teamwork competency is paramount if these intercultural differences are to be channeled into the right direction.

Similar to intercultural collaborations, interdisciplinary collaborations are also increasingly on the rise. As discussed earlier, it was an interdisciplinary collaboration between different disciplines that helped in controlling the pandemic. Though interdisciplinary collaborations can create novel solutions to complex problems, this is only possible if interdisciplinary teams work effectively. This is why effective teamwork is an imperative component in making these collaborations successful if they are to bring any meaningful outcomes (Hall & Weaver, 2001).

It is imperative to point out that for any leader to be effective, they need to possess team working skills, as the teams they are working with need the leader to relate and work with them as part of the team (Molloy, 2021). Failure to do this can result in disengagement between the leadership and the teams the leader works with. Effective teamwork during COVID-19 could only have been facilitated by the leadership who sees themselves as part of the team rather than merely a manager leading that team. However, not all leaders demonstrated these teamwork abilities. One of the significant examples of such ineffective teamwork demonstrated by world leaders could be the former U.S. president Donald Trump. Donald Trump consistently contradicted the advice of his senior health officials, such as Dr. Anthony Fauci, regarding the pandemic (Independent, 2021), and gave contrary advice such as disinfectants could be used to treat coronavirus (New York Times, 2020). This example demonstrates the disregard for the team he was working with on the pandemic issue. Trump is one of many amongst some of the world leaders who did not potentially show effective teamwork during one of the worst pandemics in decades.

Strategic Thinking

Kenneth (1980, p.18) defines Strategic thinking is an essential element of corporate strategy. Corporate strategy can be defined as

> *the pattern of decisions in a company that determines and reveals its objectives, purposes, or goals produces the principles and plans for achieving these goals and defines the range of business the company is to pursue, the kind of economic and human organization it is or intends to be, and the nature of the economic and noneconomic contribution it intends to make to its shareholders, employees, customers, and communities*

One of the main benefits of a clear corporate strategy is that it helps in reaching the organizational goals because it helps in achieving sustained competitive advantage (Porter, 1996). An effective corporate strategy does things by aligning the organization's vision, mission, and values, ensuring every employee is working in coherence to work toward the same goals. One of the main tools required for effective corporate strategy is critical thinking (Tripathy, 2020). Critical thinking is a development, reflective, mental, and issue-oriented process which aims to develop new strategies before, during, or after the strategic planning process (Moore, 2014). Strategic thinking plays an essential role in any organization's success. Leaders who demonstrate Strategic thinking have the ability to analyze any current situation and identify threats and opportunities from it. From there, leaders can strategize and develop a long-term plan which helps the organization achieve their long-term objectives. An important point to note here is that strategic thinking is associated with long-term strategic planning rather than a short-term meeting of the organizational targets.

Leadership needed to demonstrate strategic thinking due to the unprecedented uncertainty and challenges during COVID-19. During the pandemic, there was a flood of varying information coming to organizations with potentially varying degrees of effect. For this reason,leadership needed to demonstrate strategic thinking to be able to critically evaluate the information and pass it on to the employees that was critical for the survival of the organization. Scholars such as Moore and Parker (2017) reiterate this by arguing that strategic thinking plays a cardinal role in effectively analyzing, evaluating and interpreting information which is required for critical decision making.

Moreover, leadership must demonstrate critical thinking for predicting threats and navigating the organizations away from these threats. During COVID-19, approximately 600,000 businesses died (ONS, 2021), which is unprecedented and shows the extent of the damage caused by COVID-19 on businesses. Therefore, leadership needed to have critical thinking and strategic ability to make strategic decisions that could be vital for their survival.

An example of such a strategic decision would be when to keep the offices and outlets open and when to keep them closed. As offices and outlets are central to organizations, organizations inherently want to keep them open. However, a wrong short-term decision to keep the offices open could have spread the outbreak within the organization, consequently affecting the whole workings of the company. Therefore, leadership needed to show maturity and demonstrate critical thinking to make tough decisions vital for long-term survival.

Strategic thinking was also of paramount importance in the political world. Governments all around the globe were blitzed with vast amounts of contradicting information, even from different scientists (OECD, 2020). So, for them to be able to evaluate and use the information to minimize the damage on their population was critical. It also added a lot of pressure on the government leadership to make the right calls. There were governments all around the globe who managed to demonstrate critical thinking and help their country. However, there were also government leaders worldwide who did not show critical thinking and made severe mistakes. For instance, precious lives were lost in the U.K. due to the government's delay in bringing in the initial lockdown, ignoring valuable scientific advice (Independent, 2021). There is also evidence of issues noted in social care, inadequate supply of PPE (personal protective equipment), and the lack of proper health risk assessment for ethnic minority staff were some of the strategic blunders in the U.K. (O'Dowd, 2021). Robert West, professor of health psychology at University College London is also critical of the government and stated that "there is no escaping the damning conclusion that it [government] failed to take crucial public health advice on key decisions relating to test and trace and timing of restrictions, and that led many thousands of British citizens to perish" (cited in O'Dowd, 2021)

However, some countries, such as South Korea, fared much better than the United Kingdom in their pandemic response and were able to save precious lives (Bloomberg, 2022). Countries such as South Korea were able to do this because they were strategic and critical in their thinking. These countries took decisions concerning the lockdowns and markets, which helped their population and businesses ride out the pandemic much better than some of their western counterparts. For instance, from February 2020, South Korea adopted active epidemiological investigations, strict isolation of infected patients for a targeted approach and extensive public lockdowns which drastically changed the spread of the virus by the end of 2021 (Lim & Sohn, 2022).

There are important lessons to be learned by leaders of various sectors that they need to develop their critical thinking ability. The world markets are going through a turbulent time (Lonergan, 2022). The cost of doing business has increased manifolds, putting a lot of pressure on coming up with new business initiatives and models that can help businesses sustain long-term growth. These new models and initiatives need strategic and critical thinking to evaluate and analyze the various options available. Furthermore, it might only sometimes be possible to have options available. In those scenarios, strategic thinking could potentially help businesses develop innovative solutions.

Summary and Conclusion

The discussion presented in this chapter demonstrates the role of leadership during the pandemic. It highlighted how effective leaders played essential roles in business, politics, and education. It also provided some world leaders' examples, such as those of the former U.S. president, the U.K. government, and Brazil's former president Bolsonaro, who arguably demonstrated poor leadership behaviors by contradicting the valuable advice provided by their health teams and made some decisions that went entirely against the scientific advice.

The chapter also discussed the vital competencies that helped effective leaders in steering their countries and organizations through one of the most challenging times. The author highlighted how the key competencies that were required during the pandemic are an ever-important need for world leaders in helping their organizations through these tumultuous times. These key leadership competencies are communication, empathy, flexibility, responsible leadership, teamwork, and strategic thinking. It was pointed out that leaders need to show empathy to relate with the people they work with. During these uncertain times, empathy provides a level of comfort and trust between the leadership and employees, which is vital in building the trust that is critical for any organization's sustainability.

Another essential competency noted was flexibility. For organizations to adopt new agile business models that are a need of the modern times, leadership needs to be flexible and open-minded in their policy formulation and decision making so these new initiatives can be implemented in their organizations.

Another key element required in leadership is responsible leadership. The leadership needs to show that they don't only work for the shareholders in pursuit of maximizing profits and share price but considers ethics and morality, which aim to benefit the whole of the society in which it operates. This chapter also discussed the unethical practices of organizations such as the FTX and Theranos, who showed classic examples of unethical leadership so that they could maximize their profits and value. It also provided insight into how these unethical leadership practices led their founders behind bars.

Effective teamwork is another necessary competency that needs to be present in leadership. It is not enough to come across as a firm and disciplined leader; it is important that the teams the leader works with feel that he/she is part of the team and is one of them. This section discussed the benefits of effective teamwork and provided an example of interdisciplinary teams working all around the globe to develop novel solutions to the coronavirus.

Lastly, the chapter discussed the importance of leadership espousing strategic thinking. It was pointed out that strategic thinking is required to critically evaluate and analyze the critical pieces of information that are required for effective decision making. It was observed that during the COVID-19 pandemic, there was a varying amount of contradicting information available. However, it was the role of strategic leaders to decipher the information that could change the course of the pandemic.

The current times are so uncertain that a leader needs to possess strategic thinking to be able to assess different models that can help an organization attain a competitive advantage.

References

Adu-Oppong, A., & Agyin-Birikoran, E. (2014). Communication in the workplace: Guidelines for improving effectiveness. *G.J.C.M.P, 3*(5), 208–213.

Alderwick, H., Hutchings, A., Briggs, A., & Mays, N. (2021). The impacts of collaboration between local health care and non-health care organizations and factors shaping how they work: A systematic review of reviews. *BMC Public Health, 21*, 1–16.

Alvarez-Torres, F., & Schiuma, G. (2022). Measuring the impact of remote working adaptation on employees' well-being during COVID-19: Insights for innovation management environments. *European Journal of Innovation and Management*. https://www.emerald.com/insight/content/doi/10.1108/EJIM-05-2022-0244/full/html

Angelo, M, Eddy, E., & Lorenzet (2004). The importance of personal and professional leadership. *Leadership and Organisation Development Journal, 5*(6), 435–449.

Arent, R. (2009). An introduction to intercultural communication. *Speech Communication*, 306. https://www.press.umich.edu/pdf/9780472033577-ch1.pdf

Argenti, P. (2020, March 17). Communicating through the Coronavirus crisis. *Harvard Business Review*. https://hbr.org/2020/03/communicating-through-the-coronavirus-crisis. Accessed 10-12-22.

As-Saber, S., Liesch, P., & Dowling, P. (2001). *Geopolitics and its impacts on international business decisions: A framework for a geopolitical paradigm of international business*. University of Tasmania.

Avolio, B. & Gardner, W. (2005). Authentic leadership development: Getting to the root of positive forms of leadership. *The leadership quarterly, 16*, 315–338.

BBC (2020). *Cornonarius: Brazil's Bolosaro joins anti-lockdown protests*. https://www.bbc.co.uk/news/world-latin-america-52351636.

Benton, M., Davidoff-Gore., Batalova, J., Huang, L., & Zong, J. (2021). COVID-19 and the state of Global Mobility in 2021. *International Organisation for Migration, Migration Policy Institute*

Birkinshaw, J., & Gibson, C. (2020). Building organisational resilience during the coronavirus crisis. *MIT Sloan Management Review*. https://sloanreview.mit.edu/tag/resilience/

Bloomberg (2022). *The Best and worst places to be as world enters Next COVID Phase*. https://www.bloomberg.com/graphics/COVID-resilience-ranking/#xj4y7vzkg.

Cambridge Dictionary (2023). *Teamwork*. https://dictionary.cambridge.org/dictionary/english/teamwork

CambrdigeDictionary (2023). Flexibility. https://dictionary.cambridge.org/dictionary/english/flexibility

Chawla, C., & Jain, V. (2021). Teamwork on employee performance and organization Growth. *Journal of Contemporary Issues in Business and Government, 27*(3), 705–709.

Chartered Institute of Personnel and Development (CIPD) (2017). Leadership Factsheet. Accessible at: https://www.cipd.co.uk/knowledge/strategy/leadership/factsheet

CIPD (2021). *PESTLE Analysis*. https://www.cipd.co.uk/knowledge/strategy/organisational-development/pestle-analysis-factsheet#gref

CIPD (2023). *Responsible business through crisis*. https://www.cipd.co.uk/knowledge/strategy/corporate-responsibility/responsible-business-through-crisis#gref

CNBC (2021). COVID pandemic led to the loss of 22 million jobs in the US, but recovery has been swift in some sectors. *CNBC*. https://www.cnbc.com/2021/06/10/COVID-pandemic-led-to-loss-of-22-million-jobs-in-the-us.html

Cockerell, L. (2009). Creating leadership magic. *Leader to Leader, 53*, 31–36.
Contini, C., Caselli, E., Martini, F., Mariati, M., Torregiani, E., Sera, S.Vesce, F., Perri, P., Rizzo, L., & Tognon, M. (2020). COVID-19 Is a multifaceted challenging pandemic which needs urgent public health interventions. *Microorganisms, 8*(8), 1–21
Delegach, M., Klein, G., & Katz-Navon, T. (2021). Furlough and its effects on employees after returning to work: The roles of psychological contract breach and violation and perceived organizational support. *Journal of Management & Organization*, pp 1–18
Denning, S. (2021). Why business agility requires a shift from a hierarchy to a network. *Forbes*. https://www.forbes.com/sites/stevedenning/2021/08/29/why-business-agility-requires-a-shift-from-a-hierarchy-to-a-network/?sh=1ee06e021da8
Doh, J. & Quigley, N. (2014). Responsible leadership and stakeholder management: Influence pathways and organisational outcomes. *Academy of management perspectives, 28*(3) 255–274
Dutton, J. E., Workman, K. M., & Hardin, A. E. (2014). Compassion at work. *Annual Review of Organizational Psychology and Organizational Behavior, 1*(1), 277–304.
Engelsberger, A., Cavanagh, J., Bartram, T., & Halvorsen. (2021). Multicultural skills in open innovation: Relational leadership enabling knowledge sourcing and sharing. *Personnel Review, 50*(3), 980–1002.
Erburu, L., Ruz, E., & Arboledas, J. (2013). Economic crisis and communication: The role of the HR manager. *Business Systems Review. 2*(2), 278–295.
Fairlie, R., Fossen, F., Johnsen, R., & Droboniku, G. (2012). Were small businesses more likely to permanently close in the pandemic? *Small Bussiness Economics*. https://doi.org/10.1007/s11187-022-00662-1
Fry, W. (2003). Toward a theory of spiritual leadership. *The Leadership Quarterly, 14*, 693–727.
George, J. M. (2000). Emotions and leadership: The role of emotional intelligence. *Human Relations, 53*(8), 1027–1055. https://doi.org/10.1177/0018726700538001
Geraats, P. M. (2002). Central bank transparency. *The Economic Journal, 112*, 532–565.
Goleman, D. P. (1995). *Emotional intelligence: Why it can matter more than IQ for character, health and lifelong achievement*. Bantam Books.
Goleman, D., & Boyatzis, R. (2017). Social intelligence and the biology of leadership. *Harvard Business Review, 95*(5), 74–81.
Gonzalez-Roma, V. (2008). Innovation in work teams. *Papeles del Psicólogo, 29*(1), 32–40.
Guardian. (2020). *Bolsonaro says he 'wouldn't feel anything' if infected with COVID-19 and attacks state lockdowns*. https://www.theguardian.com/world/2020/mar/25/bolsonaro-brazil-wouldnt-feel-anything-COVID-19-attack-state-lockdowns.
Hall, P. & Weaver, L. (2001). Interdisciplinary education and teamwork: A long and winding road. *Medical Education, 35*, 867–875.
Independent (2021). *Trump says he didn't listen to Fauci because I was doing the opposite of what he was saying in the Fox interview*. https://www.independent.co.uk/news/world/americas/us-politics/trump-fauci-fox-news-coronavirus-b1823118.html
Independent (2021). *Report says UK's slow virus lockdown cost 1000s of lives*. https://www.independent.co.uk/news/matt-hancock-COVID-stephen-barclay-boris-johnson-sky-news-b1936715.html
Ionnidou, I., & Konstantikaki, V. (2008). Empathy and emotional intelligence: What is it really about? *International Journal of Caring Sciences, 1*(3),118–123.
Jabeen, S., Farhan, M., Zaka, M., Fiaz., & Farasat, M. (2022). COVID and world stock markets: A comprehensive discussion. *Frontiers in Psychology, 12*, 1–16.
Kahn, W. A. (1990). Psychological conditions of personal engagement and disengagement at work. *Academy of Management Journal, 33*(4), 692–724.
Karl, K. A., Peluchette, J. V., & Aghakhani, N. (2020). virtual work meetings during the COVID-19 pandemic: The good, bad, and ugly. *Small Group Research, 53*(3), 343–365.

Kenneth, A (1980). *The concept of corporate strategy* (2nd Edition). Dow-Jones Irwin.Keyton, J. (2010). *Communication and Organisational Culture*. Sage Publications.
Keyton, J. (2011). Communication and organizational culture: A key to understanding work experience. Thousand Oaks, CA: Sage.
Lajcin, D. & Porubcanova, D. (2021). Teamwork during the COVID-19 pandemic. *Emerging Science Journal*, *5*, 1–10.
Lim, S. & Sohn, M. (2022). Strategy for COVID-19, and collateral damage to cardiometabolic health. *The LANCET Regional Health*. https://www.thelancet.com/journals/lanwpc/article/PIIS2666-6065(22)00196-1/fulltext#:~:text=From%20February%202020%2C%20the%20South,until%20the%20end%20of%202021.
Lonergan, E. (2022). The volatility virus strikes again. *Financial Times*. https://www.ft.com/content/d40e9ae1-84a3-45bd-90fd-642366f82a28
Luthra, A., Dahiya, R. (2015). Effective leadership is all about communicating effectively: Connecting leadership and communication. *International Journal of Management & Business Studies*, *5*(3), 43–47
Maak, T. & Pless, N. (2008). *Responsible leadership*. Routledge.
McEvoy J. (2022). From financial ruin to jail time, here are the big billionaire downfalls that compete with Sam Bankman-Fried's $17 billion FTX collapse. *Forbes*. https://www.forbes.com/sites/jemimamcevoy/2022/11/19/sam-bankman-fried-elizabeth-holmes-and-9-other-epic-billionaire-blowups/?sh=685381724bcb
Molloy, J. (2021). Teams are Changing: Are Team Leaders and Members Keeping Up? *Harvard Business Review*. https://www.harvardbusiness.org/teams-are-changing-are-team-leaders-and-members-keeping-up/
Moore, K.D. (2014). Effective instructional strategies: From theory to practice. Sage Publications.
Morgan, G. (2006). Images of organization. Sage Publications. *Harvard Business Publishing*. https://www.harvardbusiness.org/teams-are-changing-are-team-leaders-and-members-keeping-up/
Nancarrow, A., Booth, A., Ariss, S., Smith, T., Enderby, P., & Roots, A. (2013). Ten principles of good interdisciplinary team work. *Human resources for health*, *11*(1).
New York Times (2020). *Trump's suggestion that disinfectants could be used to treat coronavirus prompts aggressive pushback*. https://www.nytimes.com/2020/04/24/us/politics/trump-inject-disinfectant-bleach-coronavirus.html.
Dowd, A (2021). COVID-19: Government's handling of pandemic had "big mistakes," MPs say. *British Medical Journal, Vol 375(2487)* https://www.bmj.com/content/375/bmj.n2487#:~:text=The%20way%20in%20which%20the,risk%20to%20protect%20their%20patients.%E2%80%9D
OECD (2020). *The territorial impact of COVID-19: Managing the crisis across levels of government*. https://www.oecd.org/coronavirus/policy-responses/the-territorial-impact-of-COVID-19-managing-the-crisis-across-levels-of-government-d3e314e1/
ONS (2023). Coronovirus (COVID-19) *latest insights*. https://www.ons.gov.uk/peoplepopulationandcommunity/healthandsocialcare/conditionsanddiseases/articles/coronavirusCOVID19/latestinsights.
ONS (2021). *Bankrupt or P\permanently closed businesses during the COVID-19 pandemic*. https://www.ons.gov.uk/aboutus/transparencyandgovernance/freedomofinformationfoi/bankruptorpermanentlyclosedbusinessesduringtheCOVID19pandemic.
Palmer, A. (2022). How does inflation impact businesses? *Henley Business School*. https://www.henley.ac.uk/news/2022/how-does-inflation-impact-businesses
Pless, N. (2007). Understanding responsible leadership: Role identity and motivational drivers. *Journal of Business Ethics*, *74*, 437–457.
Poglianich, A. & Antonek, M. (2009). *Rules of engagement in turbulent times: How Verizon Wireless uses a robust HR portal for employee communication*. Wiley InterScience.
Porter, M. E. (1996). What is strategy? *Harvard Business Review*, *74*(6), 61–78.

Ramendran, C., Raman, G., Kumar, R., Mohamed, H, Beleya, P., & Nodeson, S. (2013). Organisational Flexibility and its Implications on Employee Productivity. *Interdisciplinary Journal of Contemporary Research in Business*, *4*(10), 299–316.

Reddy, V. & Gupta, A. (2020). Importance of effective communication during COVID-19 infodemic. *Journal of Family Medicine and Primary Care*, *9*(8), 3793–3796.

Reuters (2022). *Elon Musk tells Tesla staff: Return to office or leave*. https://www.reuters.com/technology/musk-memo-tesla-staff-return-office-or-leave-company-2022-06-01/.

Ripp, J., Peccoralo, L., & Charney, D. (2020). Attending to the emotional well-being of the healthcare workforce in a New York City health system during the COVID-19 pandemic. *Academic Medicine*, *95*(8), 1136–1139. https://doi.org/10.1097/ACM.0000000000003414.

Rogoff, K. (2023). The world economy faces a huge stress test in 2023. *Guardian*. https://www.theguardian.com/business/2023/jan/05/world-economy-stress-test-2023-inflation-interest-rates-crisis.

Savić, A., & Dobrijević, G. (2022). The impact of the COVID-19 pandemic on work. *The European Journal of Applied Economics*, *19*(1), 1–15

Tripathy, M. (2020). Dimensions of critical thinking in workplace management & personal development: A conceptual analysis. *Multidisciplinary Journal for Education, Social and Technological Sciences*, *7*(2), 1–19.

Wall Street Journal (2023). *The Companies Conducting Layoffs in 2023*: *Here's the list.* https://www.wsj.com/articles/the-companies-conducting-layoffs-in-2023-heres-the-list-11673288386.

Willis. P., Nadkarny, S. (2020). Resilient leadership: Learning through crisis. *Resilient Cities Network*. https://www.resilienceshift.org/wp-content/uploads/2020/10/Resilient-Leadership-Learning-From-Crisis-Report-by-the-Resilience-Shift.pdf

Yan, Y., Zhang, J., Akhtar, M. N., & Liang, S. (2021). Positive leadership and employee engagement: The roles of state positive affect and individualism-collectivism. *Current Psychology*. https://www.ncbi.nlm.nih.gov/pmc/articles/PMC8364414/pdf/12144_2021_Article_2192.pdf

Jia Wang

Chapter 3 Was Leadership Emergency Planning Adequate? How has the Pandemic Reshaped Organizational Emergency Plans?

Abstract: COVID-19 has been recognized as one of the largest, most widespread, and deadliest pandemics in human history that have affected societies and economies worldwide. Mounting an effective response to the crisis has tested the resilience of organizational emergency plans and has demanded that leaders act with imagination, tenacity, and swift and decisive communication. This chapter reviews the effectiveness of emergency plans and looks at key learnings from the experience of operating through the COVID-19 pandemic. An action plan is also proposed to help organizations optimize their future emergency planning.

Keywords: Emergency planning, emergency plan effectiveness, communication, resilience, leadership, global economy

Emergency is a sudden unforeseen situation that calls for immediate action to avoid disaster or an urgent need for assistance or relief. Emergency is also known as a crisis – an event with a low probability of occurrence, unknown impacts, and minimal reaction time or management mechanisms (Wang et al., 2016). Emergency can also become a disaster. The World Health Organization (WHO) (2019) provided examples of a wide range of disasters, such as infectious disease outbreaks, natural hazards, conflicts, unsafe food and water, chemical and radiation incidents, building collapses, transport incidents, lack of water and power supply, air pollution, antimicrobial resistance, the effects of climate change, and other sources of risk. Based on these definitions, a novel Coronavirus Disease (COVID-19) outbreak the world has witnessed and experienced since the beginning of 2020 is an emergency, a crisis, and a disaster. For this reason, these three terms are used interchangeably to refer to the COVID-19 pandemic.

COVID-19: A Global Emergency

On December 31, 2019, WHO noted several cases of COVID-19 in Wuhan, China. On January 30, 2020, the WHO declared Public Health Emergency of International Concern, and shortly after that (on March 11, 2020), declared the global diffusion of COVID-19 a

Jia Wang, Texas A&M University, USA

https://doi.org/10.1515/9783110799101-003

pandemic (Department of Homeland Security Office of Inspector General, 2021). Beginning as a health crisis, COVID-19 rapidly evolved to become an unprecedented economic and social crisis affecting the entire world, causing severe global disruption to economies and livelihoods, especially in the earlier days. Just eight months after declaring it as a global pandemic in 2020, the WHO reported about 62 million confirmed cases and 1.5 million confirmed deaths affecting 220 countries or regions (Margherita & Heikkila, 2021). As of March 2023 (at the time of writing), there have been more than 761 million confirmed cases of COVID-19, including over 6.8 million deaths worldwide, reported to WHO (World Health Organization, 2023).

As the pandemic worsened globally, it quickly became evident that the world was dealing with an unprecedented emergency that many in our lifetime had never dreamed of, let alone dealt with. As a result, healthcare organizations, worldwide, struggled to develop protocols and communicate them across their medical professionals and patients in a timely manner. Even for countries (e.g., the United States) that have well established healthcare facilities and national emergency plans for both natural and man-made disasters, they found themselves inadequately prepared for a crisis of this magnitude and overwhelmed by a myriad of new challenges.

The private sector was not spared; many companies struggled to survive. In addition to profit losses and reduced funding opportunities, business organizations faced value chain disruptions caused by COVID-19. Face-to-face service industries such as restaurants and hotels, were hit especially hard. Meanwhile, micro, small, and medium-sized enterprises as well as women-led organizations were disproportionately affected due to their limited access to finance and digital connectivity, reducing their adaptability to changes (Susanty et al., 2022). The pandemic not only presented a major threat to business continuity, but also tested the effectiveness of organizational emergency plans and the resilience of its workforces. In addition, this extraordinary health and social emergency demanded that leaders act with imagination, tenacity, and swift and decisive communication.

The COVID-19 pandemic is unique compared to many other crises. Unlike a natural disaster or a mass trauma event, no one knew how long this health crisis would last, how the virus spread, or what interventions might quickly and effectively reduce its transmission. After what the world has suffered beyond losses of millions of lives (e.g., full lockdown, social distancing, universal masking, financial hardships, and emerging mental health crisis), COVID-19 is, no doubt, one of the largest, most widespread, and deadliest disasters in human history. Not only did it present the physical threat, but it also brought some of the fundamental societal problems to the forefront, for example, poverty and inequality. As Mr. John F. Gandolfo (the Acting Vice President, Economics & Private Sector Development, and Vice President, Treasury & Syndications of International Finance Corporation) put in, "The crisis has brought home the reality that inclusive approaches must be part and parcel of a strong and effective pandemic response" (International Finance Corporation 2021, 2021, p.11). Informed by Mr. Gandolfo's thinking, organizations must adopt holistic, strategic risk-based approaches to enable effective emergency responses. In addition, they must critically learn from past crisis management experiences and constantly seek innovative ways to deal with new threats.

The COVID-19 pandemic represents a unique opportunity to conduct a reality check for disaster preparedness. This chapter reviews the effectiveness of organizational emergency plans and draws lessons from leadership experiences of operating through the COVID-19 pandemic. The chapter consists of four sections. It begins with an introduction to the concept and common practice of emergency planning as documented in research literature. These general research-based insights inform the analysis of organizations' responses to a specific public emergency (COVID-19), which is presented in the second section. Following that are key lessons learned from leadership experiences of navigating their organizations through the pandemic. The chapter concludes with some recommendations for optimizing organizational emergency planning for the future.

Emergency Planning: Research-based Insights

Emergency management, also referred to as disaster management, is an optimized means to prevent and solve complex problems. More specifically, it involves preparing for potential calamities and responding to them as quickly, strategically, and effectively as possible, often with limited resources. The ultimate goal is to minimize disruptions, restore order, protect lives, and ensure continuous development in times of crisis. Different types of public emergencies require different measures of emergency response depending on the state, degree, and scope of impact. Different social organizations (e.g., schools, hospitals, business organizations) have different emergency management systems and mechanisms under different operational models.

Due to the variety and destructiveness of disasters, emergency management has attracted more and more public interest in recent years (Zhou et al., 2017). In the academic world, an increasing attention has been given to organizational responses to critical situations (natural or man-made) that threaten their business continuity (Margherita & Heikkila, 2021). To this end, a significant amount of research has been conducted on the topic of planning and foresight for emergency preparedness and management. As a result, various approaches have been proposed to assist organizations in their emergency management efforts, such as business continuity planning (Zsidisin et al., 2005), the Decision-Making Trial and Evaluation Laboratory (DEMATEL) method (Zhou et al., 2011). organizational learning (Wang, 2008), and crisis leadership competency building (Dirani et al., 2020).

Process of Emergency Management

Typically, effective emergency management requires following a five-stage cycle: prevention, mitigation, preparedness, response, and recovery. Below I discuss each stage briefly.

Stage 1: Prevention. The best way to address a disaster is by being proactive in stopping or avoiding a disaster, be it imminent, threatened or an actual action. This means identifying potential hazards and devising safeguards to mitigate their impact. At this pre-crisis stage, the focus is developing specific plans and measures into place that can help minimize disaster risk. For example, show employees how to quickly and safely exit the office building in the event of a fire. Emergency planning activities allow the organizations to reduce the loss of life and sustain environmental challenges.

Stage 2: Mitigation. Mitigation aims to minimize the loss of human life that would result from a disaster. At this stage, both structural and nonstructural measures may be taken. A structural measure means changing the physical characteristics of a building or an environment to curb the effects of a disaster. For example, clearing trees away from buildings nearby can ensure that dangerous storms will not knock down the trees, making them crash into the building. Nonstructural measures involve adopting or amending building codes to optimize safety for all future building construction. Mitigation related activities allow organizations to reduce the loss of life and physical assets (e,g., buildings and supplies) that will lessen the overall effect of the disaster on a facility and community as a whole.

Stage 3: Preparedness. Preparedness encompasses the continuous cycle of activities regarding what individuals, organizations, and communities will do in the event of a disaster, such as emergency planning, staff training, exercising, assessment, and remedial actions. Preparedness is about building the personal and team muscle memory that can be quickly and easily activated when emergency strikes. Fire drills, active-shooter drills, and evacuation rehearsals are a few of many examples of the preparedness stage.

Stage 4: Response. Response refers to the actions taken to address whatever challenges the event brings, for example, supply chain interruptions, changes in service delivery, or employee wellbeing. Response happens after the disaster occurs and can be either short term or long term. During the response stage, any ongoing hazards must be removed from the area. In the context of COVID for example, a severely infected patient with difficulty in breathing should receive immediate medical attention or be put on a ventilation machine. The ability to respond quickly will help save lives, protect property, safeguard the environment, and meet basic human needs in the wake of a disaster.

Stage 5: Recovery. Once the main part of the crisis is over, the recovery phase will begin. Recovery focuses on restoring and strengthening critical business functions to stabilize day-to-day services and increase capacity to continue to serve their communities after the disaster. The recovery phase allows organizations to return to a normal service level as soon as possible. However, depending on the damages caused by the disaster, recovery can take a long time, sometimes years or decades. In this sense, recovery requires prioritization, with essential services restored first (e.g., food, clean water, utilities, transportation, and healthcare).

Critical Success Factors in Emergency Management

First proposed by American scholar, Rockart, in 1979 (Rockart, 1979), the concept – Critical Success Factors (CSFs) – was first applied to project management and later extended to many other fields including organizational administration, business operation, and supply chain management. It is argued that to effectively prevent and control public emergencies, CSFs that affect the performance of emergency management must be considered. The CSFs of emergency management were explored in some previous literature. For example, Oloruntoba (2010) identified some key emergency relief chain (ERC) success factors of the Cyclone Larry based on document analyses and semi-structured interviews with emergency managers affiliated with cyclone relief management processes. Zhou et al. (2011) examined the interrelationships of 20 CSFs in emergency management using fuzzy DEMATEL method and identified five CSFs that have the most influence on the effectiveness of emergency management. Han and Deng (2018) constructed a hybrid intelligent model for assessing the CSFs of high-risk emergency systems. More recently, Mao et al. (2019) and Rivera et al., (2020) explored the challenges and risk factors of emergency and disaster risk management. These scholarly works revealed some common CSFs including both structural and nonstructural factors such as improvisation, adaptability, agility, creativity, communication, coordination, leadership, and technology application (Harrald, 2006; Zhou, Huang, & Zhang, 2011; Zhou et al., 2017).

Since the outbreak of the COVID-19 in 2020, more efforts have been made by researchers to identify the critical points and measures for managing this public emergency in various institutional contexts (e.g., business, education, and healthcare) across countries and regions. For example, Song et al. (2022) identified five CSFs that affect the emergency management of COVID-19 in colleges and universities. They are: (1) the training of emergency management professionals; (2) the cultivation of coordinating abilities; (3) the establishment of epidemic prevention and control leadership teams; (4) the development of corresponding responsibility awareness; and (5) the regulation of online public opinions. Researchers suggest that by focusing on the CSFs, it can effectively facilitate organizations to optimize their entire emergency management system. Sharmin et al. (2021) identified three CSFs that had the biggest impact on the performance of concurrent emergence management in the midst of the COVID-19. They are Incremental improvement of proactive measures, resilient supply chain and logistics network, and government leadership and military cooperation. are the most critical factors to concurrent emergency management (CEM).

Pivoting during the Pandemic: Organizational Responses

Because of the breadth and depth of the COVID-19 impact, increasing attention has been given to the ways organizations, public or private, responded to the pandemic related disruptions. To understand how organizations responded to a pandemic event such as COVID, we must first understand the impacts of a pandemic. EY Americas (2020) distinguished pandemic-related disruptions from traditional business disruptions in six dimensions: scale, velocity, duration, workforce shortage, external coordination, and infrastructure availability. First, in terms of scale, unlike business disruptions that are localized with limited impacts, pandemic-related disruptions are systemic, impacting everyone including workforce, customers, suppliers, and competitors. Second, in terms of velocity, unlike business disruptions that are typically contained and isolated quickly once the root cause of failure is identified, pandemic-related disruptions spread rapidly as a market contagion across a geography or even globally with severe cascading impacts. Third, timewise, pandemic-related disruptions last much longer (e.g., months) than business disruptions (e.g., a week). Fourth, business disruptions may result in temporary workforce shortage or repositioning of workforce; however, pandemic-related disruptions may result in significant shortage of workforce. Fifth, compared to business disruptions, pandemic-related disruptions require higher degree of coordination with public, government, law enforcement and health officials, and often more than one regional jurisdiction. Finally, as far as infrastructure is concerned, unlike business disruptions that require reliance on the availability of public infrastructure (e.g., power, internet) to complete primary business strategies, pandemic-related disruptions may constrain or restrict the availability of public infrastructure as scale and severity of event increases, especially when other organizations are influenced by the same issue.

With these differences in mind, let us examine the impacts of the COVID-19 pandemic on organizations. On the business side of management, the pandemic resulted in unprecedented challenges such as global supply chain breakdown, change of service delivery, and business process redesign. On the human side, social distancing and lockdown mandates starting in March 2020 forced leaders to abandon the traditional in-person practices and adopt digital platforms. As the COVID virus continued to spread quickly and widely, organizations across the world closely monitored the situation by taking measured approaches such as reducing output of facilities, suspending operations in affected regions, restricting business travels, and issuing work-from-home policies. These sudden drastic changes, necessary to safeguard workforce health and ensure business continuity, caused unintended consequences such as The Great Resignation, Zoom Fatigue, and the Quiet Quitting (Hirsch, 2021; Roberson, 2021). Taken together, COVID-19 related challenges exacerbated existing issues such as work-life imbalance, employee burnout, mental health crisis, health inequity, and injustice/bullying in the workplace (Roberson, 2021).

It is in this highly complex environment that organizations had to find ways to survive. It is not exaggerating to say that just about every organization and industry was blown off course by COVID. To get back on course, they had to pivot – standing their ground and shifting their positioning at the same time. Of all the terms and expressions that have been used in relation to the pandemic, such as 'flatten the curve,' 'second wave,' and 'social distancing,' none have come close to define the massive social change of this special period of human history like the word 'pivot' – arguably the defining word of the pandemic and the need for change it has forced upon organizations (McGinn, 2021). The word 'pivot' has been used to describe everything from financial markets adjusting to the pandemic, people rethinking their careers, to small business owners struggling to find ways to pay the bills, and online students battling loneliness or depression. For better or worse, like it or not, we are now living in the age of pivot and this trend will stay long after the pandemic, shaping our way of working and living. Now let's look at how organizations in different sectors forced the pivot in times of crisis.

Pivoting in Healthcare

Healthcare facilities are pivotal in responding to emergencies such as the COVID-19. To be effective, they must use all of their emergency preparedness tools, including emergency plans, policies, and procedures at hand. As the events of the COVID-19 pandemic began to unravel, many healthcare facilities found themselves dealing with things they had never seen before, such as mass fatalities and significant patient surges. Many rural or critical access facilities found that they were not able to just call the local receiving hospital that they normally use to transfer patients; instead, they had to call facilities that were hours away – or even across state borders – in order to secure placement for these critically ill patients. Some facilities even found themselves caring for critical patients without the proper resources or supplies needed to do so (Baker, 2021). These unprecedented challenges, compounded by critical staffing shortages, supply chain interruptions, and worldwide PPE shortages, forced healthcare organizations to rely on state and federal partners to help bridge the gaps, and find innovative solutions, such as the use of travel nurses.

Pivoting in Business Industries

One effort that is worth mentioning is Margherita and Heikkila's (2021) study of the strategies adopted by the 50 world-leading companies to ensure business continuity during the COVID-19 crisis (through business process changes) and to create new value beyond the crisis (through business model innovation). Through content analysis of webpages and publicly available social network posts of these companies, the authors identified a total of 77 organizational response actions in five management areas: (a) business operations and value system; (b) customer experience and support;

(c) workforce and human capital; (d) leadership and change management; and (e) community and social engagement. To the best of my knowledge, this research is one of the most extended efforts towards building an evidence-based inventory of real actions undertaken by large companies to deal with a global emergency. For this reason, I will elaborate on Margherita and Heikkila's findings in each of the five areas.

Operations and value system. Of the 50 companies included in Margherita and Heikkila's study (2021), most examined the overall impact of the COVID crisis on their business operations using advanced analytics and business intelligence systems. Many companies also focused on logistic flows to ensure both inflows of business-critical resources and processes as well as outflows of products and services to customers. In this regard, the authors identified Amazon as a good example that re-engineered more than 150 processes to enhance product supply chain and reduce risks. Furthermore, actions that would ensure the continuity of manufacturing processes were also taken by these large companies to meet new market/community needs for fighting against the pandemic. For example, General Motors got involved in face mask production and forged partnerships to provide pulmonary ventilators.

Customer experience and support. Margherita and Heikkila (2021) identified a variety of actions taken by the 50 leading world companies to enhance customer experience. Companies, like Walmart, adopted preventative measures across all customer touchpoints, such as limiting access to stores, setting sanitation stations, and implementing masking policy. Many companies also developed new training for customer teams and innovated some forms of communications with customers (e.g., AT&T). Companies such as Audi and Volkswagen even temporarily modified their well-known logos to communicate the importance of practicing social distancing.

Workforce and human capital. As revealed by Margherita and Heikkila (2021), actions taken by the 50 leading companies in this area aimed to safeguard the welfare of employees and reduce the negative impact of the COVID-19 outbreak. First, infection prevention strategies were developed to ensure the safety of the workplaces, for example, creating procedures for workplace hygiene and sanitization, redesigning office layout to allow for social distancing, and creating an online portal to communicate COVID-19 information. Second, new work rules and expectations were defined to help employees cope with "infodemic" –an overload of information, both online and offline) (Margherita & Heikkila, 2021, p. 689). Third, health related policies for leave and return to work were defined to manage employees who were exposed to or infected by COVID-19. Companies such as Costco activated premium pay and paid time off for higher-risk employees and provided protective masks and symptom screening for all employees.

Leadership and change management. According to Margherita and Heikkila (2021), the actions taken by the 50 leading companies in response to the COVID-19 emergency include defining a response plan, designating a crisis management team, forming an emergency coordination task force, and assessing the resource preparedness of the organization. Verizon Communication was a good example that senior crisis leadership and responses teams were promptly created to address the challenges caused by the pandemic. In addition to managing the current emergency, some leaders went one step further to prepare their company for the future. Margherita and Heikkila (2021) identified Honda Motors as an exemplary case where leadership injected more energy into their marketing and social media presence to maintain the trust of their customers and the larger community.

Pivoting in Education

Educational institutions are prone to become the main 'battlefield' of the pandemic prevention and control because of their dense population, concentrated activities, and the mobility of students and teachers. As any other type of organizations, schools, colleges and universities were forced to pivot; "suspension" and "online teaching" were the most widely adopted emergency management approaches because they not only helped curb the spread of COVID-19 and protect human lives, but it also allowed for continued schooling to students at all levels (Song et al., 2022).

To sum up, whether in the public or the private sector, and regardless of the size and type of services provided, all organizations had to learn how to manage the COVID-19 crisis through trials and errors, and constant pivoting. Some managed to survive by navigating the turbulence such as those showcased in this section; some, or many failed painfully, especially those that are small, family owned, or women owned. In the subsequent section, I discuss key lessons that the pandemic taught us in the past three years.

Looking Back: COVID-related Lessons Learned

COVID has arguably caused the greatest disruption to society since World War II. In just a few short weeks, it forced massive change to how organizations function – changes that might have taken years otherwise. It also changed everyone's personal priorities. In fact, our world has changed forever and we are now living in the new normal. Looking back, the conventional approaches to emergency planning fell short during the COVID-19 pandemic. This is largely because most organizations did not have an emergency plan for a viral infection of this magnitude, leaving them to scramble and develop contingency plans as the crisis events unfolded. COVID has taught the world many lessons; one of the most sobering ones is that disaster can befall any organization, community, or a country, at any time. It is important for organizations to take time and critically reflect on what they have learned from disastrous events because doing so helps leaders determine if existing measures have worked; if not, what needs to be modified and what else needs to be put in place to withstand future disasters and crises. This practice of reflection in and on action will enhance organizational resilience towards future disasters whose impacts on business operations are yet insufficiently understood. In this line of thinking, I offer four COVID-related lessons for learning and reflection.

Lesson 1: The Need for Robust Planning

Regardless of our profession, organization, sector, or geographic location, we will always have to navigate unforeseen circumstances. However, in reality, very rarely do we consider crafting a crisis management plan that takes into account all forms of calamity. As a result, we are often inadequately prepared for the scale and scope of crisis events. The COVID-19 pandemic has taught all of us, worldwide, the necessity of incorporating comprehensive, integrated emergency management plans and having various checkpoints in place. In addition, COVID has made us hyper aware of the need for a mechanism to forge our way through and beyond immediate barriers. To be able to respond to any crisis swiftly and effectively, it is a critical imperative to invest sufficient time in resilience planning and more importantly, communicating the plan clearly and frequently to all members of the organization so that each person knows whom to contact when a crisis situation occurs and quick decisions are in urgent need. As discussed earlier in this chapter, a holistic crisis management approach contains a list of actions that can be taken before, during, and after a catastrophic event that preserve lives, safeguard property, and minimize the loss of resources essential to the organization's recovery. In this sense, emergency planning should be an integral part of the organizational business strategy, the core activity during the prevention stage.

Lesson 2: The Power of Real-time Learning

During the pandemic, organizations are faced with many unfamiliar challenges that require them to constantly collect new information, make informed decisions, and then take calculated actions (pivot). The ability to do so requires being open to learn what is presented ahead, and meanwhile being willing to unlearn what is considered as the conventional or common practices. Think about the challenges facing the hospitals and EMS services – they had to quickly adapt to various new emergencies (e.g., increasing number of COVID patients, critical shortage of medical supplies, doctors and nurses, etc.) and found different ways of delivering care and treatment to patients. Looking back, healthcare leaders need to ask and determine if the five phases of emergency management (Baker, 2021) were properly in place in their facilities to deal with an event of COVID-19 magnitude. What we have learned from the past three years shows that not many facilities around the world, including developed countries such as the United States, had planned for a pandemic of this nature or duration. How we can transfer the real-time learning into concrete strategies – from procuring PPE to having solid interorganizational and cross-facility care team communication systems – will be foundational for future large-scale disaster preparedness. Going forward, cultivating the learning capacity at both the individual and organizational level will be a key to successful management of future crises.

Lesson 3: The Value of Digital Technologies (DT)

The COVID-19 pandemic has challenged organizations to adapt and redesign their processes and management practices in response to the rising emergency. Most organizational response strategies and actions have leveraged the potential of digital technologies (DT). Research shows that DT supported organizational responses to unexpected disruptions. To promote the further application of DT for emergency management, Margherita and Heikkila (2021) studied 50 world-leading corporations that confirmed the value of DT to address challenges caused by the global COVID crisis. For educational institutions, technology proved to be extremely valuable because it allowed schools to suspend traditional in-person classes (on campus) without interfering with student learning (online) (Zhang et al., 2020).

Lesson 4: The Test of Organizational Leadership

The pandemic was the ultimate test for leadership. Some organizations managed to weather the storms, and some failed. How much did leadership contribute to these outcomes? The matter of fact is: what successful leaders did before COVID enabled their organizations to bring the gap between where they were and where COVID demanded them to be. Here are some examples of the simple tasks performed by effective leaders before the pandemic: (a) creating a shared purpose within their organization; (b) establishing effective communication and decision-making systems; (c) inspiring and empowering employees in productive teamwork; (d) seeking innovative approaches for improvement; and (e) embracing change, transformation, and agility as part of daily thinking and working. It is these universal leadership qualities and attributes that ensured the organization' success before COVID, survival during COVID, and continued success post-COVID.

Going forward: Optimizing Emergency Planning

COVID-19 has sent us a clear message: the traditional resilience plans that organizations have put in place are not sufficient to address pandemic-related disruptions, because they rarely focus on pandemic management capabilities. This is understandable since pandemics are lower-probability events compared to other natural or human-made disasters. When was the last time that the WHO declared a pandemic? It was in 2009 when H1N1 influenza (swine flu) caused an estimated 284,400 deaths worldwide. While pandemic events may be experienced once in our lifetime, their impact can be long-lasting and devastating. For this reason, organizations can no longer ignore the low-frequency but high-impact threats. Going forward, they must expand beyond traditional emergency planning strategies by incorporating pandemic planning into existing resilience management activities. Doing so will enable them to provide a comprehensive response and continuity for their most critical products and services. In addition, having robust emergency plans will also facilitate crisis management efforts between the organizations and authorities at the local, state, and national levels.

As the world looks toward the post-pandemic recovery, there is a need to balance short-term relief with long-term strategy. In other words, while building back quickly, organizations must also do so in a socially and environmentally sustainable manner to ensure a resilient and inclusive recovery (International Finance Corporation, 2021). Furthermore, given the widespread implications of the COVID crisis, there is a serious need for a more customized approach to address sector-specific needs and those of vulnerable populations. In the post-pandemic era, organizations are shifting their goal from surviving to thriving. To support a faster recovery and new value creation, it is essential for organizational leaders to continue seeking innovative ways to optimize their emergency planning for the future. Based on the lessons offered above and findings from COVID research, this section proposes a few key considerations for development of robust organizational emergency plans.

Build Organizational Resilience

Organizational resilience is an organization's ability to manage uncertainty emerging from disastrous events such as natural hazards and/or man-made crises (Brown et al., 2017; Lee et al., 2013). This concept suggests that organizations consider disasters as learning opportunities (Prayag et al., 2018). Researchers have distinguished between the three types of organizations when measured by the extent of organizational resilience in the context of disaster management. According to Sawalha (2015), Type 1 organizations do the very minimum to prepare for potential disasters. Type 2 organizations go beyond the 'bare minimum' by adopting good practices in disaster prevention and mitigation, subject to budget and resource availability. Type 3 organizations take a proactive and integrated approach to disaster management by embracing best practices and engaging in continuous learning for disaster preparedness and recovery.

For example, Hall et al. (2017) found that Type 1 organizations dominate the tourism sector for at least two reasons. First, the majority of tourism businesses are small to medium sized entities with limited resources. Given the characteristics of infrequent occurrences and unpredictability of disastrous events, crisis management is typically not a key consideration when it comes to allocating resources. Second, many tourism organizations have been stuck with traditional business models. Going forward, it is important for organizational leaders to make a concerted effort to evaluate and determine which type their organization is, and more importantly, what actions to take to advance their organization into Type 3.

Enhance Emergency Management Capability

While the impact of the pandemic has been devastating, there is a silver lining – that is, it has heightened our sense of crisis/risk management in all aspects of our lives, personally and professionally. Going forward, crisis planning, and risk migration should become core skills leaders aim to develop for both their organization and people. Be open to review and modify the organizational emergency plan by engaging in open conversations with various stakeholders and learn from others' best practices. Provide periodic crisis management training to all organizational members so that they can learn about different types of crises (natural and man-made) and more importantly, appropriate strategies for mitigating the risks. Organize regular dialogue sessions (in person and virtual) to encourage members of the organization and the community to share how they are learning, healing, and growing before, during, and after the crisis. With more knowledge and skills in crisis management, we stand a better chance of weathering a very tough storm.

Organizations' struggle to lead the pandemic response efforts, especially at the early stage, was attributed partially by lack of strategic guidance, which caused confusion about roles and responsibilities in times of emergencies. To expand organizational capability to better respond to future emergencies, there is also a need to formally document the policies and procedures for making informed and consistent resource allocation decisions for critical life saving supplies and equipment. Meanwhile, there is a need to create a guidebook that defines the pandemic response roles and responsibilities of personnel at different levels of the organization.

Promote Organizational Learning

The ability to pivot and shift the emergency management approach from being reactive to preventative, and ultimately proactive, are largely dependent upon an organization's capacity to learn. The Type 3 organizations mentioned above rely on comprehensive, integrated disaster management plans and procedures and employ past disaster experiences for organizational learning and forward business/disaster planning. The concept of learning was widely discussed in crisis management literature, but it is often considered as the last action step and at the individual level. Wang (2008) argued for the importance of incorporating organizational learning as a tool before, during, and after a crisis so that a structured knowledge management system can be established to allow the organizations to draw past crisis experiences to inform their planning for future disasters. Poor organizational learning may lead to business extinction whilst 'good practices' can aid organizations in developing the necessary levels of resilience to withstand future disasters (Bhaskara & Filimonau, 2021).

Upskill Crisis Leaders

The COVID-19 pandemic has put organizational leadership under serious test. While members of organizations turned to their leaders for guidance, leaders themselves were confronted with challenges that might be beyond their current capability. Dirani et al. (2020) differentiated leadership best practices in normal times versus times of crisis. In normal times, leaders model the way, inspire a shared vision, challenge the process, enable others to act, and encourage the heart. In times of crisis, leaders are required to play very different roles, including sensemaking, enabling technology, safeguarding emotional stability and employee well-being, ensuring innovative communication, and maintaining financial health of the organization. These roles may require leaders to learn, unlearn, and relearn what they might or might not know. Going forward, leadership development programs should consider these emerging competencies leaders need to develop to meet the employee expectations of them as crisis leaders. In addition, researchers called for adaptive leadership as a response to uncertainty and ambiguity caused by major crises such as COVID. For example, Dunn (202) noted that the COVID-19 pandemic significantly increased the complexity of the environment where leaders have to face in leading their organizations. These complex environments led to considerable ambiguity around what solutions might be effective. Added to this, complexity can mean challenges may not be able to be solved with the knowledge and skills that currently exist within an organization. Complex environments require adaptive approaches as a response to uncertainty. By showing how the military cultivates adaptive practices to respond to a complex environment, Dunn (2020) proposed adaptive leadership as one possible approach organizational leaders could consider during times of significant change.

Strengthen Communication Mechanisms

At the core of crisis planning is an effective communication system. Start by establishing communication expectations by considering a number of questions. For example, what is the preferred means of communication in case of an emergency? How much information can be shared in an email? What is the proper frequency of communications based on the nature of the crisis? Who is expected to address the crisis? The list of questions can go on and on. The bottom line: every member of the organization should be prepared to answer these questions. In addition, to enhance communication requires the development of solid, trusted public and private partnerships. For example, creating partnerships among first responders, businesses and community stakeholders can ensure that the right people respond to a crisis. Collaboration across sectors also helps supply emergency management teams with the right tools they need to manage a disaster. Finally, using social media can also strengthen communication. As the world witnessed during COVID-19, government agencies and organizations across countries actively utilized social media outlets to quickly distribute information to a large number of people. However, given the vulnerability of social media to cyberattacks and outages, extra efforts must be made to ensure emergency management communication systems are secure and reliable.

Promote Digital Technology Application

During the pandemic, leaders were forced to make quick decisions about how to prevent operational interruptions and risks of infection of their workforce caused by the virus. Organizations that succeeded in these areas are those that implemented agile business processes (i.e., redesigning or adapting existing activities), utilized various digital technologies to enable different modes of working (virtual and hybrid), advanced data gathering and sense-making, and information-rich communication. When used properly and strategically, technological tools enable organizational leaders to make real-time assessment of the crisis impact and take evidence-based actions to support crisis leadership and business recovery. The good news is: there are reference tools available for organizations' consideration. For example, Margherita et al. (2021) proposed an integrative framework describing how DT can support organizational responsiveness to emergencies such as COVID-19. Derived from their analysis of 40 world-leading corporations, this model provided business leaders, managers, and HR professionals with a checklist useful to define digital-enhanced organizational emergency plans for ensuring continuing management of business operations, human resources, and customer services in crisis times.

Apply CSFs in Emergency Management

The most effective way to minimize the negative impacts of a crisis on an institution is to improve the pertinence of emergency management. Arguably the most important variables or activities that make an organization successful (Meibodi & Monavvarian, 2010), CSFs have been extensively applied in management practices, however, not so much in emergency management. For alleviating human suffering and improving the operational effectiveness of emergency management, it is essential to determine the CSFs that have the highest impact on the whole system (Sharmin et al., 2021). In the case of COVID-19, it is important for organizations to reflect on and document the CSFs at different stages – before, during, and after the pandemic. Doing so will help decision-makers pinpoint areas that are crucial to enhance EM performance (Zhou et al., 2011). For educational institutions, researchers recommend that organizational leaders adopt a phased control approach to focus on the different key points of emergency management in order to optimize the entire emergency management system (Song et al., 2022). Specifically, Song et al. (2022) recommended some actions to be taken prior to the crisis, such as establishing a sound emergency management operation mechanism and elevating leaders' awareness of their roles and responsibilities as crisis leaders. During the process of pandemic prevention and control, actions may include providing the emergency management professionals with specific training related to the characteristics of the crisis events. Meanwhile, it is essential to set up a special emergency management leadership team to monitor the emergency information flows and coordinate efforts with multiple agencies. The authors argued that, while the influencing factors after the crisis are often not identified as CSFs, they should be integrated into the overall emergency management system. Song et al. (2022) further noted that given that the CSFs may change in different fields and at different social stages, organizations then need to continuously coordinate and update the CSFs so that their emergency planning will stay current and flexibility to allow them to better cope with new challenges in the future.

Integrate SHRD in Crisis Management

Last but not the least, organizational leaders should consider adopting the strategic human resource management (SHRD) approach to crisis management. Crisis management requires the development of organization-specific capabilities and learning and performance interventions that enable stakeholders to identify, respond to, and recover from crisis events (Hutchins & Wang, 2008). Successful implementation of crisis management plans requires high-level strategic integration between organizational structure, culture, and strategy. SHRD can play a critical role in helping organizations achieve this goal because SHRD focuses on integrating HRD activities with organizational goals and values to develop core capabilities that enhance organizational competitive advantage (Garavan, 1991; 2007). Specifically, SHRD can contribute to crisis management in two areas: (a) providing organizations with operational capabilities to manage crises; and (b) inducing behaviors and practices that are likely to improve organizational responses to future crises (Wang et al., 2009). Therefore, SHRD offers a valuable set of interventions that facilitate both collective and individual learning – a key element to optimal emergency planning and management.

Conclusion

The COVID-19 pandemic response stretched the concept of modern emergency management in ways it had never been stretched before. As we continue to recover from the COVID-19 pandemic related disruptions, many of our current processes and practices for emergency management will need to be reexamined and modified. The next crisis will not necessarily be the same as the one we have just experienced, which makes it difficult to develop strategies to tackle the unknown. Nevertheless, past events have taught us that it is valuable to identify the failures in a particular crisis situation, derive important lessons, and make after-action plans. Doing so will help organizations better project and better prepare for the next challenge. With this in mind, I conclude the chapter with a call to action for organizational leaders: it is time to make serious investments in developing and improving pandemic-specific policies, procedures, infrastructures, and capabilities.

References

Baker, J. (2021, March 5). COVID-19 and the 5 phases of emergency management. https://www.pulsara.com/blog/COVID-19-and-the-5-phases-of-emergency-management

Bhaskara, G. I., & Filimonau, V. (2021). The COVID-19 pandemic and organizational learning for disaster planning and management: A perspective of tourism businesses from a destination prone to consecutive disasters. *Journal of Hospitality and Tourism Management, 46*, 364–375. https://doi.org/10.1016/j.jhtm.2021.01.011

Brown, N. A., Rovins, J. E., Feldmann-Jensen, S., Orchiston, C., & Johnston, D. (2017).Exploring disaster resilience within the hotel sector: A systematic review of literature. *International Journal of Disaster Risk Reduction, 22*, 362–370.

Delfino, G. F., & van der Kolk, B. (2021). Remote working, management control changes and Employee responses during the COVID-19 Crisis. *Accounting, Auditing & Accountability Journal, 34*(6). https://doi.org/10.1108/aaaj-06-2020-4657

Department of Homeland Security Office of Inspector General (2021, September 21). Lessons from FEMA's initial responses to COVID-19. https://www.oig.dhs.gov/sites/default/files/assets/2021-09/OIG-21-64-Sep21.pdf

Dirani, K. M., Abadi, M., Alizadeh, A., Barhate, B., Garza, R. C., Gunasekara, N., Ibrahim, G., & Majzun, Z. (2020). Leadership competencies and the essential role of Human Resource Development in times of crisis: A response to COVID-19 pandemic. *Human Resource Development International, 23*(4), 380–394. https://doi.org/10.1080/13678868.2020.1780078

Dunn, R. (2020). Adaptive Leadership: Leading Through Complexity. *International Studies in Educational Administration (ISEA), 48*(1), 31–38.

EY Americas (2020, March 19). COVID-19 and pandemic planning: How companies should respond. https://www.ey.com/en_us/COVID-19/COVID-19-and-pandemic-planning–how-companies-should-respond#chapter-1964280102

Garavan, T. N. (1991). Strategic human resource development. *Journal of European Industrial Training, 15*(1), 17–30.

Garavan, T. N. (2007). A strategic perspective on human resource development. *Advances in Developing Human Resources, 9*, 11–30.

Hall, C. M., Prayag, G., & Amore, A. (2017). *Tourism and resilience: Individual, organizational and destination perspectives*, 5. Channel View Publications.

Han, Y., & Deng, Y. (2018). A hybrid intelligent model for assessment of critical success factors in a high-risk emergency system. *Journal of Ambient Intelligence and Humanized Computing, 9*(6), 1933–1953. https://doi.org/10.1007/s12652-018-0882-4

Harrald, J. R. (2006). Agility and discipline: Critical success factors for disaster response. *The Annals of the American Academy of Political and Social Science, 604*(1), 256–272. https://doi.org/10.1177/0002716205285404

Herbane, B. (2010). The evolution of business continuity management: A historical review of practices and drivers. *Business History, 542*(6), 978–1002.

Hirsch, P. B. (2021). The Great Discontent. *Journal of Business Strategy, 42*(6), 439–442. https://doi.org/10.1108/jbs-08-2021-0141

Hutchins, H. M., & Wang, J. (2008). Organizational Crisis Management and Human Resource Development: A Review of the Literature and Implications to HRD Research and Practice. *Advances in Developing Human Resources, 10*(3), 310–330. https://doi.org/10.1177/1523422308316183

International Finance Corporation (2021). How firms are responding and adapting during COVID-19 and recovery: Opportunities for accelerated inclusion in emerging markets. https://www.ifc.org/wps/wcm/connect/08f1c445-87af-4868-a77c-29dee3e1ac4e/Report_How_Firms_Are_Responding_And_Adapting_During_COVID-19_And_Recovery_March21-web.pdf?MOD=AJPERES&CVID=nwjXW4G

Lee, A. V., Vargo, J., & Seville, E. (2013). Developing a tool to measure and Compare Organizations' resilience. *Natural Hazards Review, 14*(1), 29–41.

Mao, W., Wang, W., Luo, D., & Sun, H. (2019). Analyzing interactions between risk factors for ice disaster in Ning-Meng reach of Yellow River based on grey rough DEMATEL method. *Natural Hazards, 97*(3), 1025–1049. https://doi.org/10.1007/s11069-019-03684-3

Margherita, A. & Heikkila, M. (2021). Business continuity in the COVID-19 emergency: A framework of actions undertaken by world-leading companies. *Business Horizons, 64*, 683–695. https://doi.org/10.1016/j.bushor.2021.02.020

Margherita, A., Nasiri M., & Papadopoulos, T. (2021). The application of digital technologies in company responses to COVID-19: An integrative framework. *Technology Analysis & Strategic Management.* https://doi.org/10.1080/09537325.2021.1990255

McGinn, D. (2021, August 29). How 'pivot' became the pandemic buzzword, for better or for worse. The Globe and Mail. https://www.theglobeandmail.com/canada/article-how-pivot-became-the-pandemic-buzzword-for-better-or-for-worse/

Meibodi, L. A., & Monavvarian, A. (2010). Recognizing critical success factors (CSF) to achieve the strategic goals of SAIPA press. *Business Strategy Series, 11*(2), 124–133. https://doi.org/10.1108/17515631011026443

Oloruntoba, R. (2010). An analysis of the Cyclone Larry emergency relief chain: Some key success factors. *International Journal of Production Economics*, 126(1), 85–101. https://doi.org/10.1016/j.ijpe.2009. 10.013

Prayag, G., Chowdhury, M., Spector, S., & Orchiston, C. (2018). Organizational resilience and financial performance, *Annals of Tourism Research, 73*, 193–196. https://doi.org/10.1016/j.annals.2018.06.006.

Rivera, J., Ceesay, A. A., & Sillah, A. (2020). Challenges to disaster risk management in The Gambia: A preliminary investigation of the disaster management system's structure. *Progress in Disaster Science, 6*, 100075. https://doi.org/10.1016/j.pdisas.2020.100075

Robertson, M. B. (2021). Hindsight is 2020: Identifying missed leadership opportunities to reduce employee turnover intention amid the COVID-19 shutdown. *Strategic HR Review, 20*(6), 215–220. https://doi.org/10.1108/shr-09-2021-0045

Rockart, J.F., 1979. Chief executives define their own data needs. *Harvard business review, 57* (2), 81–93.

Sawalha, I. H. S. (2015). Managing adversity: Understanding some dimensions of organizational resilience. *Management Research Review, 38*(4), 346–366.

Sharmin, A., Rohman, M. A., Ahmed, S., & Ali, S. M. (2021). Addressing critical success factors for improving concurrent emergency management: Lessons learned from the COVID-19 pandemic. *Annals of Operations Research*, https://doi.org/10.1007/s10479-021-04447-9

Song, P., Zhao, J., Mubarak, S. M. A., & Taresh, S. M. (2022). Critical success factors for epidemic emergency management in colleges and universities during COVID-19: A study based on DEMATE method. *Safety Science, 145*. doi: 10.1016/j.ssci.2021.105498

Susanty, A., Puspitasari, N. B., Bakhtiar, A., & Prasetya, F. (2022). Assessing the impact of the COVID-19 pandemic on small and medium-sized enterprises performance. *Frontiers in Psychology, 13*, 927628. https://doi.org/10.3389/fpsyg.2022.927628

Van Wart, M., Rahman, S., & Mazumdar, T. (2021). The Dark Side of Resilient Leaders: Vampire Leadership. *Transylvanian Review of Administrative Sciences*, (SI 2021), 144–165. https://doi.org/10.24193/tras.si2021.8

Wang, J. (2008). Developing organizational learning capacity in crisis management. *Advances in Developing Human Resources, 10*(3), 425–445.

Wang, J., Hutchins, H. M., & Garavan, T. N. (2009). Exploring the strategic role of HRD in organizational crisis management. *Human Resource Development Review, 8*(1), 22–53.

Wang, J., Anne, M., & McLean, G. N. (2016). Understanding crisis and crisis management: An Indian perspective. *Human Resource Development International, 19*(3), 192–208. https://doi.org/10.1080/13678868.2015.1116242

World Health Organization. (2019). Health emergency and disaster risk management: Overview. In Health Emergency and Disaster Risk Management Fact Sheets. https://www.who.int/hac/techguidance/preparedness/health-emergency-and-disaster-risk-management-framework-eng

World Health Organization (2023). WHO Coronavirus (COVID-19) Dashboard. https://COVID19.who.int/

Zhang, W., Wang, Y., Yang, L., & Wang, C. (2020). Suspending classes without stopping learning: China's education emergency management policy in the COVID-19 outbreak. *Journal of Risk and Financial Management, 13*(552). https://doi.org/10.3390/jrfm13030055.

Zhou, Q., Huang, W., & Zhang, Y. (2011). Identifying critical success factors in emergency management using a fuzzy DEMATEL method. *Safety Science, 49*(2), 243–252. https://doi.org/10.1016/j.ssci.2010.08.005

Zhou, X., Shi, Y., Deng, X., and Deng, Y. (2017). D-DEMATEL: A new method to identify critical success factors in emergency management. Safety *Science, 91*, 93–104. https://doi.org/10.1016/j.ssci.2016.06.014

Zsidisin, G. A., Melnyk, S. A., & Ragatz, G. L. (2005). An institutional theory perspective of business continuity planning for purchasing and supply management. *International Journal of Production Research, 43*(16), 3401–3420.

Zhou, X., Shi, Y., Deng, X., and Deng, Y. (2017). D-DEMATEL: A new method to identify critical success factors in emergency management. Safety *Science, 91*, 93–104. https://doi.org/10.1016/j.ssci.2016.06.014

Zsidisin, G. A., Melnyk, S. A., & Ragatz, G. L. (2005). An institutional theory perspective of business continuity planning for purchasing and supply management. *International Journal of Production Research, 43*(16), 3401–3420.

David McGuire and Aisling Tuite

Chapter 4
Crisis Leadership in a Post-COVID World: The Need to Embrace an Ethics of Care Approach

Abstract: The COVID-19 pandemic has increased expectations that leaders will act responsibly and demonstrate an ethic of care. Such an approach upholds the value and integrity of all employees and shows a genuine concern for employee welfare. This chapter looks at how leaders can foster workplace environments built upon the pillars of compassion, support and care for others.

Keywords: Ethics of care, care, integrity, welfare, compassion, support, leadership, crisis management, leadership competencies, communication, personal attributes, organizational resilience

Introduction

The COVID-19 pandemic continues to have a significant effect on how and where work is performed. While organizations had discussed the transition to online and hybrid working for several years, the sudden arrival and rapid spread of the virus in spring 2020 forced the acceleration of such plans. With little warning, organizations were plunged into the uncertain world of lockdowns, social restrictions and disrupted supply chains, impacting upon how, where and when business could be transacted (McLean et al., 2021; Hartwell & Devinney 2021). Resilience strategies that had long been formulated, were dusted off and implemented with haste. Employees responded dutifully to the crisis, converting spare bedrooms into home offices and balancing the demands of home schooling and care giving, with the challenge of embracing new virtual working skills and work routines.

The speed and scale of the COVID-19 pandemic placed a heavy burden on leadership teams to make rapid and significant adjustments to organizational systems and practices. Faced with high levels of complexity and ambiguity, Collings et al. (2021) argues that leaders needed to reconcile a set of competing and conflicting priorities through an emergent strategy approach that was underpinned by flexible and adaptive

David McGuire, Edinburgh Napier University, Scotland
Aisling Tuite, South East Technological University, Ireland

https://doi.org/10.1515/9783110799101-004

decision-making. Yet, the pandemic also brought about a stronger realization of the importance of involving stakeholder groups and networks beyond the c-suite in framing an effective response. Maak et al. (2021) assert that the crisis response to the pandemic was characterized by an exceptionally high level of interdependence amongst organizational stakeholders to ensure business continuity and to minimize damage to individual well-being.

This chapter reflects upon the notion of leadership in a post-COVID society, with a particular emphasis on crisis leadership and how it has re-shaped notions of care. Hillyard (2000, p.9) advises that it is critical to conduct post-reflection analysis of a crisis with the intention of "learning together from the event in order to prevent, lessen the severity of, or improve upon the responses to future crises." Arguably, it is not unusual for crisis events to bring about a change in the direction of leadership theory and practice. Grant (2019) argues that the 2009–2009 global financial crisis (GFC) triggered a renewed interest in corporate social responsibility, ethics and sustainability. Indeed, Keeble-Ramsay and Armitage (2015) argue that post-GFC, there was a realization that people-focused interventions had often been circumvented by managerialistic, financialist interventions lacking a focus on people's needs. Yet, the scale, duration and global reach of the COVID-19 pandemic have ensured that the impact of the crisis on leadership approaches is substantial and sustained. Therefore, it is appropriate to reflect upon the experiences of the COVID-19 pandemic and identify improvements in leadership practices and crisis response. The chapter commences with a discussion on how the pandemic has altered the practice of leadership. It then examines crisis leadership approaches, focusing on the dawning realization of the need to embed care and compassion within crisis leadership models. It then considers why an ethic of care is a critical component of crisis leadership. Finally, the chapter concludes by highlighting some of the leadership implications from embracing an ethic of care.

How the COVID-19 Pandemic has altered the practice of leadership

Guiding an effective response to the pandemic became the primary focus of organizational leaders in the early months of 2020. Little in the existing toolkit of senior leaders prepared them for the highly stressful and uncertain conditions that required them to make radical changes to business operations arising from government imposed lockdowns. Often relying on their own judgment and wisdom as they sought to lead organizations, D'Auria and DeSmet (2020) found that leaders set out mobilizing their organizations by setting clear objectives and empowering teams to find and implement solutions. Likewise, Hope Hailey (2020) argued that the initial response to the pandemic was informed by two key objectives: first, the need to keep their businesses and organizations functioning and second, the need to address where their responsibilities lay – in relation to employees, customers, suppliers, communities, government and society as a whole.

It is important to consider why the COVID-19 pandemic was categorically different to other crises that organizations have previously faced. D'Auria and DeSmet (2020: 19) classify the pandemic as an emerging "landscape scale" crisis, comprising of "a sequence of events of enormous scale and overwhelming speed, resulting in a high degree of uncertainty that gives rise to disorientation, a feeling of lost control and strong emotional disturbance." Leonard and Howitt (2007) identify three reasons why emergent crises are difficult to address. First, emerging problems are difficult to recognise and classify. While the first cases of COVID-19 were identified in China in late December 2019, the speed of human-to-human transmission meant that the first cases in the US were detected on 13th January 2020 (CDC 2020) and the first cases in the UK were diagnosed on 31st January 2020 (Ball et al. 2020). The failure to quickly contain the initial outbreak resulted in wide-ranging health, economic and social effects globally (OECD 2020). In a few short weeks, a local outbreak became a global pandemic, with little advance warning being given to organizational decision-makers of the damaging effects this would have on their businesses. Second, Leonard and Howitt argue that emerging crises may be hard to contain if standard responses don't work or if the scale of the response is too small or too late. It was often difficult for business leaders to gauge the longevity and severity of the crisis, sometimes resulting in delay and paralysis of action. In the words of Carroll (2021: 319): "Perilous uncertainty has characterized the route, degree, and outcomes of the pandemic and this has presented a brutal cycle of business, consumer, and employee insecurity, and financial conditions being constricted. These conditions have posed significant challenges for analyzing and understanding its economic effects." Third, Leonard and Hewitt argue that emerging crises may be difficult to address as initial crisis responders may be heavily invested in a particular approach and may resent interference from external parties to the crisis. Fukuyama (2020) points to the inaction of national leaders in China, US, UK and Brazil who downplayed the dangers of the pandemic for fear of damaging their economies and in the hope that public health warnings had been overstated. As we emerge from the pandemic, it is clear from the successful approach taken by some nations that early precautionary and preventative measures are considered critical to showing decisive leadership and building confidence (McGuire et al. 2020; Wilson 2020).

The experience of the COVID-19 pandemic has left many employees tired, exhausted and overwhelmed (Hwang et al. 2020). McKinsey (2021) report that almost half of all US employees (49%) report being at least somewhat burned out and they reckon that this is an under-representation of the true figure. The experience of the pandemic and the existential threat to life has resulted in some employees looking to organizations to find greater purpose and meaning in their work (Hite & McDonald, 2020). Khan and McArthur (2021) argue that the post-pandemic environment brings a stronger awareness of the fragility of global systems and the need for appropriate leadership styles that help employees recover from the emotional toll of the pandemic. Indeed, a specially commissioned CIPD report and written by Hope Hailey (2020) highlighted the need for businesses to engage responsibly and for leaders to act with compassion, fairness and inclusion. Maak et al. (2021: 67) state, "it is the role of leaders to instill in people a sense of hope for "future goodness" and dignity, to be guardians of radical hope and see into the future."

With Amis and Janz (2020) calling for organizations post-pandemic to become more purpose-led and imbued with greater meaning for those who engage with them, the need for a change of direction in leadership theory becomes apparent. Maak et al. (2021) argue that it is time to move beyond industrial, rational, dyadic and technocratic notions of leadership towards responsible, adaptive, compassionate and communitarian-based leadership that seeks to develop strong relational bonds with employees and wider stakeholder groups. Emerging research has highlighted that supportive leadership enhances levels of hope and resilience amongst employees (Cooke et al., 2019; Siami et al., 2022), highlighting the need for leaders to build positive physical and social work environments, where employees feel engaged and valued.

A Pre-and-Post Pandemic Review of Crisis Management Approaches

Dealing effectively with a crisis is a critical test of the skills, experience and judgment of a leader. Wang et al. (2009, p. 25) define crisis events as "low probability, high-impact situations that are unexpected, unfamiliar and precipitated by people, organizational structures, technology or natural disasters". Crisis events pose three types of threat: (a) public safety (b) financial loss and (c) reputation loss, with the success of a leader being evaluated on their effectiveness in dealing with these threats. Sadiq et al. (2021, p. 66) assert that in crisis situations, leadership requires "rapid comprehension of risk, selection and processing information, timely search and exchange of information, the capacity to anticipate potential risk and the ability to make timely decisions." To prepare leaders to deal with crises, researchers have detailed the competencies that leaders should demonstrate when dealing with unpredictable and unclear contexts. It is useful to categorize and examine these competencies pre-pandemic (pre-2020 – see Table 4.1) and post-pandemic (post-2020 – see Table 4.2) to ascertain whether there has been any meaningful shift in the crisis competencies required from leaders arising from the COVID-19 pandemic.

Crisis Leadership Competencies (Pre-COVID)

Table 4.1 presents eight lists of crisis leadership competencies compiled by academics prior to the arrival of the COVID-19 pandemic. In analyzing the lists, there are four important features common to the leadership approaches being advocated to dealing with crises pre-pandemic.

1. *Organization and Resource Management Competencies*
Identifying that an organization is facing a crisis and formulating a response is a core task of leaders (D'Auria & DeSmet, 2020). In recognising the crisis and its possible impact, leaders need to seek out relevant information from reliable sources about the crisis, its likely course and possible impact (Ahern & Loh, 2021). Anticipating the scale of a crisis allows leaders to develop a plan and align systems and resources to respond effectively. Wooten and James (2008) argue that leaders have a direct responsibility for organizing the work environment through identifying the critical activities needed; ensuring employees have the competencies needed to complete these activities and possessing an understanding of the context for executing the crisis strategy. They assert that leaders are expected to anticipate and avert crises where possible, but also to contain the extent of a crisis when it occurs.

2. *Communication Competencies*
In crisis situations, leaders must demonstrate an ability to communicate clear consistent messages in an empathetic manner. A leader's communicative style in crisis situations must be confident, persuasive and empathetic as this will shape an individual's perception of the crisis and their assessment of the leader's ability to handle it (McGuire et al., 2020). It is important that leaders communicate a hopeful but realistic vision of the future in times of crisis. Where leaders adopt an open empathetic style, this has been shown to result in high levels of trust and social solidarity (Reynolds & Quinn, 2008). Indeed, through effective crisis communication, Bligh and Kohles (2005) assert that leaders have the opportunity to reframe and change existing perceptions, offer alternative solutions and infuse a new positive spirit. Haslam et al. (2021) argue that one of the key roles of a leader is to mobilize the workforce and to harness the support and energy of employees to create an us-ness or sense of shared identity in the face of a looming crisis.

3. *Personal Attribute Competencies*
An effective crisis response requires leaders to display a range of personal attributes. At a cognitive level, Combe and Carrington (2015) maintain that leaders facing crisis situations need to develop a mental model based upon their experience and schemas that will assist them in identifying causes, considerations and consequences arising from a crisis event. Wilson (2020) suggests that sensemaking provides a shared language for effective communication with employees and communities. For their part, Wooten and James (2008) argue that effective crisis leadership involves not only making sense of individual discrete events, but also necessitates the ability to make sense of a series of seemingly unrelated events. Alongside sense-making abilities, leaders are expected to demonstrate personal integrity and trust as this will help build employee confidence and improve employee well-being (Järvis & Reinhold, 2022). Yet, it

Table 4.1: Crisis Leadership Competencies (Pre-COVID).

Alexander (2004)	**Crichton et al. (2005)**	**Schoenberg (2005)**	**Wooten and James (2008)**	**Devitt and Borodzicz (2008)**	**Savaneviciene, Ciutiene and Rutelione (2014)**	**Brownlee-Turgeon (2017)**	**Wisittigars and Siengthai (2019)**
Focus on solvable problems Prioritize the elements of the problem Delegate responsibility Manage the span of control Communicate clearly and rationally Keep a level head in a crisis	Information Gathering Shared Awareness Projection/ Prediction Expectations Problem definition and diagnosis Option generation Risk and time assessment Response selection Outcome review Team and workload	Integrity Intelligence Passion Charisma Organized Analytical Vision Courage	Sense-making Perspective taking Issue Selling Organizational Agility Creativity Decision-Making Communicating Risk-taking Promoting Organizational Resilience Learning and Reflection	Task Skills comprising: Accepting New Reality Quickly, Strategic Thinking, Identifying Key Issues and Priorities, Creating Options, Decision-Making, Delegation, Meeting Skills Interpersonal Skills comprising: Emotional Intelligence, Communication Skills – Verbal and Non – Verbal, Negotiating/Influencing, Leadership Style Personal Attributes comprising: Confidence, Presence, Credibility, Pragmatism, Cognitive Skills, Effective Stress Handling, Moral Courage/ Ethics	Self-Management Competencies comprising: Trustworthiness, Agility, Adaptability, Self-Control Business Management Competencies comprising: Strategic Thinking and Planning, Creative Problem-Solving, Negotiating People Management Competencies comprising: Collaboration and teamwork,	Participatory management competencies comprising: communication, training, information, solutions and interactions Resourcefulness competencies including: decision-making, identifying opportunities, adapting to circumstances, handling information, deploying resources, systems navigation Sensemaking competencies including: identify warning signs of a	Emergency Preparedness Competencies including: Emergency Planning and Business Continuity, Law and Regulatory Issues, Risk Management, Emergency Preparedness, Fire Protection skills, Critical Incident Handling Skills, Knowledge of Safety and Security, Safety Awareness Crisis Communication Competencies including: Public Speaking, Collaboration, Press Management, Communication, Delegating, Relationships with Stakeholders Emotional Intelligence Competencies including:

management Coordination of activities Consideration and support Command Planning and replanning Provide direction Delegation Communication Communication with others		Stakeholders Awareness including: Engaging with Politics, Engaging with Media, Engaging with Strategic and Tactical Teams, Meeting Needs of a Wide Diversity of Stakeholders	Managing conflict, Empowering others	crisis and bringing the crisis to the attention of others	Self-confidence, Motivation, Stress Management, Confront Leadership Skills Competencies including: Decision-Making, Leading Teams, Leadership Skills, Management Skills, Negotiation Skills Problem-Solving Competencies including: Problem-solving, Situation Analytical Skills, Problem Analysis and Investigation, Simply Complexity

is also important that leaders display high levels of self-management as crises can take a significant personal toll on their own physical and psychological resources.

4. *Interpersonal Competencies*
Crises constitute high-pressure challenging events both for leaders and employees. McNulty et al. (2018) maintain that where a crisis exists both internal and external to the organization, the stress caused can heighten levels of anxiety and conflict. They argue that the confusion and chaos caused by crisis events can lead to ambiguity and disillusionment, requiring strong collective leadership and unity of purpose as prerequisites to an effective response. In so doing, they posit that leaders need to capitalize on the strengths and resources of individuals and departments in order to tailor operations to meet current environmental challenges. Research by Eichenauer et al. (2022) shows that effective leaders show both agentic behaviors (effective communication and project management skills) and communal behaviors (offering social support and sensitivity to workers needs). Indeed, it is critical in crisis situations that leaders can step beyond ideological positions and use their interpersonal skills to instill hope and build community amongst individuals affected by loss (Maak et al., 2021).

Crisis Leadership Competencies (Post-COVID)

Table 4.2 presents seven lists of crisis leadership competencies that were conceived and published by academics in the aftermath of the COVID-19 pandemic. While several of these frameworks contain many of the same crisis leadership competencies as those frameworks developed in pre-COVID times, there are some marked differences in the competencies being advocated for crisis leaders in the aftermath of the pandemic. It is clear that the experience of the pandemic has caused a re-evaluation of the critical competencies required of leaders in crisis situations. In this section, we will discuss three emerging features found in these new frameworks.

1. *An emphasis on organizational resilience*
The COVID-19 pandemic brought about a greater realization of the need for organizations to prepare more effectively for long, slow-moving crises. With an emphasis in the literature on fast-burning crises that have a distinct hot phase, Boin et al. (2020, p. 116) argue that organizations were ill-prepared for a slow, long-lasting creeping crisis that did not have a clear beginning or end. They argue that creeping crises have a semi-permanent character and are prone to periodic outbursts, requiring the sustained attention of decision-makers. Organizational resilience therefore has two important facets: the preparation of resilient communities and the development of resilient systems. Stern (2013) suggests that resilience is the product of investment in preparedness – ensuring that crisis and disaster plans are properly developed and regularly tested. Yet, Lombardi and colleagues (2021) maintain that resilience is the

product of improvisation, with improvisation being defined as a combination of preparation and situational responsiveness. They argue that the combination of care for the organization and its people, combined with the adoption of learning as an attitude helps leaders improve the resilience of organizational systems and avoid unwanted consequences.

2. *A focus on participatory action*
Crisis situations often trigger a unity of spirit and a willingness to engage in collective action. Exhibiting openness and encouraging participation in decision-making enables greater ownership and acceptance of the leader's vision (Petriglieri, 2020). A shared vision offers hope and the realization of goals and values as well as reassurance about the long-term viability of the company and that it possesses the resources to survive the crisis. Wilson (2020) argues that individuals should be empowered to plan for a crisis as this fosters greater trust in decisions. In so doing, she recommends that individuals should develop creative responses to minimize harm to individuals and businesses. Fostering creativity is considered essential for both leaders and followers to generate new ideas and improve business effectiveness (Wang & Li, 2022). Active, hand-on participation is also needed by leaders when working with teams remotely. Malhotra et al. (2007) assert that leaders need to engage with teams, involve everyone and encourage inclusion and involvement as this helps employees feel supported and motivated.

3. *A concern for care and compassion*
The need for leaders to connect with the emotional needs of employees and offer support during crisis situations has become a critical crisis leadership competency in a post-COVID environment. Dirani et al. (2020) maintain that a core responsibility of leaders is to assist employees to overcome emotional and personal problems. Prasongko and Capri (2021) assert that the notion of assertive, aggressive, authoritarian leaders has given way to the idea that leaders should be empathetic, caring, compassionate and willing to listen to others. Balasubramanian and Fernandes (2022) argue that leadership during a crisis involves not only securing the support of employees, but also necessitates giving support to them and showing them that the organization cares about their well-being. We will explore the need for leaders to embrace a caring approach in the following sections.

In the next section, we will examine the rationale for embracing an ethic of care within crisis leadership.

Why an Ethic of Care is Needed

The COVID-19 pandemic focused much of our attention on care, whether in work, at home or while in contact with strangers. We were expected to take care of ourselves, our families and our communities. At work, leaders and organizations responded in

Table 4.2: Crisis Leadership Competencies (Post-COVID).

Dirani et al. (2020)	Forster, Patlas and Lexa (2020)	Haslam et al. (2021)	Balasubramanian and Fernandes (2022)	Sriharan et al. (2022)	Järvis and Reinhold (2022)	Awad and Ashour (2022)
An ability to articulate strong roles and purpose A distributed leadership approach Strong communication skills Providing employee access to technology A concern for employees emotional stability A focus on organizational financial health An emphasis on organizational resilience	Assemble a network of teams Empower others Promote open discussions Encourage creativity Be flexible Act decisively and swiftly Maintain equilibrium Develop a long-term strategy Act transparently Provide clear and accurate communications Demonstrate empathy Help individuals believe in themselves	Reflect on shared social identify Represent "us" and our goals Realize shared identify in plans and policy Reinforce shared identity through ongoing action Ready the group for mobilization	Compassion and Care Openness and Communication Adaptiveness Resilience and Courage Decisiveness Consultation and Collaboration Empowerment	Task Competencies Comprising: Preparing and Planning, Communication, Collaboration Adaptive Competencies Comprising: Decision-Making, Systems Thinking/Sensemaking, Tacit Skills People Competencies Comprising: Inspiring & influencing, Leadership Presence, Empathy & Awareness	Personality Competencies including: Empathy, Flexibility, Creativity, Self-Confidence, High Integrity Leadership Competencies including: Readiness to reflect and motivate, Ability to promote organizational agility and organizational resilience, Ability to promote learning, Enhancing organizational culture where employees are involved in decision-making processes Skills-based Competencies including: High Analytical and Critical Thinking Skills, Good Team-Building Skills, Good Communications Skills, Perspective-Taking Skills, Logical Sense-Making Skills, Sound Decision-Making Skills, Issue-Selling Skills	Communication Skills Training Involvement in crisis decision-making Develop ability to handle information Adaptation to circumstances Identify warning signs of a looming crisis Bring the crisis to the attention of others Being fair and treating others fairly Encourage greater autonomy amongst employees Clarify performance goals and expectations Display care bahvior towards others Communicate about ethics Explain ethical rules Develop others

numerous ways to balance their responsibilities to their many stakeholders (Stephens, Jahn, Fox, et al., 2020) while often being simultaneously 'judged' by the public (Reed, 2022). Care is often described as being a "species activity" (Fisher & Tronto, 1990), something concomitant with human nature but also complex and personal in its meaning. Although, for the most part, outside of 'caring' environments such as health care, social care or family care it is rarely discussed as a practice. Within the caring environments of health, social care and family there are well formed philosophical discussions, models and codes of practice around an ethic of care. Yet, in some workplaces, and particularly contemporary workplaces, care often appears based around meeting legislative requirements which suggests that it has become increasingly systematized within organizational procedures. In this vein, it appears to have become directed towards the 'masculine' version of care that deals with rationalities and systems rather than 'feminist' positions that see care as relational by nature (Fisher & Tronto, 1990; Gilligan, 1982; Kittay, 1999; Lynch, 2022; Puig de la Bellacasa, 2017; Tronto, 1993; Saks, 2021).

Often care only becomes a talking point when it is missing or deemed to be lacking in some sense. The onset of the pandemic and the challenges that leaders faced surfaced the importance of care, not because it was lacking but because the way it was practiced was inadequate to meet these challenges. The distinctive and almost unique challenges brought about by the pandemic have opened up an opportunity to consider care in 'normal' work environments (beyond caring environments) and to re-examine and re-establish care as a central relationship in organizations and leadership practice. It is important that this momentum is harnessed and broader theories concerning the place of care in organizational practices are explored. The relational aspects of care, central to feminist philosophies of care, are visible in many organizations before the new-managerialism and neo-liberal economic reforms that emerged in the 1980s (Tronto, 2013). These bureaucratic reforms are underpinned by rationality and logic and resist forms of relational care due to their requirement for care to "have a clear beginning and ending" (Lynch, 2022, p. 81). This opportunity to deliberate on an ethic of care begins with a discussion on how the relational perspective of care might be re-established as a culturally embedded practice of inter and intrapersonal relations within organizations.

It is important to consider the distinction around the two predominant (philosophical or academic) categories of care. The duality between care as rational and systemic against an ethic of care as relational is often allocated to either masculine or feminine/feminist traits. It is argued that developing a feminist philosophy and tradition of care was necessitated by its traditional devaluation as being central only to domestic life and not a subject of deep philosophical discussion. The distinction is largely related to Gilligan's (1982) seminal work *In a Different Voice* that took a critical feminist perspective of work that positioned studies of morals from a largely male perspective that "tried to fashion women out of masculine cloth" (Gilligan, 1982, p.6). While some of Gilligan's findings around the masculine/feminine duality have been criticized, these categories appear to exemplify how care changed in organizations from relational to systemised throughout the latter part of the 20th century. These category shifts are often present in work that highlights the transformation of organisations and society particularly as it relates to care's place in contemporary democracy and capitalism (Lynch, 2022; Tronto, 2013). Prior to the neoliberal/new managerial ideology embedded within Thatcher and Reagan's policies in the 1980s, as described by Tronto (2013), care was evident in many places of work, especially those that offered a job for life (Tuite, 2019; Strangleman, 2019) where, although it was carefully crafted with purpose, it became deeply embedded in organization culture as a reciprocal practice and a normative expectation of working life. The strategic goal of this period of economic change was to invoke liberal ideals and to push for individual responsibility. As such, it necessitated the advancement of bureaucratic notions with workers becoming increasingly rationalized and individualized. These strategies of economic development oppose the ethic of care based on relational responsibility and reciprocity (Sander-Staudt, 2015; Tronto, 2013) and establish a work/home divide that pushes care back into the domestic sphere – a place where it is traditionally ignored as being of little consequence to society.

To say that relational care has disappeared completely from organizations would do a disservice to those who do care; to leaders who care; to colleagues who care and to organizations that care – and as Strathern (2020) says 'the words matter'. Even without a formal culture of relational or moral care, care in organizations still exists – people still care for and about each other. The sidelining of care as a relational activity and concern is a consequence of the rationalities of contemporary capitalism. In returning care to its 'natural' place, as Aristotle would have it (Tronto, 1993), in the private sphere the obligation to care in places of work beyond the legal 'duty of care' is by and large redundant. The intensification of individuality that has become embedded in workplaces has driven out the careful cultivation of caring relations and replaced it with systemised and often sub-contracted forms of care. With many organizations selecting packaged wellness and caring services from third party specialists, the rational and systemised version of care persists across management and leadership practices. The waning of relational care, then, is perhaps a de-caring of the moral duty to care for the whole person, not just their workplace identity – a consequence of which, overtime, leads to organizations, managers and leaders forgetting that care as a relational practice can benefit organizational success and lead to cohesion in times of crisis.

Although forms of care are, or should be, an integral part of leadership practice (Cunliffe & Eriksen, 2011; Gabriel, 2015; Johansson & Edwards, 2021; Rhodes, 2012; Tompkins, 2021) without a strong moral obligation or motivation to care beyond established organizational procedure, establishing an ethic of care requires disruptive thinking and actions. COVID-19 pandemic, on causing a pause or rupture in normal working ways (Bierema 2020), has created a pathway for this motivation, where it is possible to resurrect dormant notions of relational care as a new concern for good leadership practice. As described by D'Auria and DeSmet (2020) and Hope Hailey

(2020) the pandemic necessitated leaders to think differently and to re-examine their responsibilities in caring for their organization and the people around them. They appear to have achieved this by breaking away from the doctrine of individualisation and returning to community and communal relations. In upsetting the status-quo, as the contrasting pre-and post-COVID literature highlights, thoughts on care appear to move towards relational forms of care, as highlighted earlier by Maak et al. (2021).

The pre-COVID literature is laced with language that upholds the logic of systemised care, often described as being the masculine mindset of justice, rationality and a 'system of principles' (Cole & Coultrap-McQuin, 1992, p. 40). Much of this research identifies crisis leadership traits that focus on using resources effectively to achieve goals, to ensure employees can meet targets and to use empathy as a method to influence and persuade others to act towards certain goals. While collective approaches are encouraged, this often pertains to leaders standing above their employees and working towards a single purpose, rather than including employees as potential collaborators in problem solving during a crisis. The post-COVID literature surfaces a shift in this hierarchical approach towards the unstructured social relationships of communities (Turner, 1969). Such forms of social relations involve the leveling of hierarchical structures and the recognition that in a more unstructured community environment, challenges such as those arising from the pandemic can be overcome. The language in the post-COVID literature leans toward being more relational and speaks to forms of feminist care that are relational and necessitating levels of interdependence. In this work empathy is not for the purpose of persuasion – but linked with compassion and listening to others, in bringing together all stakeholders to build a caring and interdependent community. Care and ethics are discussed along with involvement, flexibility, openness, awareness and importantly sense making. As the effects of the pandemic subside, it will be necessary for organizations and leaders to assess and learn from their actions, particularly the innovative and disruptive practices that brought workplaces together in communal problem solving.

Post-COVID Leadership

Emerging from the pandemic, it is clear that crisis situations require leaders to engage with the emotional needs of employees and build social solidarity and unity amongst teams and groups. For his part, Bal (2021) identifies the three most important skills needed for a post-COVID leadership as agility, a human approach to staff and the ability to build inclusive and connected hybrid teams. It is arguable that crisis conditions demand that leaders act with moral courage. Numminen et al. (2019) provide a useful framework for understanding the concept of moral courage. They assert that moral courage comprises of four key constructs:

- compassion and true presence
- moral responsibility

- moral integrity
- commitment to good care

In relation to compassion and true presence, they argue that leaders need to recognise an employee's vulnerability in times of crisis and display genuineness and openness in responding to their specific circumstances. They maintain that leaders need to move beyond superficial emotional displays and undertake tangible actions to support employees in need. In this regard, leaders need to move beyond empathy and embrace care as a set of actions and practices that reflect an organization's values (Saks, 2021). For their part, Rocco and Shuck (2019) maintain that compassion is a tripartite concept. Leaders must first notice the person who is suffering. They must then show empathy towards the person and acknowledge their pain. Finally, they must take action that is either personal or organization that offers real genuine support to the person.

Numminen and colleagues (2019) define the notion of moral responsibility as meaning that leaders are encouraged to act with courage and move beyond narrow demarcated roles to looking at the big picture, showing an ability to adapt to the situation as conditions change. Similarly, Kayes et al. (2013) assert that leadership decision-making can carry organizational consequences and that it is critical for leaders to reflect upon the consequences of their decisions and accept responsibility for their actions. For their part, Fry and Egel (2021) consider moral responsibility as an individual ethic which extends awareness of one's actions beyond the immediate context and includes a creative ability to disengage from dominant narratives to consider and evaluate other alternatives.

Moral integrity relates to the norms and values that guide leaders in their actions, requiring moral intelligence and self-insight (Noelliste, 2013). For their part, Awad and Ashour (2002) assert that integrity behavior relates to the degree of alignment between what individuals say and what individuals do. A professional code of ethical conduct can support the moral integrity of decision-makers by offering a framework upon which to ground important decisions. Indeed, Huang and Lin (2021) maintain that leaders must pay attention to fairness, justice and ethical issues in order to ensure equitable decision-making and that their behavior and decision-making is above scrutiny.

Finally, a commitment to good care can easily be achieved by reflecting on this time and recognising that forms of care practice which emerged during this time are a valuable leadership practice that can create lasting bonds between organizational actors that can benefit the organization. In a sense, we should not be asking why an ethic of care is needed, but recognizing that this is already becoming a reality through the shared experiences of the challenges brought about by the pandemic. These experiences were not just focused on ensuring continued organizational effectiveness but on coming together to support each other and care for each other on a personal level and in supporting each other in relation to work. So, the division of work and home life, that separated care into systemised workplace care and relational home care have rejoined and the importance of relational care has become apparent for the well being of the workforce. The theoretical location of this re-visioning of care and deeper discussions of an ethic of care, including developing a notion of good care, sits well within studies of leadership. The practice and skills of leadership is imbued with emotional responsibility and in taking on this role of a champion care ethics it has potential to ensure that relational and collaborative forms of care can become culturally embedded in organization theory and practice, thereby replacing the procedural codes and rules that attempt to define care systematically.

Conclusion

It has long been argued that effective leadership has been associated with attributes such as decisiveness, strength, assertiveness and bravery and this conception of leadership shapes people's perceptions of leaders, particularly during crisis situations (Kars-Unluoglu et al., 2022). Yet the failure of many populist leaders displaying macho, control-like tendencies to deal effectively with the COVID-19 pandemic has led to a reconsideration of the true qualities needed from effective leaders in crisis situations (Bagwell 2020; Sergent & Stajkovic 2020). As a result, it can be argued that the pandemic has highlighted the importance of care, compassion and evidence-based decision-making as the basis for crisis leadership (Maak et al., 2021).

The development and transformation of workplaces that separated home spaces and work spaces consequently separated care into relational home care and systemised workplace care. The COVID-19 pandemic created a schism or rupture in this division and necessitated a pulling together of both home and work lives, and consequently a re-assessment of caring practices. In reflection, it appears that care has become a forgotten element of the workplace, through the individualisation and rationalization of organizational processes. As such, it removed the active phase of Tronto's (2015) caring process, that of the competent care giver, and the notion of how to care beyond legal requirements fades. The pandemic, with all its challenges, trauma and upheaval has reignited interest in care and debate around its role within society and places of work. The shift in the tone of language around leadership signifies that a re-evaluation of the place of care is already underway. The challenge now is to maintain this momentum and to continue to discuss meaningful care practices and how an ethic of care embedded in leadership practice might be developed.

References

Ahern, S., & Loh, E. (2021). Leadership during the COVID-19 pandemic: building and sustaining trust in times of uncertainty. *BMJ Leader*, (5), 266–269.

Alexander, D. E. (2004). Cognitive Mapping as an Emergency Management Training Exercise. *Journal of Contingencies and Crisis Management*, *12*(4), 150–160.

Amis, J. M., & Janz, B. D. (2020). Leading change in response to COVID-19. *The Journal of Applied Behavioral Science*, *56*(3), 272–278.

Awad, N.H.A. & Ashour, H.M.A. (2022). Crisis, Ethical Leadership and Moral Courage: Ethical Climate during COVID-19, *Nursing Ethics*, Earlycite.

Bagwell, J. (2020). Leading Through a Pandemic: Adaptive Leadership and Purposeful Action. *Journal of School Administration Research and Development*, *5*, 30–34.

Bal, A. (2021). 3 Essential Leadership Skills for a Post-COVID World. *Management Today*. 13th September 2021. https://www.managementtoday.co.uk/3-essential-leadership-skills-post-COVID-world/hybrid-working/article/1726827

Ball, T., Wace, C., Smyth, C., & Brown, D. (2020). Hunt for contacts of coronavirus-stricken pair in York. *The Times*. https://www.thetimes.co.uk/article/hunt-for-contacts-of-coronavirus-stricken-pair-in-york-dh363qf8k

Balasubramanian, S., & Fernandes, C. (2022). Confirmation of a crisis leadership model and its effectiveness: Lessons from the COVID-19 pandemic, *Cogent Business & Management*, *9*(1),.824–834.

Bierema, L. L. (2020). HRD research and practice after 'The Great COVID-19 Pause': The time is now for bold, critical, research. *Human Resource Development International*, *23*(4), 347–360.

Bligh, M. C., Kohles, J. C., & Pillai, R. (2005). Crisis and charisma in the California recall Election. *Leadership*, *1*(3), 323–352.

Boin, A., Ekengren, M., & Rhinard, M. (2020). Hiding in Plain Sight: Conceptualizing the Creeping Crisis. *Risks, Hazards & Crisis in Public Policy*, *11*(2), 116–138.

Brownlee-Turgeon, J. (2017). Measuring a leader's ability to identify and avert a crisis. *Journal of Management Science and Business Intelligence*, *2*(2), 9–16.

Carroll, A. B. (2021). Corporate social responsibility (CSR) and the COVID-19 pandemic: Organizational and managerial implications. *Journal of Strategy and Management*, 14(3), 315–330.

Centers for Disease Control and Prevention (CDC) (2020). *Second Travel-related Case of 2019 Novel Coronavirus Detected in the United States*. Centers for Disease Control and Prevention. https://www.cdc.gov/media/releases/2020/p0124-second-travel-coronavirus.html

Cole, E. B., & Coultrap-McQuin, S. M. (1992). *Explorations in Feminist Ethics: Theory and Practice*. Bloomington: Indiana University Press.

Collings, D. G., Nyberg, A. J., Wright, P. M., & McMackin, J. (2021). Leading through paradox in a COVID-19 world: Human resources come of age*Human Resource Journal*, *31*(4), 819–833.

Combe I. A., & Carrington D. J. (2015). Leaders' sensemaking under crises: Emerging cognitive consensus over time within management teams. *Leadership Quarterly*, *26*, 307–322.

Cooke, F. L., Wang, J., & Bartram, T. (2019). Can a supportive workplace impact employee resilience in a high pressure performance environment? An investigation of the Chinese banking industry. *Applied Psychology*, *68*(4), 695–718.

Crichton, M. T., Lauche, K., & Flin, R. (2005). Incident Command Skills in the Management of an Oil Industry Drilling Incident: A Case Study", *Journal of Contingencies and Management*, *13*, 116–128.

Cunliffe, A., & Eriksen, M. (2011). Relational Leadership. *Human Relations*, *64*(11), 1425–1449.

D'Auria, G., & De Smet, A. (2020). Leadership in a crisis: Responding to the coronavirus outbreak and future challenges. *Psychology*, *22*(2), 273–287.

Devitt, K. R., & Borodzicz, E. P. (2008). Interwoven Leadership: The Missing Link Multi-Agency Major Incident Response*Journal of Contingencies and Crisis Management*, 16(4), 208–217.

Dirani, K. M., Abadi, M., Alizadeh, A., Barhate, B. Garza, R. C., Gunasekara, N., Ibrahim, G., & Majzun, Z. (2020). Leadership competencies and the essential role of human resource development in times of crisis: a response to COVID-19 pandemic.*Human Resource Development International*, 23(4), 380–394.

Eichenauer, C. J., Ryan, A. M., & Alanis, J. M. (2022). Leadership during crisis: an examination of supervisory leadership behavior and gender during COVID-19. *Journal of Leadership & Organizational Studies, 29*(2), 190–207.

Fisher, B., & Tronto, J. (1990). Toward a feminist theory of caring. In: E. K. Abel & M. Nelson, eds. *Circles of Care*. SUNY Press, pp. 36–54.

Forster, B. B., Patlas, M. N., & Lexa, F. J. (2020). Crisis Leadership During and Following COVID-19. *Canadian Association of Radiologists Journal*, *71*(4), 421–422.

Fry, L. W., & Egel, E. (2021). Global Leadership for Sustainability. *Sustainability*, *13*, 6360–6386.

Fukuyama, F. (2020). The Thing That Determines a Country's Resistance to the Coronavirus. *The Atlantic Monthly* (March). https://www.theatlantic.com/ideas/archive/2020/03/thing-determines-how-well-countries-respond-coronavirus/609025/

Gabriel, Y. (2015). The Caring Leader – What followers expect of their leaders and why? *Leadership*, *11*(13), 316–334.

Gilligan, C. (1982). *In a Different Voice: Psychological Theory and Women's Development*. Harvard University Press.

Grant, R. M. (2019). *Contemporary strategy analysis* (10th ed). Wiley.

Hartwell, C. A., & Devinney, T. (2021). Populism, political risk, and pandemics: The challenges of political leadership for business in a post-COVID world. *Journal of World Business*, *56*(4), 101225.

Haslam, S. A., Steffens, N. K., Reicher, S. D., & Bentley, S. V. (2021). Identity leadership in a crisis: A 5R framework for learning from responses to COVID-19. *Social Issues and Policy Review*,*15*(1), 35–83.

Hillyard, M. T. (2000). *Public crisis management, how and why organisations work together to solve society's most threatening problems*. Writers Press Club.

Hite, L. M., & McDonald, K. S. (2020). Careers after COVID-19: Challenges and changes. *Human Resource Development International*, *23*(4), 427–437.

Hope Hailey, V. (2020). *Responsible Business Through Crisis: Senior leaders on trust and resilience during COVID-19*. CIPD.

Huang, T. Y., & Lin, C. P. (2021). Is paternalistic leadership a double-edged sword for team performance? The mediation of team identification and emotional exhaustion. *Journal of Leadership & Organizational Studies*, *28*(2), 207–220.

Hwang, H., W. Hur and Y. Shin (2020). Emotional exhaustion among the South Korean workforce before and after COVID-19. *Psychology and Psychotherapy: Theory, Research and Practice*, *94*, 371–381.

Järvis, M., & Reinhold, K. (2022). Crisis Management and Leadership: A Search for Competencies in SMEs. In S. Durst & T. Henschel (eds.) *Crisis Management for Small and Medium-Sized Enterprises (SMEs)* (pp. 59–76). Springer.

Johansson, J., & Edwards, M. (2021). Exploring caring leadership through a feminist ethic of care: The case of a sporty CEO. *Leadership*, *17*(3), pp. 318–335.

Kars-Unluoglu, S., Jarvis, C., & Gaggiotti, H. (2022). Unleading during a pandemic: Scrutinising leadership and its impact in a state of exception. *Leadership*, *18*(2), 277–297.

Kayes, D. C., Allen, C. N., & Self, N. (2013). Integrating learning, leadership, and crisis in management education: Lessons from army officers in Iraq and Afghanistan. *Journal of Management Education*, *37*(2), 180–202.

Keeble-Ramsay, D. R., & Armitage, A. (2015). HRD challenges faced in the post-global financial crisis period–insights from the UK. *European Journal of Training and Development*, *39*(2), 86–103.

Khan, Z. & McArthur, J. (2021). *Getting the world unstuck on the Sustainable Development Goals*. Brookings Institution, United States of America. Retrieved from https://policycommons.net/artifacts/4138009/

getting-the-world-unstuck-on-the-sustainable-development-goals/4946629/ on 01 Aug 2023. CID: 20.500.12592/4w88jm.

Kittay, E. (1999). *Love's Labour: Essays on Women, Equality and Dependency*. Routledge.

Leonard, H.B. & Howitt, A.M. (2007). Against Desperate Peril: High Performance in Emergency Preparation and Response. In D.E. Gibbons (ed.) *Communicable Crises: Prevention, Response and Recovery in the Global Arena*. Charlotte, NC: Information Age Publishing

Lombardi, S., e Cunha, M. P., & Giustiniano, L. (2021). Improvising resilience: The unfolding of resilient leadership in COVID-19 times. *International Journal of Hospitality Management, 95*, 102904.

Lynch, K. (2022). *Care and Capitalism*. Polity Press.

Maak, T., Pless, N. M., & Wohlgezogen, F. (2021). The fault lines of leadership: Lessons from the global COVID-19 crisis. *Journal of Change Management, 21*(1), 66–86.

Malhotra A., Majchrzak, A., & Rosen, B. (2007). Leading virtual teams. *The Academy of Management Perspectives, 21*(1), 60–70.

McGuire, D., Cunningham, J. E. A., Reynolds, K., & Matthews-Smith, G. (2020). Beating the virus: An examination of the crisis communication approach taken by New Zealand Prime Minister Jacinda Ardern during the COVID-19 pandemic, *Human Resource Development International, 23*(4), 361–379.

McKinsey (2021). *Employee burnout is ubiquitous, alarming — and still underreported*. https://www.mckinsey.com/featured-insights/coronavirus-leading-through-the-crisis/charting-the-path-to-the-next-normal/employee-burnout-is-ubiquitous-alarming-and-still-underreported

McLain, S., Matthews, C. M., & Paris, C. (2021). Everywhere you look, the global supply chain is a mess. *The Wall Street Journal*. https://www.wsj.com/articles/everywhere-you-look-the-global-supply-chain-is-a-mess-11616019081

McNulty, E. J., Dorn, B. C., Goralnick, E., Serino, R., Grimes, J. O., Flynn, L. B., . . . & Marcus, L. J. (2018). Swarm Intelligence: Establishing Behavioral Norms for the Emergence of Collective Leadership. *Journal of Leadership Education, 17*(2), 19–41.

Noelliste, M. (2013). Integrity: An Intrapersonal Perspective. *Human Resource Development Review*, 12(4), 474–499.

Numminen, O, Katajisto, J., & Leino-Kilpi, H. (2019). Development and validation of nurses' moral courage scale. *Nursing Ethics*, 26(7/8), 2438–2455.

Organisation for Economic Cooperation and Development (OECD) (2020). *The territorial impact of COVID-19: Managing the crisis across levels of government*. https://www.oecd.org/coronavirus/policy-responses/the-territorial-impact-of-COVID-19-managing-the-crisis-across-levels-of-government-d3e314e1/

Petriglieri, G. (2020). The psychology behind effective crisis leadership. *Harvard Business Review*, available at hbr.org (Published: April 22nd, 2020).

Prasongko, D., & Arti, W. C. Leading With Compassion: A Story of Women Grassroots Leadership Amidst COVID-19 and Coastal Flooding. *PCD Journal, 9*(1), 83–99.

Puig de la Bellacasa, M. (2017). *Matters of Care*. University of Minnesota Press.

Reed, H. (2022). When the right thing to do is also the wrong thing: Moral sensemaking of responsible business behavior during the COVID-19 crisis. *Business & Society*, 00076503221114021.

Reynolds, B., & Quinn, S. C. (2008). Effective Communication during an Influenza Pandemic: The Value of Using A Crisis and Emergency Risk Communication Framework. *Health Promotion Practice*, 9 (4), 13S–17S

Rhodes, C. (2012). Ethics, alterity and the rationality of leadership justice. *Human Relations, 65*(10), 1311–1331.

Rocco, T. S. & Shuck, B. (2019). Death and Dying: Grief, Compassion and Workplace Responses. *New Horizons in Adult Education & Human Resource Development, 32*(1), 1–4.

Sadiq, A. A., Kapucu, N., & Hu, Q. (2020). Crisis leadership during COVID-19: The role of governors in the United States. *International Journal of Public Leadership, 17*(1), 65–80.

Sander-Staudt, M. (2015). Caring Reciprocity as a Relational and Political Ideal in Confucianism and Care Ethics. In D. Engster and M. Hamington (2015), Care Ethics and Political *Theory.* Oxford University Press.
Saks, A. M. (2021). A Model of Caring in Organizations for Human Resource Development. *Human Resource Development Review, 20*(3), 289–321.
Savaneviciene, A., Ciutiene, R., & Rutelione, A. (2014). Examining Leadership Competencies during Economic Turmoil. *Procedia – Social and Behavioural Sciences, 156*, 41–46.
Schoenberg, A. (2005, Spring). Do crisis plans matter? A new perspective on leading during a crisis. *Public Relations Quarterly*, 50(1), 2–7.
Sergent, K., & Stajkovic, A. D. (2020). Women's leadership is associated with fewer deaths during the COVID-19 crisis: Quantitative and qualitative analyses of United States governors. *Journal of Applied Psychology, 105*(8), 771–783
Siami, S., Gorji, M., & Martin, A. (2022). Psychosocial Safety Climate and Supportive Leadership as Vital Enhancers of Personal Hope and Resilience during the COVID-19 Pandemic. *Stress and Health*. Earlycite.
Sriharan, A., Hertelendy, A. J., Banaszak-Holl, J., Fleig-Palmer, M. M., Mitchell, C., Nigam, A., . . . & Singer, S. J. (2022). Public health and health sector crisis leadership during pandemics: a review of the medical and business literature. *Medical Care Research and Review, 79*(4), 475–486.
Stephens, K. K., Jahn, J. L. S., Fox, S., Charoensap-Kelly, P., Mitra, R., Sutton, J., Waters, E. D, Xie, B., & Meisenbach, R. J. (2020). Collective Sensemaking Around COVID-19: Experiences, Concerns, and Agendas for our Rapidly Changing Organizational Lives. *Management Communication Quarterly, 34*(3), 426–457.
Stern, E. (2013). Preparing: The sixth task of crisis leadership. *Journal of Leadership Studies, 7*(3), 51–56.
Strangleman, T. (2019). *Voices of Guinness: An Oral History of the Park Royal Brewery*. Oxford University Press.
Strathern, M. (2020). *Relations: An Anthropological Account*. Duke University Press.
Tomkins, L. (2021). Caring leadership as Nietzschean slave morality. *Leadership, 11*(3), 316–334.
Tronto, J. C. (1993). *Moral boundaries: a political argument for an ethic of care*. Routledge.
Tronto, J. C. (2013). *Caring Democracy: Markets, Equality and Justice*. New York University Press.
Tronto, J. C. (2015). *Who Cares? How to Reshape a Democratic Politics*. Cornell University Press.
Tuite, A. (2019). *The Lost Art of Banking*. Palgrave Macmillan.
Turner, V. (1969). *The Ritual Process: Structure and Anti-Structure*. Aldine Transaction.
Wang, J., Hutchins, H. M. & Garavan, T. N. (2009). Exploring the Strategic Role of Human Resource Development in Organisational Crisis Management. *Human Resource Development Review, 8*(1), 22–53.
Wang, Y., & Li, M. (2022). Leadership, creativity, and recovery from the crisis in rural tourism. *Asia Pacific Journal of Tourism Research, 27*(6), 652–670.
Wilson, S. (2020). Pandemic leadership: Lessons from New Zealand's approach to COVID-19. *Leadership, 16*(3), 279–293.
Wisittigars, B., & Siengthai, S. (2019). Crisis Leadership Competencies: The Facility Management Sector in Thailand. *Facilities, 37*(13/14), 881–896.
Wooton, L. P., & James, E. H. (2008). Linking Crisis Management and Leadership Competencies: The Role of Human Resource Development. *Advances in Developing Human Resources, 10*(3).

Marie-Line Germain

Chapter 5
Narcissistic Leadership Through the COVID-19 Pandemic: The importance of empathy for leadership effectiveness

Abstract: The chapter examines the characteristics of dysfunctional leaders as they encounter crises such as pandemics. The author focuses on highly narcissistic leaders who often flourish in emergency and tumultuous situations. Despite their apparent competence, their notorious lack of empathy can harm their colleagues and organization. The chapter emphasizes the toxicity of narcissistic leaders in times of crisis and argues that leadership effectiveness is best achieved by cultivating empathetic leadership.

Keywords: Leadership in crisis, destructive leadership, compassionate leadership, compassion, empathy, narcissism, narcissistic leadership, dysfunctional leadership, toxic leadership, responsible leadership, leadership effectiveness, COVID-19, pandemic

Introduction

The COVID-19 pandemic and the actions implemented to contain it have resulted in substantial impacts on individuals, organizations, the economy, and society (Garcia-Sanchez et al., 2021). Leaders in business and politics possess the influence and power to establish policies and integrate them into corporate or national strategies. During the COVID-19 pandemic, the moral values and convictions of these leaders were paramount, as they were responsible for instilling confidence and demonstrating control over the crisis.

The pandemic brought about a period of tremendous uncertainty and difficulties for both business leaders and employees, resulting in significant changes to organizational strategies, remote work, restructuring, and the implementation of workplace safety protocols such as distancing and mask-wearing. As a result, the pandemic had both short- and long-term impacts on the way businesses operate. This heightened level of uncertainty also resulted in increased stress and anxiety among employees, who were left with unanswered questions regarding the impact of COVID on their work arrangements and how they would be impacted. This widespread fear of mortality caused by the pandemic added to the anxiety experienced by employees, leading

Marie-Line Germain, Western Carolina University, USA

https://doi.org/10.1515/9783110799101-005

to reduced job engagement, motivation, and prosocial behavior (Belmi & Pfeffer, 2016; Hu et al., 2020; Sliter et al., 2014). This uncertainty also had negative effects on information processing and created distractions (Eysenck & Byrne, 1992; Gino et al., 2012). In such a context, the ability of business and political leaders to make quick and effective decisions was crucial (McKinsey & Company, 2020), and their behaviors and personalities had a direct impact on the outcomes of their organizations and countries (Hambrick, 2007). The pandemic demonstrated that extraordinary crises require extraordinary leaders, rather than extraordinary institutions (Hartwell, 2021).

The COVID-19 pandemic presents a unique opportunity to examine leadership behavior and crisis management. Literature on crisis management often focuses on leaders' attributes, personality traits, styles, and characteristics to determine their ability to prepare for and deal with various crises (Ansell et al., 2010; Blondel, 1987; Boin & Bynander, 2015; Boin & 't Hart, 2010; Boin et al. 2010; DeLeo, 2018). Effective leadership is heavily influenced by personality traits (Kirkpatrick & Locke, 1991), and negative traits are often ignored since they do not lead to positive outcomes for organizations and individuals (Campbell & Campbell, 2009; Cleese & Skynner, 1996). However, as the author posits in this chapter, extreme leader narcissism, which is characterized by a lack of empathy, arrogance, self-absorption, entitlement, and hostility (Rosenthal & Pittinsky, 2006), is considered a "dark side of leadership" (Conger, 1990), which can result in poor decision-making and negatively impact countries, organizations and individuals. Therefore, it is crucial to examine these negative traits of leaders and their effects on crisis management. The chapter also delves into the contrasting perspective of crisis leadership, which emphasizes compassion and empathy. By analyzing how extreme narcissism can undermine a leader's ability to engage with stakeholders and provide responsible leadership during a defining moment (Maak & Pless, 2006), such as a pandemic, this chapter highlights the significance of relational work for effective crisis response. The author concludes by exploring specific crisis leadership practices that can provide insights into responsible leadership (Clegg, et al., 2021).

Defining Narcissistic Personality Disorder

The American Psychological Association DSM-IV-TR and the DSM-5 (2022) describe narcissistic personality disorder as a type of personality disorder characterized by the following characteristics: (a) a long-standing pattern of grandiose self-importance, and an exaggerated sense of talent and achievements; (b) fantasies of unlimited sex, power, brilliance, or beauty; (c) an exhibitionistic need for attention and admiration; (d) either cool indifference or feelings of rage, humiliation, or emptiness as a response to criticism, indifference, or defeat; and (e) various interpersonal disturbances, such as feeling entitled to special favors, taking advantage of others, and inability to empathize with the feelings of others.

Narcissism and Leadership

The impact of leadership styles and personality traits on organizational functioning is a well-established topic of research. Scholars have examined how certain disordered traits can have negative effects on leadership roles and organizational effectiveness (Davies, 2004; Fox & Spector, 2005; Galvin et al., 2010; Goldman, 2005; Harms, Spain, & Hannah, 2011; Judge et al., 2006). Due to their need for power, prestige, and charisma, many narcissists end up in leadership positions, and CEO narcissism is characterized by traits such as self-inflation, self-centeredness, self-righteousness, indifference to others, and attention-seeking, among other traits (Hochwarter & Thompson, 2012). These leaders' ability to create drama, manipulate people, and form superficial relationships can serve them well in organizational life, where such characteristics are often rewarded (Camm, 2014; Germain, 2017; Kets de Vries, 2003, p. 23).

Positives Aspects of Leaders with Extreme Narcissistic Traits

As aforementioned, employees in management and leadership positions often possess qualities that overlap with those of highly narcissistic individuals, such as charisma, risk-taking propensity, self-assurance, entrepreneurial spirit, ambition, and strong motivation to succeed. These traits have been noted in various studies (Galvin et al., 2010; Germain, 2017; Grijalva et al., 2015; Kohut, 1996; Maccoby, 2000; Maccoby, 2003; Miller, 1991). When these traits are utilized positively, they can help narcissistic individuals achieve impressive outcomes, even under difficult circumstances. This section presents how charisma, vision, and entrepreneurial spirit manifest themselves in narcissistic leaders.

Charisma

Individuals with narcissistic tendencies often hold themselves in high regard and possess the ability to sway others into believing the same. They may also possess strong oratory skills and exhibit a natural charm and charisma, which can facilitate their persuasion of others. Narcissistic individuals initially create a positive impression (Germain, 2017). However, their negative qualities such as arrogance, exploitation, and self-centeredness can erode relationships over time. This is especially true in workplace settings, where these qualities can become more apparent as people work closely with narcissistic individuals. This can have negative impacts on their effectiveness and success in the workplace (Back et al., 2010; Paulhus, 1998; Robins & Beer, 2001).

Vision

Narcissistic leaders often strive for attention and admiration, motivating them to pursue ambitious and attention-grabbing strategies and policies that showcase their leadership and vision, inspiring awe in others (Buyl et al., 2019; Gerstner et al., 2013; Wales et al., 2013). However, their excessive self-assurance and feelings of superiority can cause them to have unrealistically positive expectations about the outcomes of their decisions (Emmons, 1987). They may perceive themselves as more competent than others and believe that their decisions are inherently more likely to succeed, leading them to make overly optimistic or unrealistic decisions.

Entrepreneurial Spirit

According to Finkelstein and Hambrick (1996), leaders with narcissistic traits often engage in grandiose acts that result in big wins or big losses. They may consider their organizations as entrepreneurial and demonstrate behaviors such as innovation, proactiveness, and risk-taking. These actions may serve to establish their dominance and control over the organization and allow them to pursue new or untested technologies and strategies to gain an advantage over competitors. While such behaviors may lead to success, they are also inherently risky and may not always yield positive outcomes, as research suggests. Indeed, highly narcissistic CEOs may be more prone to adopting risky technologies or strategies, even when the risks are not fully understood or outweigh the potential benefits (Buyl et al., 2019; Gerstner et al., 2013; Wales et al., 2013). Such a course of action can be precarious and may not always be successful in the long term.

In essence, charisma can manifest as an ability to persuade others and make a strong impression, while vision may involve an ability to identify opportunities and inspire others to follow a particular course of action. Also, entrepreneurial spirit may involve a willingness to take risks and pursue innovative ideas. However, when these traits are used in a self-centered manner, they may lead to negative consequences for a country, an organization, and employees.

Negatives Aspects of Leaders with Narcissistic Personality Disorder

Extreme narcissism can be detrimental to responsible leadership in various ways, especially crisis leadership (Maak et al., 2021). The potential downsides to having extreme narcissistic individuals lead people and organizations encompass personal flaws, a need for control and power, relationship difficulties, and risk-taking behaviors.

Personal Flaws

Individuals with extreme narcissistic tendencies may struggle with empathy and may prioritize self-promotion, which can hinder their ability to work effectively in a team and relate to others. The toxic leadership of these individuals can result in numerous negative consequences for both the organization and its employees, especially in crisis situations. This includes high levels of stress and burnout, decreased morale and productivity, absenteeism, presenteeism, reduced commitment to the organization, job satisfaction, psychological well-being, and affective commitment (Ashford, 1994; Benson, 2006; Benson & Campbell, 2007; Benson & Hogan, 2008; Duffy, Ganster, & Pagon, 2002; Goldman, 2005). Toxic leadership can also lead to high turnover rates as employees seek to leave the unhealthy environment (Benson & Hogan, 2008). Moreover, it can foster a culture of fear and distrust, impeding communication and idea-sharing within the organization. Finally, toxic leadership can have severe reputational consequences for the organization or a country, including negative publicity and legal repercussions resulting from the unethical behavior of its leaders (Gladwell, 2002; Hogan et al., 1994; Post, 1993).

Need for Control and Power

Leaders who display extreme narcissistic traits often have a strong need for control and may be unwilling to consider input or feedback from others, leading to a toxic work environment and potential conflicts with team members (Germain, 2017). These leaders often seek to dominate and control their employees and the organization, using tactics such as micromanaging, belittling or criticizing employees, or manipulating situations to make themselves look good at the expense of others. They may also take credit for the work of their employees or fail to acknowledge their contributions, creating a demoralizing work environment. These behaviors can be seen as a way to manipulate others to meet their own needs.

Difficulty with Relationships and Infliction of Pain on Coworkers

Narcissistic leaders' conceit, manipulation, and self-centeredness may emerge and gradually sour their relationships with others, especially in a workplace setting where their colleagues interact with them closely over an extended period. Research by Back and colleagues (2010), Paulhus (1998), and Robins and Beer (2001) has demonstrated that narcissistic individuals often encounter difficulties in maintaining positive relationships, which can adversely impact their effectiveness as leaders. They often set high expectations for their employees or constituents and demand significant time and effort from them. They may also react negatively, displaying anger or frustration, when these expectations are not met. This behavior is often driven by the belief that any failure is a personal attack on their leadership capabilities. Furthermore, narcissistic leaders may undervalue the input and contributions of the people who report to them, seeing them as inferior or unable to make meaningful contributions (Kets de Vries & Miller, 1985; Maccoby, 2000; Rosenthal & Pittinsky, 2006).

Additionally, extreme narcissistic leaders may project an impression of confidence and proficiency, but this may merely be a front created to conceal their insecurities and weaknesses. They might be compelled by an incessant need to uphold this facade, even if it harms others. They may face difficulties accepting criticism and may resort to deflecting the blame onto others to protect their image and reputation. This preoccupation with maintaining their image can often prove to be a hindrance and can impede their leadership and management skills. Consequently, their appearance of being competent and in control may be misleading, and they may be grappling with the demands of their role.

Leaders with extreme narcissistic traits who prioritize their personal goals and desires over those of their team or their country or organization may be inclined to engage in actions that undermine the success of important initiatives. Additionally, they may adopt riskier or unscrupulous methods to attract attention or admiration, which can lead to the failure of these important initiatives (Pinto & Patanakul, 2015; Higgs & Rowland, 2008; Wallace & Baumeister, 2002).

Risk-taking Behavior

The excessive self-confidence of leaders with narcissistic tendencies can lead them to engage in risky behavior that can result in both positive and negative outcomes. CEOs and country leaders with narcissistic tendencies may be more motivated to boost firm or country performance in order to achieve their personal goals. This is because their narcissism combines overconfidence with a strong desire for personal rewards, leading them to take greater risks in pursuit of these rewards. Research suggests that narcissistic CEOs may pursue risky business strategies or investments to achieve short-term gains (Buyl et al., 2019; Wowak & Hambrick, 2010). Organizations and countries led by narcissistic individuals may encounter more erratic and extreme performance, characterized by more notable victories and failures and more significant annual fluctuations (Chatterjee & Hambrick, 2007). This could be attributed in part to the preference of narcissistic leaders for high-risk, high-reward approaches, which can result in increased performance variability (Wales et al., 2013). Additionally, narcissistic leaders may have a lower inclination to hedge against potential threats or to monitor signs of economic decline attentively, which can heighten the risks and volatility faced by their country or organizations (Patel & Cooper, 2014).

For instance, a study by Foster and colleagues (2011) reveals that highly narcissistic individuals may experience greater losses after a financial crash, possibly due to their more aggressive and risky decision-making prior to the crash. Narcissistic leaders tend to prioritize short-term gains over long-term performance and sustainability, leading them to make decisions that deplete resources or otherwise negatively impact the country or organization. This tendency, referred to by O'Reilly et al. (2014) as "opportunistic exploitation," can harm the long-term health of the country or organization. Additionally, according to Wales et al. (2013), narcissistic leaders can be labeled as "resource hogs" because they may acquire resources without considering the potential negative impacts on the country or organization's objectives. Moreover, their lack of concern for others can make them less effective as stewards of country or organizational resources (O'Reilly et al., 2014; Patel & Cooper, 2014).

According to a study conducted by Buyl et al. (2019), banks led by narcissistic CEOs experienced slower recoveries after the September 2008 financial crisis. Narcissistic leadership may be linked to a greater risk of financial instability and slower recovery during times of crisis. Their lack of consideration for potential risks can render organizations or countries more susceptible to external shocks and less resilient in the face of extreme events such as a pandemic.

Michael Maccoby (2003) has dedicated considerable attention to the perils and potential adverse outcomes associated with narcissistic leadership. He warns that while narcissistic leaders may possess the ability to elevate an organization to the next level, it can come at a price. He suggests that narcissistic leaders may be more prone to making impetuous or hazardous decisions, resulting in negative repercussions for the organization in the long term. His work underscores the significance of weighing the potential risks and outcomes of narcissistic leadership and striving to balance the advantages of visionary leadership with the imperative for stability and lasting progress.

Narcissistic Leaders during Crises

Individuals with extreme narcissistic tendencies are more likely to have encountered crises in their personal lives, which makes them more familiar and adept at dealing with such situations in their professional lives. They tend to be poised and assertive in tumultuous settings, capable of assuming control and maintaining authority. Narcissistic leaders may also possess crisis management skills, given their confidence, assertiveness, and ability to take charge in challenging circumstances, making them adept at portraying themselves as "heroes" (Heinitz, 2018). All-in-all, one may think that extreme narcissistic leaders are best suited to handle crises. In practice, the extreme narcissist's shortcomings can outweigh their qualities.

In times of crisis, it is vital for leaders to instill hope and offer a clear path forward for their team or organization. Narcissistic leaders tend to engage in negative, harmful behaviors towards others, such as being self-centered, abusive, or deficient in empathy. Such leadership practices can be particularly destructive during a crisis, as employees or constituents may be grappling with difficulties and seeking guidance and encouragement from their leaders (Padilla et al., 2007).

As aforementioned, leaders who display narcissistic traits tend to portray themselves as highly competent and proficient, often taking credit for their team or organization's achievements. They possess the ability to manipulate others and convince them that they possess exceptional talents, which can be attractive to individuals who are drawn to their self-assuredness and charm. This behavior can have short-term benefits by creating unity and order within a group, particularly during a crisis (Kets de Vries, 1993). Nevertheless, the long-term ramifications of narcissistic leadership may not be sustainable. Such leaders might continually require crises to satisfy their desire for attention and adoration, causing fatigue among employees or constituents and negatively affecting the work environment. Although narcissistic leaders may be effective in managing crises in the short run, their long-term influence on organizations or countries may be detrimental.

When the welfare of people is in jeopardy, as it was the case during the COVID-19 pandemic, exceptional relational intelligence and ethical principles are crucial for leaders to thrive (Maak & Pless, 2006). An effective leadership strategy should involve the amalgamation of leaders' traits and qualities with a comprehensive comprehension of the multifaceted leadership dilemmas presented by a worldwide pandemic, and adopting a relational approach.

In essence, during crises, leader narcissism can affect organizational outcomes both positively (Patel & Cooper, 2014) and negatively (Buyl et al., 2019; O'Reilly et al., 2018). Leaders are faced with urgent demands from various stakeholders and must make decisions amidst high levels of uncertainty. Narcissistic leaders often respond to these pressures by focusing on their own needs and seeking control and approval. These tendencies can significantly impact how organizations or countries respond to crises (Maak et al., 2021).

Lack of Empathy and Concern for People: The examples of Donald J. Trump and Jair Bolsonaro

The characteristics of narcissistic leaders, such as a lack of integrity, empathy, self-centeredness, and a need for attention, can have negative consequences in life-or-death situations (Gaskell, 2020; Senior, 2020; Simmons, 2020). These traits are in direct conflict with what is expected of leaders during a crisis (Kim et al., 2021). Leaders are expected to make decisions based on evidence and show genuine concern for their employees (Bell, 2020; Sergent & Stajkovic, 2020) or constituents. When there is a cognitive mismatch between the ideal and actual characteristics of a leader, people may feel uncertain about the future of their organization (Kim et al., 2021) or country. Leaders may respond to this uncertainty in two ways: by avoiding taking on a leadership role and not reacting to situations, or by managing their own image and exercising control. Leaders such as former U.S. President Donald J. Trump and former Brazilian president Jair Bolsonaro can be cited as examples of such leaders. They viewed themselves as excellent leaders who could deal with the COVID-19 pandemic. Yet, Trump prioritized advancing his own interests during his presidency. In typical narcissistic fashion, those who refused to comply with their demands were demeaned, ridiculed, and often fired. Extreme narcissistic leaders have an altered sense of reality and indulge in fantasies of limitless success. Despite overseeing a country with over 500,000 COVID-related deaths and the worst economic slump in decades, Trump believed he was "special" regardless.

It could be argued that Trump's narcissistic behavior worsened the COVID-19 crisis by hindering a timely and concerted response. Despite being aware of the deadly threat the virus posed in February 2020, Donald J. Trump repeatedly gave false assurances, such as "We've done a great job . . . Everything is really under control". He censored officials who publicly disclosed information about possible community spread and the disruption of daily life without his approval. Additionally, he delayed the preparation and implementation of mitigation measures that might have been unpopular. This behavior likely was an "accelerant" that fueled the spread of the virus.

During the surge of COVID cases and deaths in the U.S., the President's egocentric tendencies intensified instead of responding to the unfolding crisis and the needs of the American people with a national strategy. He refused to take responsibility for what he called the "Chinese virus", bragged about being number one on social media, and complained that Dr. Anthony Fauci, the director of the National Institute of Allergy and Infectious Diseases and the chief medical advisor to the President, was better liked than him (CNBC, 2020). Trump excluded health experts from his COVID press briefings, twisted rhetoric to demonstrate the success of his administration's COVID-19 response, and blamed various groups (the World Health Organization, China, the Obama administration, governors, and Democrats) for the rising case numbers in the U.S. while complaining about the media's unfair treatment of him. Over the course of five weeks, he self-congratulated 600 times on the handling of the crisis. Trump's behavior was characteristic of narcissism and demonstrated his lack of concern for others or national unity.

Jair Bolsonaro, the former president of Brazil, may have exhibited a more covert form of extreme narcissism, but its impact was arguably as disastrous. Bolsonaro's disregard for Brazil's constitution was apparent, and his response to the COVID-19 pandemic was lackluster. When questioned about the rising death toll, he callously replied, "So what? Sorry, but what do you want me to do?" (Londono et al., 2020a). He made unfounded claims that Brazilians were uniquely equipped to handle the pandemic because "God is Brazilian" and "because they can be dunked in raw sewage and don't catch a thing," and if some did get sick, "some will die [. . .], such is life" (Londono et al., 2020b). Bolsonaro ignored crucial statistics and publicly ridiculed quarantine measures.

Trump and Bolsonaro are extreme examples of narcissistic leaders whose erratic behaviors and neediness can have severe consequences during crises. In times of crisis, such leaders often neglect people's emotional needs and concerns, revealing a lack of relational intelligence that can be highly detrimental to organizations or countries.

As a result, narcissistic individuals may not be suitable leaders during a crisis, as they are unable to inspire people to work towards long-term goals and heal broken social bonds. In fact, studies have consistently shown a negative correlation between narcissism and long-term leadership effectiveness. Narcissistic leaders' struggle to maintain positive relationships with others can hinder their ability to lead effectively. Effective leadership requires the skill of building and nurturing positive relationships with team members, stakeholders, and others, which can be difficult for narcissistic individuals. They are more focused on their own interests and objectives and may not recognize or value the perspectives and contributions of others. This can create a hostile work environment, low morale, high employee turnover, and other undesirable outcomes.

Additionally, individuals with extreme narcissistic traits may have fragile egos and exhibit vindictive behavior when their self-image is threatened. While the negative impacts of narcissistic leadership may be limited during ordinary times, they can create chaos and division during crises such as pandemics when projecting hope and unity is crucial. Their self-centeredness and the prioritization of their own needs and desires can result in catastrophic consequences for organizations and the broader community. Their lack of empathetic concern for others may lead to perilous situations. In contrast, in the next section, the leadership of Jacinda Ardern, Prime Minister of New Zealand, during the COVID-19 pandemic is discussed as an example of responsible crisis leadership based on evidence-based thinking and decision-making, and compassion (Maak et al., 2021).

Leadership qualities for effectiveness in crises

As discussed throughout this book, in highly stressful situations, leaders must be able to provide clear and consistent communication, set a vision for navigating the crisis, and take decisive action to address challenges. They must also be able to inspire confidence and trust among team members and provide support and resources to help them cope with the difficulties deriving from the crisis. Ultimately, effective leaders must present an image to the external world that there will be a positive outcome to the crisis. These attributes are found in servant leaders who focus on serving the needs of others. Servant leaders are motivated by a desire to help others and use their power to empower others and make the world a better place. Servant leaders are typically humble, compassionate, and empathetic. They are good listeners, and they can build strong relationships with others. They are also good at delegating tasks and giving credit to others. Servant leadership has been shown to be an effective leadership that can lead to increased employee engagement, productivity, innovation, and organizational performance (Greenleaf, 1970).

Servant Leadership

During a crisis, leaders who prioritize their people's emotional needs and unite them under a common goal have a significant impact on their followers' response (Mainiero & Gibson, 2003). Servant leadership, which is rooted in fulfilling others' needs, attending to employees' emotional distress, empowering them, and serving the community, was critical in guiding people who suffered from anxiety related to the COVID-19 pandemic (Greenleaf, 1970; Hu et al., 2020). By acknowledging their uncertainties and concerns, empathizing with their anxiety, and affirming their confidence in them, servant leaders can improve their followers' wellbeing, making them feel valuable contributors to the organization or country and more willing to invest in their roles (Isabella, 1990; Judge et al., 1999; Rich et al., 2010). During COVID, servant leaders' attention to their people's needs led to a better understanding of their situations, and they provided support and resources to help them cope with the crisis, reducing their anxiety and increasing engagement within and beyond the organization (Cheng & McCarthy, 2018; Hu et al., 2020; Kahn, 1990) or country. According to Greenberg and colleagues (1986), feeling valued can mitigate the negative impacts of anxiety related to mortality. Therefore, organizational and political leaders played a critical role in reducing death-related anxiety (Bligh et al., 2004).

Empathy vs. Narcissism: The example of Prime Minister Jacinda Ardern

According to Merriam-Webster (2022), empathy is the act of comprehending, being conscious of, being responsive to, and experiencing vicariously the emotions, ideas, and experiences of another person, either from the past or present, without having them explicitly communicated in an objective manner.

As further mentioned in Chapters 4 and 8 in this book, Jacinda Ardern's leadership style during the COVID-19 pandemic has been highly regarded for her compassionate and successful approach. In her own words, "Please be strong, be kind, and unite against COVID-19" (Ardern, 2020a). She communicated clearly and honestly with the public, emphasized the importance of unity and kindness, and demonstrated her willingness to take decisive action by implementing strict measures to control the spread of the virus (McGuire, 2021). Her comprehensive approach included swift measures such as testing, contact tracing, quarantine, and public education and engagement (Jefferies et al., 2020), all of which were designed to limit the spread of the virus and protect the health and safety of New Zealanders. Through the rigorous and consistent implementation of these measures, her government was successful in eliminating the virus from New Zealand and shielding its citizens from the pandemic's worst consequences. To address pains and fears during crises, leaders should be capable of mitigating polarization and encouraging unity and empathy. Ardern's leadership provides an excellent example of compassionate leadership and social bonding during such times. She urged New

Zealanders to come together as a "team of 5 million" to protect lives and exemplified the importance of compassionate leadership, stating "What we need from you, is support one another. Go home tonight and check in on your neighbours" (Ardern, 2020b). Instead of acting as an aloof and self-serving leader, Ardern prioritized the unity of New Zealanders through compassionate and inclusive actions, personally connecting with them (Maak et al., 2021).

Compassionate leadership is crucial during crises when individuals require guidance, direction, and encouragement. Leaders who exhibit empathy and compassion can understand and address the emotional requirements of their followers, fostering a supportive and nurturing atmosphere that makes people feel valued and cared for. This is particularly relevant in times of crisis, when individuals may experience anxiety, stress, or uncertainty. Through showcasing empathy and compassion towards their followers, leaders can establish trust, promote a sense of solidarity, and instill optimism and resilience in the face of adversity. This can be a vital aspect of a leader's "relational intelligence," enabling them to effectively connect with and support their followers. Leaders like Prime Minister Jacinda Ardern demonstrate empathy, have a clear understanding of their role as representatives of their nation, and acknowledge their shared responsibilities with others. They can understand and share the feelings of others and take responsibility for their wellbeing. They recognize the needs, feelings, interests, and opinions of stakeholders and demonstrate accountability.

As further discussed in Chapter 8, studies have indicated that female leaders may handle crises in a different manner than their male counterparts. Typically, female leaders are more inclined to collaborate, display empathy, and engage in communication, and they may prioritize the wellbeing and needs of their employees and constituents. While this might seem like anecdotal evidence, during the COVID-19 pandemic, several female world leaders were applauded for their compassionate and decisive leadership. They took prompt action to safeguard the health and safety of their citizens, trusted science, and enforced measures such as mask mandates and lockdowns (The New York Times, 2020). These female leaders included Jacinda Ardern in New Zealand, Angela Merkel in Germany, Tsai Ing-wen in Taiwan, Mette Fredriksen in Denmark, Sanna Marin in Finland, Erna Solberg in Norway, and Karin Jakobsdottir in Iceland. Their leadership style may have played a role in their ability to manage the crisis and lessen its impact on their countries. However, it is crucial to note that effective leadership can come from leaders of any gender and that each leader's personality and style can also influence their response to crises.

In contrast, leaders such as Trump and Bolsonaro, who engaged in polarizing and often careless communication, may have contributed to their countries' struggles in managing the pandemic. Extreme narcissistic leaders may find it difficult to demonstrate compassionate behavior, as they may be unwilling or unable to empathize with the struggles of others. Their focus is primarily on their own needs and goals, making it challenging for them to connect with others and demonstrate care and compassion.

This lack of empathy and compassion can make it difficult for them to effectively lead and support their team or organization during times of crisis (Cassell, 2017).

Responsible and Compassionate Leadership

Crises, such as pandemics, present leadership challenges that are distinct from those of more typical situations. They are significant events that upset the normal functioning of a social system and frequently involve considerable uncertainty. In such scenarios, responsible leadership is of particular importance. Responsible leadership theory emphasizes that leaders should consider the interests of all stakeholders, rather than solely focusing on shareholders' interests. During times of crisis, it is essential for leaders to be aware of the potential consequences of their actions and to weigh the impact on all stakeholders, including employees, customers, constituents, and the broader community. By adopting a responsible and ethical approach to leadership, leaders can help reduce the adverse effects of crises and establish trust with their stakeholders.

During crises, people may face various challenges and require emotional support and guidance, making compassionate leadership particularly essential (Hallowell, 1999). Leaders must be present both intellectually and emotionally, demonstrating empathy and compassion toward those who are struggling. This entails listening to and comprehending the needs and concerns of others and taking actions to relieve their suffering or support them in coping with the crisis. In times of isolation or lockdown, physical presence may not always be feasible, but virtual presence can still provide others with support and connection. Compassionate behavior can enhance the wellbeing of others, helping them cope with challenging situations, cultivate resilience, and regain control over their lives (Frost, 2003).

Conclusion

The COVID-19 pandemic has emphasized the significance of effective and responsible leadership. In times of crisis, leaders must acknowledge the reality and collaborate with experts to devise an action plan. Additionally, they should exude confidence and empathy, prioritize evidence-based decision-making, and adhere to their values. Leaders need to inspire hope and instill confidence in others that a post-crisis world is possible. Responsive leadership during crises necessitates a willingness to adapt and change to address the situation's needs.

The COVID-19 pandemic exhibited the extraordinary potential of certain leaders while others failed to fulfill people's expectations. As discussed in this chapter, narcissistic leaders may struggle to manage crises effectively due to their self-centeredness and lack of empathy. They may overlook others' emotional needs and fail to foster the sense of community and connection essential for people to unite and navigate temporary hardships. Conversely, compassionate and responsible leaders who exhibit empathy can lay the groundwork for broad-based support for crisis management efforts. Effective communication, instilling hope, and creating human moments can help develop trust and a sense of community.

Also, leaders who can handle risks competently may be preferred by countries or organizations, as it is frequently regarded as a critical component of effective leadership (Graham et al., 2013). Taking sensible and measured risks can be a fundamental element of successfully navigating challenges and achieving desired outcomes, particularly in times of ambiguity or crisis such as pandemics. However, leaders must balance the need to take risks with the requirement to exercise caution and consider the potential consequences of their actions. Effective leaders should possess the capacity to evaluate risks and make informed decisions about how to proceed, even when confronted with limited data or uncertainty (Hoskisson, Chirico, Zyung, & Gambeta, 2017; Scheuerlein & Chládková, 2022). Ultimately, the ability to take calculated and thoughtful risks can be a crucial aspect of effective leadership.

Effective leadership centers around meeting the needs of followers and stakeholders rather than prioritizing the leader's interests. Therefore, leaders must be aware of their roles and work towards aligning their duties as citizens, servants, stewards, and visionaries to be effective. During the COVID-19 crisis, the role of an orchestrator of effective crisis response became particularly significant. This required taking action to coordinate a complex, evidence-based response that was compassionate and considered the needs of all stakeholders (Maak & Pless, 2006). Servant leaders who prioritize constituents and employees' or constituents' wellbeing and exhibit compassion can help keep people engaged during crises and contribute to the broader community (Hu et al., 2020).

There is an ongoing debate about the potential positive and negative consequences of narcissism in leadership (Buyl et al., 2019; Germain, 2017; Wales et al., 2013). Some studies have suggested that narcissistic leaders may exhibit confidence, assertiveness, and charisma, which can be advantageous in specific situations. However, other research has demonstrated that narcissistic leaders typically have unfavorable long-term effects on organizations (e.g., Chatterjee & Hambrick, 2007; Gerstner et al., 2013) or countries. Although they may be proficient in handling crises and devising survival strategies, their long-term impact on organizations or countries may not be favorable. Additionally, narcissistic leaders may be more likely to engage in unethical behaviors, such as manipulating or exploiting others for their benefit, which can harm the team or organization's reputation and credibility. Overall, the drawbacks of narcissistic leadership during crises such as COVID-19 appear to far outweigh the potential benefits, and organizations should exercise caution when promoting narcissistic individuals to leadership positions.

Post-Pandemic Practical Implications

As we navigate through a post-pandemic world, it is critical to evaluate the leadership style of any potential executive carefully and consider the potential risks and downsides of narcissistic leadership. Narcissistic tendencies in leaders can have diverse effects on how they may address crises. Some of the ways in which narcissistic traits can influence leadership include:

- Less compassion: Individuals with narcissistic tendencies may struggle to empathize and may prioritize their own interests, making it challenging for them to exhibit compassion towards others.
- Limited receptiveness: Narcissistic leaders may be reluctant to entertain novel concepts or viewpoints that do not align with their own beliefs.
- Limited integrative thinking: Narcissistic leaders may concentrate on their own objectives and may not be as willing to contemplate the opinions and needs of others, which has shown to be crucial in successfully overcoming the COVID-19 pandemic.

Several steps can be taken to curb narcissism in leaders and promote more effective leadership:

- Examine a leader's emotional profile – It is essential to examine a leader's emotional traits, such as malignant narcissism and other abnormal characteristics, in detail to identify possible areas for development (Germain, 2017).
- Foster critical followership: Promoting open communication and critical thinking throughout the organization or government team can offset a leader's narcissistic inclinations and enhance the effectiveness of decision-making.
- Introduce checks and balances: Creating mechanisms to enforce transparency and honesty and hold leaders responsible can help prevent narcissistic conduct and foster more effective leadership.

In general, it is crucial for leaders to possess self-awareness and seek a more balanced and healthy approach to leadership that considers the views and requirements of all stakeholders who must be able to express their concerns. Organizations and governments should thoroughly evaluate their executives' leadership styles and implement appropriate measures to manage the potential risks associated with narcissistic leadership, particularly during crisis situations.

While some may contend that narcissistic leaders can effectively handle crises, evidence suggests that the relationship between narcissism and leadership effectiveness is not straightforward. Rather, there may be an optimal level of leader narcissism, falling within a midrange, that can benefit both employees and organizations (Grijalva & Harms, 2014) or governments. In the end, we expect our leaders to guide us in the right direction. And leaders who exhibit extreme narcissistic behavior through their words and deeds are seldom able to fulfill this role, despite being admired and rewarded in many organizations or elected in government leadership roles. To strengthen an organization or a country's long-term resilience, implementing sound corporate governance practices may help mitigate the negative consequences of leader narcissism (Buyl et al., 2019).

References

American Psychological Association (2022). *Narcissistic Personality Disorder*. https://dictionary.apa.org/narcissistic-personality-disorder

Ansell, C., Boin, A., & Keller, A. (2010). Managing transboundary crises: Identifying the building blocks of an effective response system. *Journal of contingencies and crisis management, 18*(4), 195–207.

Ansell, C., Sørensen, E., & Torfing, J. (2020). The COVID-19 pandemic as a game changer for public administration and leadership? The need for robust governance responses to turbulent problems. *Public Management Review*, 1–12. https://doi.org/10.1080/14719037.2020.1820272

Ardern, J. (2020a, March 21). *Prime Minister Address: COVID-19 Update*. https://www.beehive.govt.nz/speech/pm-address-COVID-19-update

Ardern, J. (2020b, March 23). *Prime Minister Address: COVID-19 Alert Level increased*. https://www.beehive.govt.nz/speech/prime-minister-COVID-19-alert-level-increased

Ashford, B. E. (1994). Pretty tyranny in organizations. *Human Relations, 47*(4), 755–778.

Back, M. D., Schmukle, S. C., & Egloff, B. (2010). Why are narcissists so charming at first sight? Decoding the narcissism–popularity link at zero acquaintance. *Journal of Personality and Social Psychology, 98*(1), 132.

Baker, M. G., Wilson, N., & Anglemyer, A. (2020). Successful elimination of COVID-19 transmission in New Zealand. *New England Journal of Medicine, 383*(8), e56. https://doi.org/10.1056/NEJMc2025203

Bell, D. A. (2020, August 20). Why female leaders are faring better than "wartime presidents" against COVID-19. *Fortune*. https://fortune.com/2020/08/20/women-female-leaders-vs-wartime-president-trump-jacinda-ardern-angela-merkel-COVID-19-coronavirus/

Belmi, P., & Pfeffer, J. (2016). Power and death: Mortality salience increases power seeking while feeling powerful reduces death anxiety. *Journal of Applied Psychology, 101*, 702–720. http://dx.doi.org/10.1037/apl0000076

Benson, M. J. (2006). New explorations in the field of leadership research: *A Walk on the Dark Side of Personality and Implications for Leadership (in) Effectiveness*. University of Minnesota.

Benson, M. J., & Campbell, J. P. (2007). To be, or not to be, linear: An expanded representation of personality and its relationship to leadership performance. *International Journal of Selection and Assessment, 15*, 232–249.

Benson, M. J., & Hogan, R. (2008). How dark side leadership personality destroys trust and degrades organizational effectiveness. *Organisations and People, 15*(3), 10–18.

Bligh, M. C., Kohles, J. C., & Meindl, J. R. (2004). Charisma under crisis: Presidential leadership, rhetoric, and media responses before and after the September 11th terrorist attacks. *The Leadership Quarterly, 15*, 211–239. http://dx.doi.org/10.1016/j.leaqua.2004.02.005

Blondel, J. (1987). Political leadership: Towards a general analysis. Sage Publishing.

Boin, A., & Bynander, F. (2015). Explaining success and failure in crisis coordination. Geografiska Annaler: Series A. *Physical Geography, 97*(1), 123–135.

Boin, A., & 't Hart, P. (2010). Organising for effective emergency management: Lessons from research. *Australian Journal of Public Administration, 69*(4), 357–371.

Boin, A., 't Hart, P., McConnell, A., & Preston, T. (2010). Leadership style, crisis response and blame management: The case of Hurricane Katrina. *Public Administration, 88*(3), 706–723.

Bojar, A., & Kriesi, H. (2020). Action repertoires in contentious episodes: What determines governments' and challengers' action strategies? A cross-national analysis. *European Journal of Political Research*. https://doi.org/10.1111/1475-6765.12386.

Buyl, T., Boone, C., & Wade, J. B. (2019). CEO narcissism, risk-taking, and resilience: An empirical analysis in US commercial banks. Journal of Management, *45*(4), 1372–1400.

Camm, T. W. (2014). The Dark side of Leadership: Dealing with a narcissistic boss. *Mining Engineering*. Paper 2. http://digitalcommons.mtech.edu/mine_engr/2

Campbell, W. K., & Campbell, S. M. (2009). On the self-regulatory dynamics created by the peculiar benefits and costs of narcissism: A contextual reinforcement model and examination of leadership. *Self and Identity*, *8*, 21–232.

Cassell, E. J. (2017). Compassion. In C. R. Snyder, S. J. Lopez, L. M. Edwards, & S. C. Marques (Eds.), *The Oxford Handbook of Positive Psychology* (3rd ed.), 434–445.

Chatterjee, A., & Hambrick, D. C. (2011). Executive personality, capability cues, and risk taking: How narcissistic CEOs react to their successes and stumbles. *Administrative Science* Quarterly, 56, 202–237.

Cheng, B. H., & McCarthy, J. M. (2018). Understanding the dark and bright sides of anxiety: A theory of workplace anxiety. *Journal of Applied Psychology*, *103*, 537–560. http://dx.doi.org/10.1037/apl0000266

Clegg, S., Crevani, L., Uhl-Bien, M., & By, R. T. (2021). Changing leadership in changing times. *Journal of Change Management*, *21*(1), 1–13.

Cleese, J., & Skynner, D. R. (1996). *Life and how to survive it*. Cedar Books.

Conger, J. A. (1990). The dark side of leadership. *Organizational Dynamics*, *19*(2), 44–55. https://doi.org/10.1016/0090-2616(90)90070-6

Cowen, A. P., & Montgomery, N. V. (2020). To be or not to be sorry? How CEO gender impacts the effectiveness of organizational apologies. *Journal of Applied Psychology*, *105*(2), 196–208. https://doi.org/10.1037/apl0000430

Davies, M. R. (2004). *Prediction of transformational leadership by personality constructs for senior Australian organizational executive leaders*. (Unpublished doctoral dissertation). Griffith University, South Brisbane, Australia.

DeLeo, R. A. (2018). Indicators, agendas and streams: analysing the politics of preparedness. *Policy & Politics*, *46*(1), 27–45.

Duffy, M. K., Ganster, D. C., & Pagon, M. (2002). Social undermining in the workplace. *Academy of Management Journal*, *45*(2), 331–351.

Emmons, R. A. (1987). Narcissism: Theory and measurement. *Journal of Personality and Social Psychology*, *52*, 11–17.

Engelen, A., Neumann, C., & Schmidt, S. (2016). Should entrepreneurially oriented firms have narcissistic CEOs? *Journal of Management*, *42*, 698–721.

Eysenck, M. W., & Byrne, A. (1992). Anxiety and susceptibility to distraction. *Personality and Individual Differences*, *13*, 793–798. http://dx.doi.org/10.1016/0191-8869(92)90052-Q

Finkelstein, S., & Hambrick, D. C. (1996). *Strategic leadership: Top executives and their effects on organizations*. West Publishing Company.

Foster, J. D., Reidy, D. E., Misra, T. A., & Goff, J. S. (2011). Narcissism and stock market investing: Correlates and consequences of cocksure investing. *Personality and Individual Differences*, *50*, 816–821.

Fox, S., & Spector, P. E. (Eds.). (2005). *Counterproductive work behavior: Investigations of actors and targets* (Vol. 151). Washington, DC: American Psychological Association.

Frost, P. (2003). *Toxic emotions at work: How compassionate managers handle pain and conflict*. Harvard Business School Press.

Galvin, B. M., Waldman, D. A., & Balthazard, P. (2010). Visionary communication qualities as mediators of the relationship between narcissism and attributions of leader charisma. *Personnel Psychology*, *63*, 509–537.

García-Sánchez, I.-M., Amor-Esteban, V., & García-Sánchez, A. (2021). Different Leaders in a COVID-19 Scenario: CEO Altruism and Generous Discourse. *Sustainability*, *13*, 3841. https://doi.org/10.3390/su13073841

Gaskell, A. (2020, May 19). How Narcissistic leaders can destroy organizations during COVID-19. *Forbes*. https://www.forbes.com/sites/adigaskell/2020/05/19/how-narcissistic-leaders-can-destroy-organizations-during-COVID-19/?sh=2e2f30ed2ea9

Germain, M.-L. (2017). *Narcissism at work: Personality Disorders of Corporate Leaders*. Palgrave MacMillan.

Germain, M.-L., & McGuire, D. (2014). The role of swift trust in virtual teams and implications for human resource development. *Advances in Developing Human Resources*, *16*(3), 356–370.

Gerstner, W. C., König, A., Enders, A., & Hambrick, D. C. (2013). CEO narcissism, audience engagement, and organizational adoption of technological discontinuities. *Administrative Science Quarterly*, *58*, 257–291.

Gino, F., Brooks, A. W., & Schweitzer, M. E. (2012). Anxiety, advice, and the ability to discern: Feeling anxious motivates individuals to seek and use advice. *Journal of Personality and Social Psychology*, *102*, 497–512. http://dx.doi.org/10.1037/a0026413

Gladwell, M. (2002). *The Talent Myth*. The New Yorker, *22*, 28–33.

Goldman, A. (2005). *Leadership pathology as a nexus of dysfunctional organizations*. Academy of Management, Honolulu, Hawaii, August.

Graham, J. R., Harvey, C. R., & Puri, M. (2013). Managerial attitudes and corporate actions. *Journal of Financial Economics*, *109*, 103–121.

Grant, A. M. (2020, March 19). *Bad leaders believe people work for them. Good leaders believe people work with them. Great leaders believe they work for [Tweet]*. Twitter. https://twitter.com/adammgrant/status/1240654620252418050?lang=en

Greenberg, J., Pyszczynski, T., & Solomon, S. (1986). The causes and consequences of a need for self-esteem: A terror management theory. In R. F. Baumeister (Ed.), *Public self and private self* (pp. 189–212). Springer. http://dx.doi.org/10.1007/978-1-4613-9564-5_10

Greenleaf, R. K. (1970). *The servant as leader (an essay)*. Robert K. Greeleaf Center.

Grijalva, E., & Harms, P. D. (2014). Narcissism: An integrative synthesis and dominance complementarity model. *Academy of Management Perspectives*, 28(2), 108–127.

Grijalva, E., Harms, P. D., Newman, D. A., Gaddis, B. H., & Fraley, R. C. (2015). Narcissism and leadership: A meta-analytic review of linear and nonlinear relationships. *Personnel Psychology*, *68*(1), 1–47.

Hallowell, E. M. (1999). *The human moment at work* (pp. 1–8). Harvard Business Review.

Hambrick, D. C. (2007). Upper echelons theory: An update. *Academy of Management Review*, *32*(2), 334–343. https://doi.org/10.5465/amr.2007.24345254

Harms, P. D., Spain, S. M., & Hannah, S. T. (2011). Leader development and the dark side of personality. *The Leadership Quarterly*, *22*(3), 495–509.

Hartwell, C. A. (2021). *What Drove the First Response to the COVID-19 Pandemic? The Role of* Institutions and Leader Attributes. https://mpra.ub.uni-muenchen.de/110563/

Hays, J. N. (2009). *The Burdens of disease: Epidemics and human response in Western history* (2nd ed.). Rutgers University Press.

Heinitz, K. (2018). *Can dark triad leaders be a good choice for a leadership position?* https://www.egonzehnder.com

Higgs, M., & Rowland, D. H. (2008). Change leadership that works: The role of positive psychology. *Organisations and People*, *15*(2), 12.

Hochwarter, W. A., & Thompson, K. W. (2012). Mirror, mirror on my boss's wall: Engaged enactment's moderating role on the relationship between perceived narcissistic supervision and work outcomes. *Human Relations*, *65*(3), 335–366. https://doi.org/10.1177/0018726711430003

Hoffman, B. J., Woehr, D. J., Maldagen-Youngjohn, R., & Lyons, B. D. (2011). Great man or great myth? A quantitative review of the relationship between individual differences and leader effectiveness. *Journal of Occupational and Organizational Psychology*, *84*, 347–381.

Hogan, R., Curphy, G. J., & Hogan, J. (1994). What we know about leadership: Effectiveness and personality. *American Psychologist, 49*(6), 493.

Hoskisson, R. E., Chirico, F., Zyung, J., & Gambeta, E. (2017). Managerial risk taking: A multitheoretical review and future research agenda. *Journal of Management, 43*, 137–169.

Hu, J., He, W., & Zhou, K. (2020). The mind, the heart, and the leader in times of crisis: How and when COVID-19-triggered mortality salience relates to state anxiety, job engagement, and prosocial behavior. *Journal of Applied Psychology, 105*(11), 1218.

Isabella, L. A. (1990). Evolving interpretations as a change unfolds: How managers construe key organizational events. *Academy of Management Journal, 33*(1), 7–41. http://dx.doi.org/10.2307/256350

Jarvenpaa, S. L., Knoll, K., & Leidner, D. E. (1998). Is anybody out there? Antecedents of trust in global virtual teams. Journal of Management Information Systems, 14, 29–64.

Jefferies, S., French, N., Gilkison, C., Graham, G., Hope, V., Marshall, J., McElnay C., McNeill A., Muellner P., Paine S., Prasad N., Scott J., Sherwood J., Yang L., Priest P., & Prasad, N. (2020). COVID-19 in New Zealand and the impact of the national response: A descriptive epidemiological study. *The Lancet Public Health, 5*(11), e612–e623. https://doi.org/10.1016/S2468-2667(20)30225-5

Judge, T. A., LePine, J. A., & Rich, B. L. (2006). Loving yourself abundantly: Relationship of the narcissistic personality to self- and other perceptions of workplace deviance, leadership, and task and contextual performance. *Journal of Applied Psychology, 91*, 762–776.

Judge, T. A., Thoresen, C. J., Pucik, V., & Welbourne, T. M. (1999). Managerial coping with organizational change: A dispositional perspective. *Journal of Applied Psychology, 84*, 107–122. http://dx.doi.org/10.1037/0021-9010.84.1.107

Kahn, W. A. (1990). Psychological conditions of personal engagement and disengagement at work. *Academy of Management Journal, 33*(4), 692–724. http://dx.doi.org/10.5465/256287

Kets de Vries, M. F. K., & Miller, D. (1985). Narcissism and leadership: An object relations perspective. *Human Relations, 38*(6), 583–601.

Kets de Vries, M. F. R. (1995). *Life and Death in the Executive Fast Lane: Essays on Irrational Organizations and their Leaders*. Jossey-Bass.

Kets de Vries, M. F. K. (2003). *Dysfunctional leadership*. INSEAD.

Kim, J., Lee, H. W., Gao, H., & Johnson, R. E. (2021). When CEOs are all about themselves: Perceived CEO narcissism and middle managers' workplace behaviors amid the COVID-19 pandemic. *Journal of Applied Psychology, 106*(9), 1283.

Kirkpatick, S. A., & Locke, E. A. (1991). Leadership: Do traits matter? *The Executive, 5*(2),48–60.

Kohut, H. (1996). Forms and transformations of narcissism. *Journal of the Americas Psychoanalytical Association, 14*, 243–272.

Londono, E., Andreoni, M., & Casado, L. (2020a). Bolsonaro, isolated and defiant, dismisses coronavirus threat to Brazil. *The New York Times*, April 1. https://www.nytimes.com/2020/04/01/world/americas/brazil-bolsonaro-coronavirus.html

Londono, E., Andreoni, M., & Casado, L. (2020b). President Bolsonaro of Brazil Tests Positive for Coronavirus. *The New York Times*. July 7. https://www.nytimes.com/2020/07/07/world/americas/brazil-bolsonaro-coronavirus.html

Maak, T., & Pless, N. M. (2006). Responsible leadership in a stakeholder society – a relational perspective. *Journal of Business Ethics, 66*(1), 99–115. https://doi.org/10.1007/s10551-006-9047-z

Maak, T., Pless, N. M., & Wohlgezogen, F. (2021). The fault lines of leadership: Lessons from the global COVID-19 crisis. *Journal of Change Management, 21*(1), 66–86.

Maccoby, M. (2000). Narcissistic leaders: The incredible pros, the inevitable cons. *Harvard Business Review, 78*(1), 68–78.

Maccoby, M. (2003). *The productive narcissist – The Promise and Peril of visionary leadership*. Broadway.

Mainiero, L. A., & Gibson, D. E. (2003). Managing employee trauma: Dealing with the emotional fallout from 9–11. *The Academy of Management Perspectives*, *17*, 130–143. http://dx.doi.org/10.5465/ame.2003.10954782

Mayer, R. C., Davis, J. H., & Schoorman, F. D. (1995). An integration model of organizational trust. *Academy of Management Review*, *20*(3), 709–729.

McGuire, D. (2021, February 9). *New Zealand's Prime Minister Jacinda Ardern's Success in Eliminating COVID-19*. Episode 4. Podcast show, Dear Human Resources.

McKinsey & Company. (2020, July 21). *The CEO moment: Leadership for a new era*. https://www.mckinsey.com/featured-insights/leadership/the-ceo-moment-leadership-for-a-new-era

Merriam-Webster.com (2022). Empathy. https://www.merriam-webster.com/dictionary/empathy

Miller, D. (1991). Stale in the saddle: CEO tenure and the match between organization and environment. *Management Science*, *37*(1), 34–52.

O'Reilly, C. A., Doerr, B., Caldwell, D. F., & Chatman, J. A. (2014). Narcissistic CEOs and executive compensation. *Leadership Quarterly*, *25*(2), 218–231.

O'Reilly, C. A., III, Doerr, B., & Chatman, J. A. (2018). "See you in court": How CEO narcissism increases firms' vulnerability to lawsuits. *The Leadership Quarterly*, *29*(3), 365–378. https://doi.org/10.1016/j.leaqua.2017.08.001

Pablo, A. L., Sitkin, S. B., & Jemison, D. B. (1996). Acquisition decision-making processes: The central role of risk. *Journal of Management*, *22*(5), 723–746.

Padilla, A., Hogan, R., & Kaiser, R. B. (2007). The toxic triangle: Destructive leaders, susceptible followers, and conducive environments. *The Leadership Quarterly*, *18*(3), 176–194.

Patel, P. C., & Cooper, D. (2014). The harder they fall, the faster they rise: Approach and avoidance focus in narcissistic CEOs. *Strategic Management Journal*, *35*(10), 1528–1540.

Paulhus, D. L. (1998). Interpersonal and intrapsychic adaptiveness of trait self-enhancement: A mixed blessing? *Journal of Personality and Social Psychology*, *74*(5), 1197.

Pearson, C. M., & Clair, J. A. (1998). Reframing crisis management. *Academy of Management Review*, *23*(1), 59–76. https://doi.org/10.5465/amr.1998.192960

Pinto, J. K., & Patanakul, P. (2015). When narcissism drives project champions: A review and research agenda. *International Journal of Project Management*, *33*(5), 1180–1190.

Post, J. M. (1993). Current concepts of the narcissistic personality: Implications for political psychology. *Political Psychology*, 99–121.

Rich, B. L., Lepine, J. A., & Crawford, E. R. (2010). Job engagement: Antecedents and effects on job performance. *Academy of Management Journal*, *53*(3), 617–635. http://dx.doi.org/10.5465/amj.2010.51468988

Robins, R. W., & Beer, J. S. (2001). Positive illusions about the self: short-term benefits and long-term costs. *Journal of Personality and Social Psychology*, *80*(2), 340.

Rosenthal, S. A., & Pittinsky, T. L. (2006). Narcissistic leadership. *Leadership Quarterly*, *17*(6), 617–633.

Scheuerlein, J., & Chládková, H. (2022). Leadership and effectiveness: a content analysis of letters to shareholders during the financial crisis. *International Journal of Business Communication*, *59*(3), 385–405. DOI: 10.1177/23294884/8804044

Senior, J. (2020, April 5). This is what happens when a narcissist runs a crisis. *The New York Times*. https://www.nytimes.com/2020/04/05/opinion/trump-coronavirus.html

Sergent, K., & Stajkovic, A. D. (2020). Women's leadership is associated with fewer deaths during the COVID-19 crisis: Quantitative and qualitative analyses of United States governors. *Journal of Applied Psychology*, *105*(8), 771–783. https://doi.org/10.1037/apl0000577

Simmons, L. (2020, April 30). How narcissistic leaders destroy from within. *Stanford Business*. https://www.gsb.stanford.edu/insights/how-narcissistic-leaders-destroy-within

Sliter, M. T., Sinclair, R. R., Yuan, Z., & Mohr, C. D. (2014). Don't fear the reaper: Trait death anxiety, mortality salience, and occupational health. *Journal of Applied Psychology, 99*(4), 759–769. http://dx.doi.org/10.1037/a0035729

The New York Times. (2020). *In a crisis, true leaders stand out.* The Editorial Board, April 30. www.nytimes.com/2020/04/30/opinion/coronavirus-leadership.html

Wales, W. J., Patel, P. C., & Lumpkin, G. T. (2013). In pursuit of greatness: CEO narcissism, entrepreneurial orientation, and firm performance variance. *Journal of Management Studies, 50*(6), 1041–1069.

Wallace, H. M., & Baumeister, R. F. (2002). The performance of narcissists rises and falls with perceived opportunity for glory. *Journal of Personality and Social Psychology, 82*(5), 819.

Wowak, A. J., & Hambrick, D. C. (2010). A model of person-pay interaction: How executives vary in their responses to compensation arrangements. *Strategic Management Journal, 31*(8), 803–821.

Part III: **Sectoral Leadership Lessons for a Post-COVID World**

Marie-Line Germain and David McGuire

Chapter 6
An Overview of Leadership Changes in Retail, Technology, Hospitality, and Healthcare post-COVID-19

Abstract: This chapter provides an overview of how the COVID-19 pandemic has profoundly changed the way leaders lead in four industries: business in general, technology, hospitality, and healthcare.

Keywords: Retail, hospitality, healthcare, technology, leadership, remote work, training, collaboration, communication, teamwork, innovation, telemedicine, digital transformation, cybersecurity, adaptability, flexibility, health, restaurant, hotel, cruise line

Introduction

The COVID-19 pandemic had a profound effect on businesses and industries of all sizes across the world, requiring leaders to adapt quickly and make difficult decisions. The devastating impact of the pandemic took form in the stock market crash of March 2020 (March 9, 2000; March 12, 2000; March 16, 2000) with the Dow Jones index losing approximately 26% of its overall value (Mazur et al., 2021). The stock market crash of March 2020 precipitated a series of national lockdowns, travel bans and stimulus packages, resulting in widespread changes in how business was performed and transacted (Chen & Weh, 2021). International markets and supply chains were severely impacted with resource shortages affecting access to essential medicines, personal protective equipment and a range of everyday products and services (Hernandez & Wagh, 2022; Ranney et al., 2020). Alongside human illness and loss, this cocktail of circumstances created a potent mix that strongly inhibited organizations from fulfilling their ambitions and achieving their stated goals. The economic slowdown that followed the arrival of the pandemic led to a loss of jobs with many employees experiencing significant mental health problems arising from financial insecurity and health anxieties. Yet, while disruption was experienced across all sectors, the COVID-19 pandemic had heterogeneous effects on different industries. This chapter provides an overview of how the COVID-19 pandemic has profoundly changed the way leaders lead in four sectors: retail, technology, hospitality, and healthcare.

Marie-Line Germain, Western Carolina University, USA
David McGuire, Edinburgh Napier University, Scotland

https://doi.org/10.1515/9783110799101-006

The Effect of the COVID-19 Pandemic on the Retail Sector

The COVID-19 pandemic had a profound impact on retail businesses of all sizes from small family businesses to large multinational chains, requiring leaders to adapt quickly and make difficult decisions. The rapid spread of the pandemic forced retailers to make significant changes to the physical layout of stores, accompanied by social distancing and mask mandates to protect both customers and employees. The accompanying fear of product and food shortages led to panic buying and stockpiling, adding pressure to already overstretched supply chains (Prentice et al., 2022). With the need to minimize in-person interactions, larger retailers faced increased demand to service customers directly at home, requiring immediate investment in online ordering and transportation systems (Roggeveen & Sethuraman, 2020).

Two key employee-related challenges faced by retail leaders during the pandemic were employee safety and employee resourcing. Gaining access to personal protective equipment (PPE) and regular sanitisation of the workplace became critical aspects of providing a safe working environment. In many countries, retailers were expected to pay for additional signage, visors, masks, gloves and disinfectant (Precioso et al., 2021). House of Commons reports (2020) commissioned during the pandemic indicated that death rates amongst retail workers were 75% higher amongst men and 60% higher amongst women than across the general population. With high rates of illness and death caused by the pandemic, sudden store closures and reduced operating hours became common with many retailers struggling to find additional staff to meet customer demand. Indeed, retail workers were considered key workers (UK) or essential workers (U.S.) during the pandemic – ensuring that food and essential supplies were made available to the population.

The pandemic also brought about a focus on financial management and cost control. With many businesses facing a decline in revenue, arising from reduced footfall, some retailers engaged in forced experimentation to reach their customers remotely (Panzone et al., 2021). This sometimes took the form of searching for alternative suppliers, altering modes of sale and delivery and stronger engagement with social media platforms as a way of communicating with customers. In other instances, retailers reduced levels of variety within a product category, allowing them to build up inventory of a staple product more quickly (Jaravel & O'Connell, 2020). In many countries, retailers were also reliant on government support programs to make up revenue shortfalls arising from reduced sales and increased operating costs.

The long duration of the pandemic offered many consumers an opportunity to acclimate and gain familiarity with online shopping. For many individuals, the transition to virtual retailing accompanied an increased level of working from home, requiring individuals to show agility in adjusting to new technological work systems and processes (Baig et al., 2020). In the post-COVID environment, it is clear that a greater investment in IT infrastructure, data analytics and customer-facing digital solutions is needed in order to attract, retain and meet customer needs in the digital marketplace.

Overall, the pandemic brought a significant amount of challenges to the retail sector, requiring the display of significant leadership skills. This period was marked by significant hardship in relation to employee health and well-being, resourcing challenges and inventory shortages to the fore. Retail leaders had to work closely with other businesses, government agencies, and community organizations to mitigate the impact of the crisis. This required leaders to be open-minded, creative, and to think outside the box in order to find new ways of operating and generating revenue.

The Effect of the COVID-19 Pandemic on the Technology Sector

One of the most significant changes brought about by the pandemic has been the digital transformation of organizations and economies. In the technology sector, COVID-19 forced the acceleration of new software and technologies due to the increased demand for digital services and rapid growth of e-commerce. This required technology companies to be agile and responsive in order to meet this demand and work collaboratively bringing together people, information systems and infrastructure to share knowledge and expertise (Datta & Nwankpa, 2021). Technology industry leaders have had to be able to quickly adapt their product offerings and services to meet the changing needs of their customers, and to be able to lead their teams through this process. Bennett and McWhorter (2021) argue that the pandemic ushered in an era of reskilling and upskilling, requiring employees to demonstrate agility, problem solving, and strategic thinking. They call for leaders to become "learning leaders" (p. 16) who invest and support the growth of employees, recognizing that it is through the application of learning and experience that organizations will navigate new conditions to achieve successful outcomes.

Another important change brought about by the pandemic is the emphasis on cybersecurity and data privacy. With more businesses and individuals working remotely, the risk of cyberattacks has increased, and technology leaders have had to ensure that their products and services are secure and that their customers' data is protected (Al-Qahtani & Cresci, 2022). The rapid transition to digital platforms, messaging apps and new communication methods left individuals and organizations vulnerable to such attacks as the transition to largely insecure and unmanaged environments occurred, with individuals receiving little training on how to work remotely in a secure way. The reliance on online environments thus left organizations (and governments) open to data breaches and service disruption, underlining the need for leaders to have a deep understanding of cybersecurity and data privacy laws, as well as the ability to manage and mitigate risk. Indeed, Farooq and colleagues (2023) argue that remote work environments make it more challenging for organizations to protect sensitive and confidential information from unauthorized access and disclosure.

The pandemic has also brought about a renewed focus on innovation and research and development. With many businesses struggling to survive, technology leaders have had to find new ways to create value and generate revenue. This required leaders to be creative and to think outside the box, and to be able to identify and capitalize on new opportunities.This includes being able to pivot and develop products and services that can support businesses and individuals during the pandemic and developing a culture that supports employees to take risks and try out new ideas. Indeed, in their research, Thi Minh Ly et al. (2023) found that online platform use and an organizational innovation culture are positively related to levels of creativity. For some organizations, innovation can take the form of external collaborations and partnerships. During the pandemic, many technology companies opted to work closely with other companies and organizations to develop new products and services, and to find new revenue streams. From a leadership perspective, this requires a level of open-mindedness and an ability to engage collaboratively with other stakeholders.

Finally, the pandemic has also brought about changes in the way technology companies operate and the skills required of their leaders. With the shift to remote work, technology leaders have had to be able to effectively manage and lead remote teams. This has required leaders to be able to communicate effectively, to be able to build trust and maintain morale (Germain & McGuire, 2022), and to be able to provide their employees with the necessary support and resources. Kucherov et al. (2023) found that many employers moved employer branding initiatives online during the COVID-19 pandemic, making greater use of social media and offering flexible working practices to recruit and retain professionals.

The Effect of the COVID-19 Pandemic on the Hospitality Sector

In the hospitality industry, the pandemic brought about major changes in the way hotels, restaurants, cruise lines, and other hospitality businesses operate. With travel restrictions and stringent social distancing measures in place, the pandemic caused significant financial, job security and psychological well-being stress on the labor-intensive hospitality sector (Lai & Cai, 2023). Many front-line staff were furloughed, while other staff were made redundant as demand across the sector dropped over a sustained period of time. One major change brought about by the pandemic was the emphasis on health and safety protocols. With the need to prevent the spread of the virus, hospitality leaders have had to implement a wide range of measures, including increased cleaning and sanitation, social distancing, and mask-wearing. Many hospitality organizations also turned to technological solutions such as artificial intelligence, contactless payments and sophisticated mobile ordering systems to protect both customers and employees health (Pillai et al., 2021). Yet, despite digital improvements, research shows that employees reported that the pandemic had taken a physical toll on them, leading in some cases to more difficult family dynamics and relationship conflicts (Agarwal, 2023). The experience of significant, pandemic-related job losses within the hospitality sector, combined with the casual and insecure nature of employment and poor working conditions caused many employees to rethink their longer-term career plans and seek employment in other sectors (Popa et al., 2023). In the U.S. the term Great Resignation became a household word. This is likely to have a lasting impact as hospitality organizations rebuild in a post-pandemic environment. Much work thus remains for the industry to rebuild talent pipelines and to attract new employees with relevant skills to vacant positions.

The pandemic highlighted the importance of flexibility and adaptability in hospitality leadership. With the constantly changing nature of the crisis, leaders had to be able to quickly pivot their strategies and operations in response to new information and guidelines. Research by Lai and Cai (2023) indicates that transparent decision-making and an empathetic leadership style can reduce employee anxiety and encourage employees to take innovative action to cope with organizational and environmental uncertainty. For their part, Popa et al. (2023) assert that there is an onus on hospitality trade associations and employers' groups to rebuild trust with hospitality employees and capture and communicate what has been learned from the experience of the COVID-19 pandemic. They recommend that the industry use the pandemic experience to produce clearer and more effective crisis management and crisis recovery plans with a stronger emphasis on employee welfare.

In addition, the pandemic also underscored the importance of financial management and cost control. With the decline in tourism and travel, many hospitality businesses have faced significant financial challenges. Leaders have had to find ways to cut costs and generate revenue while still maintaining high levels of service and safety. Yet, research by Bagheri et al. (2023) has shown that the social responsibility of leaders and organizations has become a critical factor in attracting employees in a post-COVID environment. In other words, employees are looking to see that potential employers will prioritize health and well-being issues and engage more proactively with employees even if this means reducing physical capacity within organizations and sacrificing revenue maximization. This has required a willingness to experiment with new ideas and balance out competing priorities in the business. An example of a new idea includes a four-day workweek.

Finally, the pandemic has also brought about the need for strong communication and collaboration. With many businesses shutting down and others operating at reduced capacity, leaders had to work closely with other businesses, government agencies, and community organizations to mitigate the impact of the crisis. The provision of government stimulus programs, tax reductions, wage subsidies and public health messaging was crucial to supporting hospitality organization survival during the pandemic (Salem et al., 2021). For Canhoto and Wei (2021), the pandemic highlighted the interdependencies between hotel owners, employees, customers, government and communities and they argue that collaboration with stakeholders can lead to new business opportunities and stronger relationships.

The Effect of the COVID-19 Pandemic on the Healthcare Sector

Without a doubt, the pandemic had a massive disruptive effect on healthcare delivery across the world. With the rapid spread of COVID-19 and the need to free up hospital space and recalibrate medical priorities, millions of patients living in the UK with health problems, including cancer, had their treatments postponed or canceled (British Medical Association, 2020). The suddenness of the pandemic brought about significant resource challenges for hospitals, which faced staffing shortages due to increased patient loads and staff themselves falling ill from the virus (Rossman et al., 2021). At the same time, healthcare providers struggled to gain sufficient access to medication and supplies of personal protective equipment (PPE) and COVID-testing kits (Coto et al., 2020). A key lesson from the pandemic is that it required leaders to face new challenges, perform unaccustomed tasks and demonstrate an ability to learn on the fly (Abdi et al., 2022). It placed an emphasis on crisis management skills and an ability to make decisions under conditions of uncertainty. For their part, Abdi et al. (2022) argue that a hospital leader needs to show psychological stability and balance to inspire his/her team, have confidence and self-assurance to confront the crisis, handle stress and remain calm and focused amid chaos. Likewise, Al Saidi et al. (2020) maintain that hospital leaders need to respond quickly to developing situations, show good coordination, adopt an evidence-based approach, demonstrate good communications and work from plans that are well communicated, and demonstrate partnership spirit.

One major change brought about by the pandemic was the increased importance of telemedicine. With the need for social distancing, the use of virtual consultations and remote appointments became crucial in providing healthcare services. As Vidal-Alaball et al. (2020) point out, telemedicine offers convenience, low-cost, and accessible health information, which can be relayed to patients and their families over the internet and through the use of telemonitoring, sensors, and chatbots. These new communications channels helped improve efficiency and drive cost-savings during the pandemic, whilst also reducing infection risk to doctors and healthcare providers. For healthcare leaders, key challenges included the provision of a secure technological infrastructure and ensuring that staff remains adequately trained to use the new technologies effectively (Jumreornvong et al., 2020).

The pandemic has presented healthcare leaders with an unprecedented challenge, requiring them to make quick and difficult decisions in the face of rapidly evolving information. This has highlighted the need for leaders who can remain calm under pressure and effectively communicate with their staff, patients, and the public. Abdi et al. (2022) argue that a range of specific managerial competencies are needed by healthcare leaders to deal with pandemics and major public health emergencies and that these skills may be best developed through the provision of competency-based training courses. They argue that healthcare leaders need to be able to engage in environmental scanning, be self-disciplined, have a sense of urgency, demonstrate emotional intelligence, tolerate ambiguity and work collaboratively with good communication skills to reach valued goals. For his part, Barton (2008) underlines the importance of preparedness and training simulations in order to ensure that organizational leaders have the skills to cope with unexpected and unanticipated challenges. He stresses the importance of crisis management and business continuity plans, which set out ways to protect organizational assets and mission-critical infrastructure.

Lastly, the pandemic also highlighted the importance of collaboration and teamwork in healthcare. In order to effectively respond to the crisis, healthcare leaders had to work closely with other healthcare providers, government agencies, and community organizations. This required strong leadership skills, including the ability to build and maintain positive relationships, delegate responsibilities, and coordinate efforts. Moreover, the pandemic underlined the need for collaboration at local, national and global levels, where knowledge-sharing and strategic action-planning helped form the basis of an effective response to the pandemic (Khalili et al., 2021). Indeed, research emerging since the start of the pandemic has focused on the importance of collaborative practice and the need to remove barriers to the quick dissemination of evidence-informed discoveries and the integration of key findings into scientific and public health approaches (Lackie et al., 2020; Schot et al., 2020).

Conclusion

The COVID-19 pandemic has brought about significant changes in the way businesses operate, requiring leaders to be adaptable, flexible, and able to make quick decisions under uncertainty. As Datta and Nwankpa (2021) remark, COVID-19 highlighted an open, global world system networked and distributed across different countries and economies. A key lesson from the pandemic has been the increased realization and recognition being given to critical national infrastructure and that a focus on cost efficiency should not come at the expense of investing in national resilience (Coyle, 2022). Organizations are encouraged to incorporate resilience indicators into system stress tests and business continuity evaluations, so that better benchmarking of crisis readiness can be established.

It is clear that the pandemic has accelerated the transition to remote work and digital transformation. Driven by necessity, it sparked a period of innovation, marked by the emergence of new software, technologies, and online systems. It is clear across many sectors in the post-pandemic environment that there is a marked shift away from rigid office-based work, to more flexible hybrid work arrangements, where employees can attain a healthier work-life balance. By necessity, this means that organizations will need to redesign work systems and support mechanisms to ensure that employees remain engaged and connected to the organization. An overview of the key leadership challenges faced by organizational leaders is provided in Table 6.1.

Table 6.1: Key Leadership Challenges in the Post-Pandemic Environment.

Strategic Priorities	– Focus on environment scanning – Development of robust crisis management and business continuity plans – Responsibility in relation to workplace safety
Logistics and Transportation	– Stronger emphasis on cost control – Greater embedding of contingency planning in Inventory management systems – Increased investment in transportation systems – Protection of critical national infrastructure
Technology	– Prioritization of online ordering and customer service systems – Stronger emphasis on cybersecurity and data protection and privacy – Provision of training to upskill employees in new technological systems – Transition to new online communication and messaging platforms
Human Resource	– Reorienting employer branding for the hybrid working environment – Online recruitment plans and job redesign – Redrafting of recruitment plans in relation to talent attraction – Emphasis on employee health, welfare and work-life balance
Collaboration	– Effective communication and support for remote teams – Fostering an organizational innovation culture within an online environment – Knowledge sharing with key partners (businesses, government agencies, community organizations)

Looking specifically at the four sectors examined in this chapter, the experience of the pandemic has yielded significant changes in how organizations within these sectors operate. In a post-pandemic environment, there is an increased focus on logistics and cost and inventory control within the retail sector. Online and home delivery services have grown significantly, requiring retail leaders to make greater investments in technological infrastructure. The heavy demands made by the pandemic on the sector to continue to service the needs of customers have left many employees shattered and exhausted. In a sector where many staff are poorly paid, organizations are placing a greater emphasis on employee wellbeing and engagement initiatives.

The pandemic also brought about significant changes in the way technology companies operate and the skills required of their leaders. Technology industry leaders have had to be agile, responsive, and able to quickly adapt to the changing needs of their customers, as the demand for new systems and software products increases in the post-pandemic environment. Aside from the demands of customers, technology leaders have to be able to lead their own teams through the process of digital transformation, to ensure the security of their products and services, and to be able to identify new opportunities and generate revenue.

In a post-pandemic world, the hospitality industry has been working hard to recover from the disastrous effects of the pandemic. WIth national lockdowns, restrictions on travel and the need for social distancing, hospitality leaders needed to demonstrate new levels of adaptability, creativity, and leadership. From the introduction of new health and safety protocols, contactless and digital experiences, to new mobile ordering apps, hospitality organizations worked hard to survive and thrive in this harsh new environment. In a sector characterized by long hours and low pay, hospitality organizations are needing to attract new talent through a competitive employee value proposition that balances hard intensive work with an equitable salary and favorable employee wellbeing initiatives.

Finally, the pandemic has brought about significant changes in healthcare leadership, including the increased importance of telemedicine, crisis management, and forward-thinking. It has highlighted the need for leaders to partner more effectively with other healthcare providers, government agencies, and community organizations to engender collaborative practice and underlined the need to remove barriers to knowledge sharing across the sector. It recognizes the need for healthcare leaders to develop relevant competencies to cope with crisis situations, including the need to be adaptable, flexible, and able to effectively communicate and work with others in order to provide the best possible care for patients.

References

Abdi, Z., Lega, F., Ebeid, N., & Ravaghi, H. (2022). Role of hospital leadership in combating the COVID-19 pandemic. *Health services management research, 35*(1), 2–6.

Agarwal, B. (2021). Reflections on the Less Visible and Less Measured: Gender and COVID-19 in India. *Gender & Society, 35*(2), 244–255.

Agarwal, P. (2023). Shattered but Smiling: Human Resource Management and the Wellbeing of Hotel Employees During COVID-19. *International Journal of Hospitality Management, 93*, 102765.

Al Saidi, A. M. O., Nur, F. A., Al-Mandhari, A. S., El Rabbat, M., Hafeez, A., & Abubakar, A. (2020). Decisive leadership is a necessity in the COVID-19 response. *The Lancet, 396*(10247), 295–298.

Al-Qahtani, A. F., & Cresci, S. (2022). The COVID-19 Scamdemic: A Survey of Phishing Attacks and Their Countermeasures during COVID-19. *IET Information Security, 16*(5), 324–345.

Bagheri, M., Baum, T., Mobasheri, A.A., & Nikbakht, A. (2022). Identifying and Ranking Employer Brand Improvement Strategies in post-COVID 19 Tourism and Hospitality. *Tourism and Hospitality Research*. Earlycite.

Bagheri, M., Baum, T., Mobasheri, A. A., & Nikbakht, A. (2023). Identifying and ranking employer brand improvement strategies in post-COVID 19 tourism and hospitality. *Tourism and Hospitality Research, 23*(3), 391–405.

Baig, A., Hall, B., Jenkins, P., Lamarre, E., & McCarthy, B. (2020). The COVID-19 recovery will be digital: A plan for the first 90 days. McKinsey and Company. https://www.mckinsey.de/~/media/mckinsey/business%20functions/mckinsey%20dig

Barton, L. (2008) *Crisis Leadership Now. A Real-World Guide to Preparing for Threats, Disaster, Sabotage and Scandal.* McGraw Hill.

Bennett, E. E., & McWhorter, R. R. (2021). Virtual HRD's Role in Crisis and the post COVID-19 Professional Lifeworld: Accelerating Skills for Digital Transformation, *Advances in Developing Human Resources, 23*(1), 5–25.

British Medical Association (2020). *The Hidden Impact of COVID-19 on Patient Care in the NHS in England.* https://www.bma.org.uk/media/2840/the-hidden-impact-of-COVID_web-pdf.pdf

Canhoto, A. I., & Wei, L. (2021). Stakeholders of the World: Unite! Hospitality in the time of COVID-19. *International Journal of Hospitality Management, 95*, 102922.

Chatterjee, K., Dangi, A., Prakash, J., Srivastava, K., Chauhan, V., & Yadav, P. (2020). Critical Supply Shortages – The Need for Ventilators and Personal Protective Equipment during the COVID-19 Pandemic. *New England Journal of Medicine, 382*, e41.

Chen, H. C., & Yeh, C. W. (2021). Global financial crisis and COVID-19: Industrial reactions. *Finance Research Letters, 42*, 101940.

Coto, J., Restrepo, A., Cejas, I., & Prentiss, S. (2020). The impact of COVID-19 on allied health professions. *PLoS One, 15*(10), e0241328.

Coyle, D. (2022). Healthcare as social infrastructure: productivity and the UK NHS during and after COVID-19. The Productivity Institute, Working Paper No.017. https://www.productivity.ac.uk/wp-content/uploads/2022/02/WP017-Healthcare-as-a-social-infrastructure-FINAL-170222.pdf

Datta, P., & Nwankpa, J.K. (2021). Digital Transformation and the COVID-19 Crisis Continuity Planning. *Journal of Information Technology Teaching Cases, 11*(2), 81–89.

Farooq, R., Dash, D., Vij, S., & Bashir, M. (2023). Guest editorial: Role of knowledge management in turbulent times. *VINE Journal of Information and Knowledge Management Systems, 53*(2), 205–209.

Germain, M.-L., & McGuire, D. (2022). Using Developmental Relationships to Foster Trust in Effective Virtual Teams: Lessons in Emergency Preparedness from the COVID-19 Pandemic. In H. Hutchins and R. Ghosh (Eds), *Connecting and Relating: HRD Perspectives on Developmental Relationships*. Doi: 10.1007/978-3-030-85033-3_12

Hernandez, D., & Wagh, M. (2022, september 23). These 19 Items Are in Short Supply Due to COVID-Related Supply Chain Issues. *Popular Mechanics*. https://www.popularmechanics.com/culture/g38674719/COVID-shortages/

House of Commons. (2020, July 14). *Coronavirus update*. Vol. 678, Col. 1395. https://hansard.parliament.uk/commons/2020-07-14/debates/93B43A96-E240-4E02-994D-1E6ED3A405DC/CoronavirusUpdate

Jaravel, X., & O'Connell, M. (2020). Real-time Price Indices: Inflation Spike and Falling Product Variety during the Great Lockdown. *Journal of Public Economics, 191*, 140270.

Jumreornvong, O., Yang, E., Race, J., & Appel, J. (2020). Telemedicine and medical education in the age of COVID-19. *Academic Medicine*, 12, 1838–1843.

Khalili, H., Lising, D., Kolcu, G., Thistlethwaite, J., Gilbert, J., Langlois, S., . . . & Pfeifle, A. (2021). Advancing health care resilience through a systems-based collaborative approach: Lessons learned from COVID-19. *Journal of interprofessional care, 35*(6), 809–812.

Kucherov, D. G., Alkanova, O. N., Lisovskaia, A. Y., & Tsybova, V. S. (2022). Employer branding orientation: effects on recruitment performance under COVID-19. *The International Journal of Human Resource Management*, 1–29.

Kucherov, D. G., Alkanova, O. N., Lisovskaia, A. Y., & Tsybova, V. S. (2023). Employer branding orientation: effects on recruitment performance under COVID-19. *The International Journal of Human Resource Management, 34*(10), 2107–2135.

Lackie, K., Najjar, G., El-Awaisi, A., Frost, J., Green, C., Langlois, S., . . . & Khalili, H. (2020). Interprofessional education and collaborative practice research during the COVID-19 pandemic: considerations to advance the field. *Journal of Interprofessional Care, 34*(5), 583–586.

Lai, Y. L., & Cai, W. (2023). Enhancing post-COVID-19 Work Resilience in Hospitality: A micro-level Crisis Management Framework. *Tourism and Hospitality Research, 23*(1), 88–100.

Popa, I., Lee, L., Yu, H., & Madera, J. M. (2023). Losing talent due to COVID-19: The roles of anger and fear on industry turnover intentions. *Journal of Hospitality and Tourism Management, 54*, 119–127.

Mazur, M., Dang, M., & Vega, M. (2021). COVID-19 and the march 2020 stock market crash. Evidence from S&P1500. *Finance research letters, 38*, 101690.

Pillai S. G., Haldorai, K., & Seo W. S. (2021) COVID-19 and hospitality 5.0: redefining hospitality operations. *International Journal of Hospitality Management*, *94*, 102869. PubMed.
Precioso, J., Samorinha, C., & Alves, R. (2021). Prevention measures for COVID-19 in retail food stores in Braga, Portugal. *Pulmonology*, May-Jun, *27*(3), 260–261
Panzone, L. A., Larcom, S., & She, P. W. (2021). Estimating the Impact of the First COVID-19 Lockdown on UK Food Retailers and the Restaurant Sector. *Global Food Security*, *28*, 100495.
Prentice, C., Quach, S., & Thaichon, P. (2022). Antecedents and Consequences of Panic Buying: The Case of COVID-19. *International Journal of Consumer Studies*, *46*(1), 3–18.
Ranney, M. L., Griffeth, V., & Jha, A. K. (2020). Critical supply shortages—the need for ventilators and personal protective equipment during the COVID-19 pandemic. *New England Journal of Medicine*, *382*(18), e41.
Roggeveen, A. L., & Sethuraman, R. (2020). How the COVID-19 pandemic may change the world of retailing. *Journal of Retailing*, *96*(2), 169–179.
Rossman, H., Meir, T., Somer, J., Shilo, S., Gutman, R., Ben Arie, A., . . . & Gorfine, M. (2021). Hospital load and increased COVID-19 related mortality in Israel. *Nature communications*, *12*(1), 1904.
Salem, I. E., Elbaz, A. M., Elkhwesky, Z., & Ghazi, K. M. (2021). The COVID-19 Pandemic: The Mitigating Role of Government and Hotel Support of Hotel Employees in Egypt. *Tourism Management*, *85*, 1–6.
Schot, E., Tummers, L., & Noordegraaf, M. (2020). Working on working together. A systematic review on how healthcare professionals contribute to interprofessional collaboration. *Journal of interprofessional care*, *34*(3), 332–342.
Thi Minh Ly, P., Tien Thanh, P., Duy, L. T., Nghi, C. N. P., Giao, N. D. P., & Nghi, T. M. (2023). Online knowledge sharing and creativity in the context of working from home during the COVID-19 pandemic. *VINE Journal of Information and Knowledge Management Systems*, *53*(2), 292–314.
Vidal-Alaball, J., Acosta-Roja, R., Hernández, N. P., Luque, U. S., Morrison, D., Pérez, S. N., . . . & Seguí, F. L. (2020). Telemedicine in the face of the COVID-19 pandemic. *Atencion primaria*, *52*(6), 418–422.

Siham Lekchiri and Barbara A. W. Eversole

Chapter 7
Higher Education Leadership in a Post-Pandemic World: Dealing with and Adjusting to a New Normal

Abstract: Leadership is a continuous learning journey that requires a shift in leadership decisions and behaviors. Since March 2020, we have seen higher education leaders scramble amid the pandemic. Some of the most substantial changes included the necessary move to a new era of remote versus in-person learning, vaccinations and mask mandates, and the shift to the Work From Anywhere movement, among others. These decisions required swift and visionary leadership. As Tom Peters wrote in 1988, "The most obvious benefit of unsettled times is the unique opportunity they afford to create rapid change. For those of vision, chaos can facilitate innovation." Such is the case for higher education during the pandemic: It required specific leadership abilities characterized by strategic planning, effective communication, and supportive leadership. In this chapter, we look into the reality of change in higher education leadership during the COVID-19 pandemic and we address the leadership expectations for an effective change in leadership.

Keywords: Colleges, COVID-19, deanship, higher education, hybrid learning, leadership abilities, universities, work from home

Leadership and learning are indispensable to each other. –John Kennedy, former U.S. President

Even before the COVID-19 pandemic turned the world upside down, higher education was perceived as going through neverending changes and unrest. Traditional systems and values often dominate the operational and governance models. The pandemic forced higher education institutions to reconsider almost every facet of their regular operations, and higher education leadership had to remain at the foreground in order to acclimate to the post-pandemic new normal. In March 2020, routine pre-pandemic decision-making was no longer working in a changing environment. Higher education leaders made drastic changes and learned lessons as they went. These pressures were also faced by the faculty and staff who had to quickly adjust and alter their working models within a short period of time. Students were sent home, instruction was moved to online settings, and staff had to adjust to find ways to work from home. Stakeholders

Siham Lekchiri, Western Carolina University, USA
Barbara A. W. Eversole, Indiana State University, USA

https://doi.org/10.1515/9783110799101-007

stepped-up to ensure the transition was done as rapidly as possible. Fast forward to spring 2022, as we were turning the corner, institutions started going back to their normal/traditional operations. In retrospect, the pandemic has forced higher education institutions to challenge their traditional ways of operating. In this chapter, we look into the reality of change in higher education leadership during the pandemic, and we address the leadership expectations for an effective change in leadership.

Leadership

Daft states that "defining leadership has been a complex and elusive problem, largely because the nature of leadership itself is complex" (2015, p. 4). The term leadership has several definitions and remains an evolving discipline. There are various styles and approaches to leadership, which makes it difficult to identify a single definition. According to Newton (2021), "Leadership is getting things done through others, by creating a common purpose where all concerned believe that the goals can credibly be achieved and that they, individually, have the wherewithal to do so in the context of a shared culture, marked by mutual professional and personal respect" (p. 3). In other words, leadership has to do with a person's talent in influencing others to accomplish common goals and objectives. The first significant element of leadership is influence geared toward meaningful changes that constitute shared determinations by both the leader and followers. Daft (2016) asserts that for leadership to be successful, it has to be reciprocal, meaning that the leader influences the followers and vice versa. In an ever changing environment, understanding and expectations of leadership also continue to evolve. Xie (2020) notes the importance of leadership style to organizational learning culture. The future is often uncertain and the pace is obstinate, thus requiring a transformative leadership that can adjust easily to these changes as opposed to the traditional models. In the new leadership model, leaders should be change managers, facilitators, collaborators and diversity promoters (Daft, 2016). After analyzing the tweets of leaders during the pandemic, Goel and Sharma (2021) found that fear and sadness predominated, along with a concern with trying to attain the trust of the public.

Higher Education Leadership

Universities are some of the oldest establishments in the world –the University of Al-Quarawiyin in Fez, Morocco is known to be the oldest (El Fasi, 1962). It was founded by Fatima Al-Fihri's inheritance to benefit and educate the occupants of the city of Fez. It initially started with Quranic instruction, and through Fatima's vision and leadership, the university began to diversify its curriculum including math, medicine, sciences, medicine, and astronomy, among other topics (Azad, 2021). It is reported that Fatima was enthusiastically devoted to ensuring that the university continues to grow. Through her vision, she established the framework for higher education as we know it today (Azad, 2021).

Universities and colleges – higher education institutions (HEIs) – are foundational elements in every country. They have an important direct influence on countries' national development by delivering education to shape the upcoming generations (Bor & Shute, 1991). Moreover, education is perceived as being a catalyst to human and continuous countries development (Hamlin & Patel, 2015). Higher education institutions provide an educated workforce and generate knowledge through research (Blankenberger & Williams, 2020).They are, therefore, considered practical tools necessary to foster any country's economic growth and intellectual abilities, making it possible for nations to unlock their potential for promised future development (Lekchiri et al., 2018). Hence, a great emphasis is placed on the leadership and management of higher education institutions that need to stay abreast of the constantly changing environment and address the needs for continuous improvement transformations. In higher education, there is a significant difference between HEI management and HEI leadership. The management side focuses on performing duties related to the operational features of academia, while the leadership side focuses on the strategic aspects regarding the general direction of the institution (Denney, 2021). In the context of this chapter, leadership is construed as the sphere of senior leadership that assumes the strategic direction of the institution as it relates to various aspects of academic education, research and partnerships. This is distinct from the leadership occurring at the department level as studied by Bryman (2007). According to Smith and Hughey (2006),

> *Leadership in academia is complicated by the dynamic social, economic and policy contexts in which most colleges and universities operate. To be successful in higher education, leaders must be intuitively cognizant of the unique factors that characterize most campus environments* (p.159).

Leadership in HEIs is distinct from leadership in other contexts in its use of power (Lumby, 2019). HEI leaders must use power judiciously as its use is frowned upon in a context where leadership itself is not welcomed. As they continue to evolve, deal with an uncertain future, and move into the digital age, higher education leaders will be relentlessly faced with challenges related to strategic planning, staffing, adapting institutional structures and budgeting. Nica (2013) also emphasizes the importance of considering the needs and necessities of the different stakeholders in academia, especially during turbulent times. Nica (2013) states that "decision-makers should view leadership as a "process" that requires innovation and input from all relevant stakeholders" (p.192). School leadership influences the quality of the learning and teaching that takes place at the institution primarily by maintaining and improving classroom and other conditions (Leithwood, et al., 2020).

Impact of the COVID-19 Pandemic on HEIs

In March 2020, as the COVID-19 pandemic was quickly spreading, the world stood still. Higher education was vulnerable to the external pandemic environment, which led to conflicts and dilemmas around institutional policies and reduced resources (Nugroho, 2021). Higher education leadership was faced with a mountain of challenges and uncertainty as all normal operations were halted and radical changes were made as a result of the spread of the pandemic. Students were sent home in the middle of the spring semester; faculty were left scrambling on how to transition their traditional, in-person courses to online settings in a very short period of time (Fernandez & Shaw, 2020); and staff were sent to work from home. It is not unusual for higher education to experience waves of disruptions, but the COVID-19 pandemic was the biggest unprecedented crisis ever experienced. According to Ewing (2021), the pandemic affected "more than 1.6 billion students [. . .], representing 91% of all students" (p. 39) in over 200 countries (Pokhrel & Chhetri, 2021). It forced all institutions to adopt remote education as the only alternative to safely deliver instruction to students. Discussions began taking place regarding the fate of higher education during the pandemic and more uncertainty developed post-pandemic. Higher education leadership was also faced with the cumbersome task of restructuring their traditional operating system with considerably diminished resources (Kruse et al., 2020). The quality of education and the stakeholders' health safety remained the top two priorities. According to Lamm et al. (2022), higher education leadership was strained to redesign various operational aspects, which included a transition to online education, running with considerably decreased resources, and finding creative ways for staff to operate while ensuring that health and safety were priorities. Additionally, Clabaugh et al. (2021) revealed that the pandemic resulted in significantly amplified levels of stress and anxiety among students as they were forced to deal with the new challenges. Clabaugh et al. (2021) adds that the pandemic intensified the difficulties already experienced by higher education institutions.

Most higher education institutions have emergency response strategies in place to deal with a variety of potential crises. These emergency plans are normally created along with various stakeholders in HEIs to address specific emergency situations (e.g., campus shooting, tornadoes, etc.) (Miller, 2021). Nonetheless, the COVID-19 pandemic created an unprecedented emergency. No emergency plans in place could apply to this new situation, and new urgent measures had to be made abruptly, with a heavy reliance on state and country policymakers. The pandemic showed that HEIs were vulnerable and unprepared to deal with such external threats (Lemoine & Richardson, 2020). Liu and colleagues (2022) found that while 84% of their HEI leaders' participants had crisis management plans, none of those plans were helpful. One participant in their study reported that dealing with the COVID situation for HEI leaders felt like "building the plane while it's in the air" (Liu et al., 2022, p. 358). The most important part of managing the crisis was to maintain clear and prompt communication protocols with all the concerned stakeholders. Therefore, following a major worldwide lockdown, higher education institutions' responses included the following: First, moving all instruction to remote settings to maintain the safety and health of HEI stakeholders; second, shutting down all campus offices and residence halls; and third, sending faculty and staff to work from home. Mask and vaccination mandates came at a later time, as HEIs attempted to slowly go back to in-person operations in the fall of 2021.

The following represents a list of emergency response strategies implemented by HEI in the wake of the COVID-19 pandemic.

Campus closures/ Learning interruption. The first response to the pandemic was to immediately shut down all campus operations and buildings, prompting an instant shift from in-person to online instruction. The health and safety of university stakeholders was the first priority. Nonetheless, the disruption of traditional on-campus instruction and the move to online-only instruction was a substantial undertaking. The quality of education had to remain at the forefront, and by the fall of 2020, institutions had to determine plans to continue online instructions, and in special cases, develop a plan for a blended-learning model with the appropriate social distancing. Online education triggered concerns about the quality of instruction, along with issues of access and equity, particularly for students struggling with online instruction, and for those who did not have access to high-speed internet or computers Routledge (2021).

Student enrollment. The abrupt closures of all higher education institutions led to a significant disruption to student enrollment, as campus visits and admission examinations had to be temporarily paused. Many institutions extended admission deadlines and temporarily waived certain admission requirements (Smalley, 2021). Despite that, student admission and enrollment took a deep dive compared to previous years. It was reported that "undergraduate enrollment fell 4.4% in the fall. This includes an unprecedented 13% drop in first-year enrollment" (Kovacs, 2022, para. 4).

International Admissions. International students' admissions is a significant revenue generator for higher education institutions (NAFSA, 2020). The impact of the pandemic and new federal regulations implemented drastically impacted international students' admissions and enrollment. In fact, according to the Association of International Educators, international students' enrollment dropped by a staggering 43% (NAFSA, 2020), leading to a loss of at least three billion dollars in the fall of 2020. The same report also revealed that this significant revenue loss impacted decisions related to staffing and study abroad programs.

Financial troubles and uncertain budgets. Higher education leaders were not only faced with growing concerns over decreased enrollment revenue and potential budget cuts, but also with challenges over increased online instruction resources. Hiring freezes and furloughs had to be implemented to stay afloat. The higher education model is typically based on a business model that relies heavily on revenue auxiliary services, from housing, dining services, and others (Liu et al., 2022). Even though those services were abruptly suspended, HEIs still had to cover those costs, in addition to covering refunds for room and board and other services.

Remote work. The pandemic forced higher education institutions to reimagine the status of their employees then and in the future. It became some sort of forced remote work experiment that could help HEIs get unstuck from past traditional work practices (Dagiene et al., 2022; Green et al., 2020; Zackal, 2021). Before COVID-19, the possibility of a remote work arrangement would not have been imaginable for most HEIs. That brusquely changed and leaders had to make the health and safety of their workforce a top priority, prompting an unprecedented Work From Anywhere (WFA) model. A common expression to refer to this phenomenon is "Maslow before Bloom," indicating that students need to be safe, having basic needs met before they can begin to learn virtually (Pokhrel & Chhetri, 2021). Institutions had to be flexible with assessments, allowing resubmissions, consultations with professors, and due dates (Kele & Mzileni, 2021).

Inclusivity Suffers. The pandemic was a difficult time for everyone. However, it was particularly difficult on women scholars' research agendas (Lekchiri et al., 2022; Stadnyk, 2020). While their male counterparts increased their productivity during the pandemic, women took an increased domestic load and their research productivity decreased. Other marginalized academic groups such as differently-abled persons, those from the Global South, and those in precarious employment situations were also disproportionately affected by the COVID-19 pandemic (Maas et al., 2020; Watermeyer et al., 2021).

During the crisis, HEI leadership involved three main approaches (Nugroho et al., 2021): First, leaders had to be effective at communicating in several directions; second, leaders needed to use cooperation; and third, leaders needed to be empathetic to be encouraging and they had to promote health and productivity. Fernandez and Shaw (2020) noted that servant leadership, including emotional intelligence and stability, along with distributing leadership throughout networks and communicating frequently and clearly throughout the crisis, were important. In this book, Dr. Marie-Line Germain's chapter further explores the importance of servant leadership and leader empathy during the pandemic. In their study of a South African university, Menon and Motala (2021) found that leaders relied on values of teaching excellence, equity, social justice, and access to lead during the pandemic. Another South African study of HEIs during the pandemic (Sonn et al., 2021) also found that global citizenship and social justice through education were important. Gigliotti (2020) further noted the importance of preparation, perception (identifying the crisis), and the principles in leading through crises such as pandemics.

Now that the pandemic dust has somewhat settled, the International Monetary Fund (IMF) has determined that the impact of the pandemic worldwide has been worse than the Great Depression of the 1930's, accelerating the need for digital transformation (Nair, 2021). Many international students deferred their studies abroad and stayed local instead (Nair, 2021). Declining student enrollments may cause universities to close or merge (Nair, 2021). Accessibility and affordability for online learners is a worldwide issue, depending on their economic backgrounds (Pokhrel & Chhetri, 2021). One of the most radical changes that the pandemic has brought to higher education is the reliance on distance education or e-learning and hybrid campuses (Ashour et al., 2021). Considering that students and parents have an information deficit when it comes to the higher education experience (i.e. they do not really know what they need to know or how their knowledge will be assessed), the crisis upsets a fragile balance (Blankenberger, & Williams, 2020).

Higher Education Leadership Post-Pandemic

The COVID-19 pandemic has radically changed the way that HEIs operated globally (El Aref, 2020). Some of these changes are here to stay, and may ultimately improve it (Fernandez & Shaw, 2022a; Marmolejo & Groccia, 2022; Zhao, 2020). The pandemic has actually offered an opportunity for higher education. Roy (2020) calls that opportunity a "portal" and Hollander (2021) notes that, "the pandemic is taking higher education back to school." Kandri (2021) further asserts that, "yesterday's disruptors can become today's lifeguards"; the pandemic "could be driving a long-overdue revolution in education worldwide" (para. 4).

Lethargy, as Rosowsky (2022) describes it, is "the path of least resistance and returning as much as possible to pre-pandemic conditions, is the easy way out" (para. 1). This would be the backward approach that fails to take into account that the post-pandemic environment will be much different than what we know. Thus, returning to old habits will be a big strategic misstep. Hence, the pandemic provided an opportunity for higher education leadership to embrace new forms of distributive, transformational, and instructional leadership approaches (Dagiene et al., 2022; Jansa & Anderson, 2021). Moreover, as the university becomes more digital since it can operate at a distance, it is dependent on platforms like social media (Carrigan & Jordan, 2021). Benhayoun (2021) envisions a new global university unbound by place or government. We know how important effective HEI leadership is to the success of academic institutions (Rehbock, 2020). However, what will leadership in HEIs look like in what Fleener (2021) calls "post-pandemic times (PPT)" (p. 1)?

Eringfeld (2021) imagines the following for the post-coronial university: online learning as the predominant mode of delivery will lead to a loss of HE as an "embodied and communal" experience (p. 147). Yet, it will be more accessible by allowing more participation. The challenge is to create a hybrid, blended higher education experience that combines face-to-face with distance/online so that it is inclusive. Indeed, the pandemic seemed tailor-made to destroy what HEIs have always promised students: closeness between faculty and students, students and students, and community (Rosenberg, 2020). Califano (2022) notes the importance for the post-pandemic HEI experience to be tailored to each learner's needs for delivery, adapting to a shared digital platform that is independent of time or place.

Bebbington (2021) offers several strategies for higher education leadership post-pandemic: moving toward hybrid delivery of courses; a teaching schedule throughout the year; blended learning campus; making externally collaborative a norm; moving away from capital investments to digital transformation and online teaching; and going back to full-time salaried faculty and away from the contingent workforce. Rapanta (2021) similarly advises that investment in faculty needs to be made to improve online instructional skills. HEI leadership should also focus on obtaining more scholarships, fellowships, and endowed chairs from donors, and increased government funding for domestic and international students (Bebbington, 2021).

The pandemic created a new kind of academic leader – the allostatic leader (Fernandez & Shaw, 2020; 2022b), a transformative leader who was able to learn from the pandemic and adopt new behaviors to create positive change. Allostatic leaders distribute leadership, connect people, and are clear communicators. They are resilient and adaptive, able to strategically evolve. Remote work and distance education meet the needs of post-pandemic learners, offering more choices for students, while delivering content more leanly and with more agility.

Bakir and Dahlan (2022) noted the need for training and development for HEI leaders in PPT in order to provide the flexible student and industry-focused curriculum required. Leaders need to have vision and foresight, be persuasive, good communicators, skilled at using power, and flexible to be able to lead in volatility, uncertainty, changeability, and ambiguity (VUCA) (Edmondson, 2021; Purcell & Lumbreras, 2020). They need to be self-aware collaborators who can lead in complexity. Edmondson (2021) noted that leaders who can lead in VUCA marketplaces can navigate among six different types of leaders: architect, curator, humanist, pioneer, advocate, and conductor. They need to be savvy, authentic, dynamic, and agile. The architect function enables the leader to adjust the institution's mission statement in order to stay appropriate for the ever-changing context. The curator takes the time to examine the volatile higher education environment and assess the risks associated with it to grow as an agile leader (Edmondson, 2021). The humanist style of the agile leader is characterized by empathy and great consideration for the diverse nature of their employees. In this role, the leader takes time to appreciate the unique potential of their team members to nurture and promote a culture that encourages employee engagement and productivity (Thompson, 2019). The pioneer leader is an-out of the box strategic thinker that explores novel ideas and concepts that could potentially advance their institutions. In this role, the agile leader encourages discussions among all stakeholders to assess, develop and implement the novel concepts. In the advocate role, the agile leader encourages and promotes the employees, the work, and the values the organization stands for to both internal and external stakeholders (Edmondson, 2021). Finally, the conductor is committed and invested in the employees' growth through access to skill development programs to integrate that talent in driving positive changes within their institutions.

Fung and Gordon (2022) propose a new model of academic leadership based on seven principles. They note the importance of collaboration between faculty and staff with what they call a "culture of consent to cooperate." They describe their post-pandemic strategy focused on research-based education, the student experience, and community and inclusion. Gunawan et al. (2022) suggest a model of "e-caring" for leaders in PPT to both engage and retain employees with technology.

Ünal (2022) further suggests that leaders need to be altrocentric, resonant, and have emotional, social and cognitive competencies. A number of international institutions used different approaches to deal with the impact of the pandemic. Shah (2022), who studied leaders in Pakistani HEIs in PPT, found that the pandemic led them to innovate and reform their universities. Reforms included hybrid teaching, professional development for staff, focusing on critical thinking of students, cybersecurity for virtuality, Research and Development financial support, and globalization. Sethi and Roy (2022), who studied Indian universities, found a drop in student satisfaction in course content and teaching delivery. Gurukkal (2020) argues that HEI may become split into two types: social sciences and humanities that may be taught online to the general public, while sciences and engineering may be taught on campus. This would leave about 30% of students who would not have access to online education and 30% of instructors who would not be needed. Disciplinary lines will be blurred, and studies will be more student-directed.

Blankenberger and Williams (2020) note the importance of integrity and accountability for HEI leadership post-pandemic. Social equity may be one of the casualties of the pandemic due the financial pressures, the increase in virtual platforms, and the decrease in enrollments. According to Rapanta (2020), it is "time to rethink the practices of [higher education]: moving towards a more harmonious integration of physical and digital tools and methods for the sake of more active, flexible and meaningful learning" (p. 738).

Coll and Ruch (2021) offered a vision for the post-pandemic dean: she or he will need to lead refocused, reorganized, and newly resourced colleges. Departmental leadership will also have to take on strategic responsibility in a post-pandemic world (Floyd, 2022). College deans will need to act as CEOs of their colleges, aligning their mission with the institution, being innovative, and planning in a scenario style. They will need to move from a student retention focus to a recruitment focus, and to market-driven programming with all delivery modalities (remote, hybrid, and face-to-face). Finally, they will need to focus on a budget that has multiple revenue streams.

Fisher and Seamster (2022) noted that leadership in PPT will require leaders to engage with stakeholders to discuss the current state of the institution and its future around a series of honest critical questions. These questions need to be around the institution's values and purpose (the why), the engagement of stakeholders (the who), and the orientation of their operations (the what and how). All of these areas represent risks to HEIs, including liabilities, cost of debt, demographic changes, digitization, the value of higher education, and effectiveness. Gardner-McTaggart and Charles

(2020) note that HEI leadership needs to be globally-minded and intersubjective, and act communicatively.

Acosta (2021) suggests that HEI leaders not delay the transformation in PPT, encouraging leaders to re-emphasize the human element in education, to be more ethical in reorganizing, to fully engage in digitization and a new hybrid norm without sacrificing quality, and to commit to distributed leadership and innovation. Leaders must also influence public policy, ally with other universities, and serve larger populations since leadership is key to HEI success and critical to the success of the community.

HEI leaders need to consider that even in a post-pandemic world, people may still get the coronavirus, so burnout is a very real threat (Lapke & Lapke, 2022). Burnout is also occurring because of the stress of coping with transforming to a digital course delivery mode (El Aref, 2020). Despite the opportunities, the pandemic could still have devastating consequences such as cuts in funding from public sources, loss of tuition, HEIs closing, and lower access and higher dropout rates of disadvantaged student groups (Farnell et al., 2021).

Implications

Per Benhayoun (2020), the HEIs' responses to the global pandemic has been a "prelude to the beginning of a new era in the history of higher education," which is a striking statement for an industry marked by tradition and resistance to change. Mukaram et al. (2021), in their study of Pakistani HEIs, found that an adaptive leadership style was better able to deal with uncertainties and helped the institution be ready for change. They also found that it was important to invest in digitization and in learning capacity. Academic leadership is bound by academic structures, while adaptive leadership is flexible and dynamic, changing with the situation, and is best in complex situations undergoing rapid changes (Dunn, 2020; Sunderman et al., 2020).

Fleener (2021) developed a list of financial stressors for higher education as a result of the pandemic. These stressors led the author to conclude that large research and small private universities are most at risk in PPT. Erhan and Gümüş (2020) similarly noted that many HEIs worldwide are weak financially and may not survive. The continuing growth of distance education will also dislocate where learning takes place. Fleener (2021) suggests a shift away from the individual emphasis in learning institutions to a more dynamic, collective one, using the metaphor of the nautilus. To thrive in PPT, HEIs need to invest in digitization that is inclusive and provides equitable access. They also need to be externally focused and provide professional development for their staff (Alexander et al., 2020). As Acosta (2021) notes, "without determined leadership, all may be lost for higher education institutions" (p. 186). HEI leadership will not be able to face PPT alone. They will need assistance from government and other stakeholders globally (Farnell et al., 2021).

Conclusion

If the pandemic has taught us anything, it is that the future is unpredictable and that not staying stuck in the past is important. Leading higher education institutions has never been a smooth undertaking, but it is pivotal for leaders to continue to find ways to learn from the COVID-19 pandemic and identify new ways to operate more effectively and efficiently. As Wesley (2022) points out, "we're trying to tread a middle ground between an utterly exhausted executive team and a hawk-eyed board" (p. 26). Leaders in HEIs had to manage their own challenges, dealing with brusque changes. Many of them have faced these trials with remarkable responsiveness by espousing innovation and by spearheading a speedy transformation. Now that we are turning the corner, leaders of higher education institutions need to ensure that new ways of operation are adopted, while making sure to remain open to innovative modes of operations that are appropriate for the unforeseeable future (Kuusisto-Ek, 2022). Most importantly, HEI leadership needs to maintain open communication channels and dialogue with various stakeholders. This has been the norm during the pandemic and a significant factor to the success of various interventions. There has also been great agility in adopting digital transformation and integration from educational and operational perspectives, which has further proven that new modes of learning and operating using digital formats are not impossible. That said, the future of higher education rests in leaders' openness to adapt and maintain the levels of flexibility imposed by the internal and external environments.

References

Acosta, S. (2021). Leadership and opportunities for sustainable higher education vis-à-vis the pandemic. In S. Bergan, T. Gallher, I. Harkavy, R. Munck and H. van't Land (Eds.) *Higher Education's Response to The COVID-19 Pandemic*, 181–186. Council of Europe Higher Education Series No. 25.

Alexander, B., Darby, F., Fischer, K., Jack, A. A., Staisloff, R., Le Sane II, C. B., & Stout, K. A. (2020). *The Post-pandemic College: And the Future of The Academic Enterprise, Teaching and Learning, The Student Experience, Disadvantaged Students, Business Models, Enrollment, Community Colleges*. Chronicle of Higher Education.

Ashour, S., El-Refae, G. A., & Zaitoun, E. A. (2021). Post-pandemic higher education: Perspectives from university leaders and educational experts in the United Arab Emirates. *Higher Education for the Future*, *8*(2), 219–238. https://doi.org/10.1177/23476311211007261

Azad, R. (2021). *Founder of the world's first university: Fatima al-Fihri set the foundation of higher education recognized today*. https://thetempest.co/2021/03/03/history/fatima-al-fihri-founder-of-the-worlds-first-university/

Bakir, A., & Dahlan, M. (2022). Higher education leadership and curricular design in industry 5.0 environment: A cursory glance. *Development and Learning Organizations: An International Journal*, Ahead of print, https://doi.org/10.1108/DLO-08-2022–0166

Bebbington, W. (2021). Leadership strategies for a higher education sector in flux. *Studies in Higher Education*, *46*(1), 158–165. https://doi.org/10.1080/03075079.2020.1859686

Benhayoun, J. E. (2020). The new global university in the post-COVID–19 world. *University World News, 4.*

Blankenberger, B., & Williams, A. M. (2020). COVID and the impact on higher education: The essential role of integrity and accountability. *Administrative Theory & Praxis, 42*(3), 404–423. https://doi.org/10.1080/10841806.2020.1771907

Bor, W., & Shute, J. (1991). Higher education in the third world: Status symbol or instrument for development? *Higher Education, 22*(3), 1–15.

Bryman, A. (2007). Effective leadership in higher education: A literature review. *Studies in Higher Education, 32(*6), 693–710. https://doi.org/10.1080/03075070701685114

Califano, S. K. (2022). People, place, and purpose: Emergent post–pandemic higher education and employment needs in the future of work. In S. Ramlall, T. Cross, & M. Love, (Eds.) *Handbook of Research on Future of Work and Education: Implications for Curriculum Delivery and Work Design.* pp. 55–70. IGI Global

Carrigan, M., & Jordan, K. (2022). Platforms and institutions in the post-pandemic university: A case study of social media and the impact agenda. *Postdigital Science and Education*, *4*, 354–372. https://doi.org/10.1007/s42438-021-00269-x

Clabaugh, A., Duque, J. F., & Fields, L. J. (2021). Academic stress and emotional well-being of United States college students following onset of the COVID-19 pandemic. *Frontiers in Psychology*, 12. https://doi.org/10.3389/fpsyg.2021.628787

Coll, K. M., & Ruch, C. P. (2021). Academic deanship in a post–pandemic institution. *International Journal of Higher Education*, *10*(5), 132–137.

Daft, R. F. (2016). *The Leadership Experience*. Cengage Learning.

Dagiene, V., Jasute, E., Navickiene, V., Butkiene, R., & Gudoniene, D. (2022). Opportunities, quality factors, and required changes during the pandemic based on higher education leaders' perspective. *Sustainability*, *14*(3), 1933. https://doi.org/10.3390/su14031933

Denney, F. (2021). The 'golden braid' model: Courage, compassion and resilience in higher education leadership. *Journal of Higher Education Policy and Leadership Studies*, *2*(2), 37–49. https://dx.doi.org/10.52547/johepal.2.2.37

Dunn, R. (2020). Adaptive leadership: Leading through complexity. *International Studies in Educational Administration (Commonwealth Council for Educational Administration and Management (CCEAM)*, *48*(1), 31–38.

Edmondson, M. (2021). Agile leadership in a volatile world: It calls for self-awareness, thinking differently, and creating organizational change. *Planning for Higher Education*, *49*(3).

El Aref, N. (2020). Post Pandemic Paradigm of Higher Education. *EFMD Global.* https://blog.efmdglobal.org/2020/07/07/post-pandemic-paradigm-of-higher–education/

El Fasi, M. (1962). *L'Université Marocaine au Tournant de son Histoire*. Le Monde Diplomatique.

Erhan, Ç., & Gümüş, Ş. (2020). Opportunities and risks in higher education in the post pandemic period. In M. Seker, A. Ozer, and C. Korkut, (Eds). *Reflections on the Pandemic in the Future of the World*, 179–194.Turkish Academy of Sciences.

Eringfeld, S. (2021). Higher education and its post-coronial future: Utopian hopes and dystopian fears at Cambridge University during COVID–19, *Studies in Higher Education*, *46*(1), 146–157. https://doi.org/10.1080/03075079.2020.1859681

Ewing, L. A. (2021). Rethinking Higher Education Post COVID–19. Chapter 3, 37–54. https://doi.org/10.1007/978-981-33-4126-5

Farnell, T., Skledar Matijević, A., & Šćukanec Schmidt, N. (2021). *The impact of COVID-19 on higher education: A review of emerging evidence: Analytical report*, European Commission, Directorate–General for Education, Youth, Sport and Culture Publications Office. https://data.europa.eu/doi/10.2766/069216

Fernandez, A.A., & Shaw, G. P. (2020). Academic leadership in a time of crisis: The coronavirus and COVID-19. *Journal of Leadership Studies*, *14*(1), 39–45.

Fernandez, A. A., & Shaw, G. P. (2022a). Higher education leadership in a changing world: The coronavirus pandemic and COVID–19. In *Leadership and Management Strategies for Creating Agile Universities*, 1–15. IGI Global. https://doi.org/10.4018/978-1-7998-8213-8.ch001

Fernandez, A. A., & Shaw, G. (2022b). Higher education leadership in uncertain times: Navigating the coronavirus pandemic toward positive change. In *INTED2022 Proceedings* (pp. 2031–2035). IATED.

Fisher, J. K., & Seamster, J. (2022). Exiting the pandemic: A leadership approach to critical engagement and change. *The Vermont Connection, 43*(1), 222–236. https://scholarworks.uvm.edu/tvc/vol43/iss1/22

Fleener, M. J. (2021). A social inquiry analysis of post-pandemic higher education: A futures perspective. *Journal of Higher Education Theory & Practice, 21*(10).

Floyd, A. (2022). Departmental leadership in a post-pandemic world: Taking collective responsibility for our future success. In *Leadership and Management Strategies for Creating Agile Universities*. https://doi.org/10.4018/978-1-7998-8213-8.ch002

Fung, D., & Gordon, C. E. (2022). Leadership, vision, and values in a time of change and crisis: A perspective from a UK research-intensive university. In *Leadership and Management Strategies for Creating Agile Universities*. IGI Global. https://doi.org/10.4018/978-1-7998-8213-8.ch005

Gardner–McTaggart, A. C., & Charles, A. (2020). Educational leadership and global crises; Reimagining planetary futures through social practice. *International Journal of Leadership in Education, 25*(4), 1–17. https://doi.org/10.1080/13603124.2020.1811900

Goel, R., & Sharma, R. (2021). Studying leaders & their concerns using online social media during the times of crisis – A COVID case study. *Social. Network. Analysis and Mining, 11*, 46. https://doi.org/10.1007/s13278-021-00756–w

Gigliotti, R. A. (2020). *Crisis leadership in higher education: Theory and practice*. Rutgers University Press.

Green, W., Anderson, V., Tait, K., & Tran, L. T. (2020). Precarity, fear and hope: Reflecting and imagining in higher education during a global pandemic. *Higher Education Research & Development, 39*(7), 1309–1312. https://doi.org/10.1080/07294360.2020.1826029

Gunawan, J., Marzilli, C., & Aungsuroch, Y. (2022). Sustaining e-caring leadership in a post–pandemic world. *Belitung Nursing Journal, 8*(1), 1–3. https://doi.org/10.33546/bnj.2039

Gurukkal, R. (2020). Will COVID 19 Turn higher education into another mode? *Higher Education for the Future, 7*(2), 89–96. https://doi.org/10.1177/2347631120931606

Hamlin, R. G., & Patel, T. (2015). Perceived managerial and leadership effectiveness within higher education in France. *Studies in Higher Education, 1–23.* https://doi.org/10.1080/03075079.2015.1045480

Hollander, J. B. (2021). The pandemic is taking higher education back to school. *University World News*, 23 January. https://www.universityworldnews.com/post.php?story=20210118070559840

Jansa, T., & Anderson, D. L. (2021). Socially responsive leadership for post-pandemic international higher education: Theoretical considerations and practical implications. *Institute of International Education.* https://iie.widen.net/s/smjqvmzkc9/socially-responsive-leadership-white-paper

Kandri, S. E. (2020 May 12). How COVID-19 is driving a long-overdue revolution in education. *World Economic Forum*. https://www.weforum.org/agenda/2020/05/how-COVID-19-is-sparking-a-revolution-in-higher-education/

Kele, K., & Mzileni, P. (2021). Higher education leadership responses applied in two South African comprehensive universities during the COVID-19 pandemic: A critical discourse analysis. *Transformation in Higher Education, 6*(0), a114. https://doi.org/10.4102/the.v6i0.114

Kovacs, K. (2022). *The Pandemic's Impact on College Enrollment*. https://www.bestcolleges.com/blog/COVID19-impact-on-college-enrollment/

Kruse, S. D., Hackmann, D. G., & Lindle, J. C. (2020). Academic leadership during a pandemic: Department heads leading with a focus on equity. *Frontiers in Education, 5*. https://doi.org/10.3389/feduc.2020.614641

Kummitha, H. R., Kolloju, N., Chittoor, P., & Madepalli, V. (2021). Coronavirus Disease 2019 and its effect on teaching and learning process in the higher educational institutions. *Higher Education for the Future, 8* (1), 90–107. https://doi.org/10.1177/2347631120983650

Kuusisto-Ek, H. (2022). Strategic management of higher education institutions in a European context: A literature review. In *Leadership and Management Strategies for Creating Agile Universities*. IGI Global. https://doi.org/10.4018/978-1-7998-8213-8

Lamm, K. W., Powell, A., Sapp, L., & Lamm, A. (2022). Higher education leadership development during the COVID–19 pandemic: An exploration of online learner readiness. *Journal of International Agricultural and Extension Education, 29*(1), 22–39. https://doi.org/10.4148/2831–5960.1016

Lapke, S. M., & Lapke, M. S., (2022). Effectively leading the new normal for higher education in a post pandemic world. *Digital Culture & Education, 14*(1), 38–55. https://www.digitalcultureandeducation.com/volume-14–1

Leithwood, K., Harris, A., & Hopkins, D. (2020). Seven strong claims about successful school leadership revisited. *School Leadership and Management, 40*(1), 5–22.

Lekchiri, S., Chuang, S., Crowder, C. L., Eversole, B. A. W. (2022). The disappearing research agendas of mother-scholars in academia during the COVID–19 pandemic: Autoethnographic studies. *New Horizons in Adult Education and Human Resource Development, 34*(3), 40–53. https://doi.org/10.1002/nha3.20357

Lekchiri, S., Eversole, B. A. W., Hamlin, R. G., & Crowder, C. (2018). Perceived managerial efficacy within a Moroccan higher education institution. *Human Resource Development International, 21*(4), 340–361. https://doi.org/10.1080/13678868.2018.1433394

Lemoine, P. A., & Richardson, M. D. (2020). Planning for higher education institutions: Chaos and the COVID–19 pandemic. *Educational Planning, 27*(3), 43–57.

Liu, B. F., Shi, D., Lim, J. R., Islam, K., Edwards, A. L., & Seeger, M. (2022). When crises hit home: How U.S. higher education leaders navigate values during uncertain times. *Journal of Business Ethics, 179*, 353–368. https://doi.org/10.1007/s10551-021-04820–5

Lumby, J. (2019). Leadership and power in higher education, *Studies in Higher Education, 44(*9), 1619–1629. https://doi.org/10.1080/03075079.2018.1458221

Maas, B., Grogan, K. E., Chirango, Y., Harris, N., Liévano-Latorre, L. F., McGuire, K. L., . . . Toomey, A. (2020). Academic leaders must support inclusive scientific communities during COVID-19. *Natural Ecology & Evolution, 4*, 997–999. https://doi.org/10.1038/s41559-020-1233-3

Marmolejo, F. J., & Groccia, J. E. (2022). Reimagining and redesigning teaching and learning in the post-pandemic world. *New Directions in Teaching and Learning, 169*, 21–37. https://doi.org/10.1002/tl.20480

Menon, K., & Motala, S. (2021). Pandemic leadership in higher education: New horizons, risks and complexities. *Education as Change, 25*(1), 1–19. https://dx.doi.org/10.25159/1947–9417/8880

Miller, M. T. (2021). Do learning organizations learn? Higher education institutions and pandemic response strategies. *The Learning Organization, 28*(1), 84–93. https://doi.org/10.1108/TLO-09-2020-0159

Mukaram, A.T., Rathore, K., Khan, M. A., Danish, R. Q., & Zubair, S. S. (2021). Can adaptive–academic leadership duo make universities ready for change? Evidence from higher education institutions in Pakistan in the light of COVID–19. *Management Research Review, 44*(11), 1478–1498. https://doi.org/10.1108/MRR-09-2020-0598

NAFSA. (2020). *NAFSA financial impact survey: a brief summary*. NAFSA Financial Impact Survey.

Newton, R. (2021). Rediscover joy at work. *Harvard Business Review*. https://hbr.org/2021/09/rediscover-joy-at-work

Nair, P. (2021). Reimagining higher education in the post-pandemic world. In *Transforming Curriculum Through Teacher-Learner Partnerships* (pp. 1–9). IGI Global.

Nica, E. (2013). The importance of leadership within higher education. *Contemporary Readings in Law and Social Justice, 5*(2), 189–194.

Nugroho, I., Paramita, N., Mengistie, B. T., & Krupskyi, O. P. (2021). Higher education leadership and uncertainty during the COVID–19 pandemic. *Journal of Socioeconomics and Development*, *4*(1), 1–7.

Peters, T. J. (1987). *Thriving on Chaos: Handbook for a Management Revolution*. Harper Perennial.

Pokhrel, S., & Chhetri, R. (2021). A literature review on impact of COVID-19 Pandemic on teaching and learning. *Higher Education for the Future*, *8*(1), 133–14. https://doi.org/10.1177/2347631120983481

Purcell, W. M., & Lumbreras, J. (2021). Higher education and the COVID-19 pandemic: Navigating disruption using the sustainable development goals. *Discover Sustainability*, *2*(6). https://doi.org/10.1007/s43621-021-00013-2

Rapanta, C., Botturti, L., Goodyear, P. Guardia, L., & Koole, M. (2021). Balancing technology, pedagogy and the new normal: Post–pandemic challenges for higher education. *Postdigital Science and Education*, *3*, 715–742. https://doi.org/10.1007/s42438-021-00249–1

Rehbock, S. K. (2020), Academic leadership: Challenges and opportunities for leaders and leadership development in higher education, In M. Antoniadou and M. Crowder, (Eds). *Modern Day Challenges in Academia*, pp. 252–264. Edward Elgar Publishing.

Rosowsky, D. (2022). Learn, leverage, and leap? Or lethargy, lapse, and languish? Higher education's post-pandemic posture. https://www.forbes.com/sites/davidrosowsky/2022/03/27/learn-leverage-and-leap-or-lethargy-lapse-and-languish-higher-educations-post-pandemic-posture/?sh=10d6f4ca3f7a

Routledge. (2021). How COVID-19 has changed higher education. https://www.routledge.com/blog/article/how-COVID-19-has-changed-higher-education

Rosenberg, B. (2020, April 3). How should colleges prepare for a post-pandemic world? *The Chronicle of Higher Education*. https://docs.bartonccc.edu/about/administration/presidents-blog/how-should-colleges-prepare-for-post-pandemic-world.pdf

Roy, A. (2020). The pandemic is a portal. *Financial Times*, 3 April. https://www.ft.com/content/10d8f5e8-74eb-11ea-95fe-fcd274e920ca

Sethi, K., & Roy, M. (2022). Gaining a better understanding of higher education: During and post-pandemic scenario. *International Review of Business and Economics*. *7*(1), Article 5. https://digitalcommons.du.edu/irbe/vol7/iss1/5

Shah, A. M., Anjum, T., Niazi, S., Ahmed, S. T., Hussain, M. K., & Haider, S. (2022). Post pandemic reforms in education and role of leadership in critical situation at higher education institutions of Pakistan. *Webology* (ISSN: 1735-188X), *19*(2).

Smalley, A. (2021). Higher education responses to Coronavirus (COVID-19). https://www.ncsl.org/research/education/higher-education-responses-to-coronavirus-COVID–19.aspx#:~:text=The%20outbreak%20of%20the%20coronavirus,moving%20to%20online%2Donly%20instruction

Smith, B. L., & Hughey, A. W. (2006). Leadership in higher education–its evolution and potential: A unique role facing critical challenges. *Industry & Higher Education*, *20*(3) 157–163.

Sonn, I. K., Du Plessis, M., Jansen Van Vuuren, C. D., Marais, J., Wagener, E., & Roman, N. V. (2021). Achievements and challenges for higher education during the COVID-19 pandemic: A rapid review of media in Africa. *International Journal of Environmental Research and Public Health*, *18*(24), 12888. https://doi.org/10.3390/ijerph182412888

Stadnyk, T., & Black, K. (2020). Lost ground: Female academics face an uphill battle in post–pandemic world. *Hydrological processes*, *34*(15), 3400–3402. https://doi.org/10.1002/hyp.13803

Sunderman, H. M., Headrick, J., & McCain, K. (2020). Addressing complex issues and crises in higher education with an adaptive leadership framework. *Change: The Magazine of Higher Learning*, *52*(6), 22–29. https://doi.org/10.1080/00091383.2020.1839322

Thompson, J. (2019). Public administrators: The relevance of teaching the agility model for efficacious sector leadership. *American Society for Public Administration*. https://patimes.org/public-administrators-the-relevance-of-teaching-the-agility-model-for-efficacious-sector-leadership/

Ünal, Z. M. (2022). Need for leadership in times of crises: Integration of modern and post-modern leadership approaches. In *Leadership and Management Strategies for Creating Agile Universities*. IGI Global. https://doi.org/10.4018/978-1-7998-8213-8.ch004

Watermeyer, R., Crick, T., Knight, C. & Goodall, J. (2021). COVID–19 and digital disruption in UK universities: Afflictions and affordances of emergency online migration. *Higher Education, 81*, 623–642. https://doi.org/10.1007/s10734-020-00561-y

Wesley, J. (2022). COVID-19: A Catalyst of HEI Leadership. *Saxton Bampfylde*.

Xie, L. (2020). Leadership and organizational learning culture: A systematic literature review, *European Journal of Training and Development, 43*(1–2), 76–104. https://doi.org/10.1108/EJTD-06-2018-0056

Zackal, J. (2021). Remote work is more of a possibility beyond the pandemic. https://www.higheredjobs.com/Articles/articleDisplay.cfm?ID=2600

Zhao, Y. (2020). COVID-19 as a catalyst for educational change. *Prospects: Quarterly Review of Comparative Education, 49*(1–2), 29–3. https://doi.org/10.1007/s11125-020-09477-y

Cliodhna MacKenzie and Thomas Garavan

Chapter 8
Political Leadership during the COVID-19 Pandemic: Paradox, Politics, Power and Compassion

Abstract: The COVID-19 pandemic was a once-in-100 year event that presented significant leadership challenges for leaders across the world including effective crisis leadership. In this chapter we critique crisis leadership utilizing a paradox theory lens, and unpack whether embracing paradoxical thinking provides clues to why some leaders were more successful than others in responding to the COVID-19 pandemic. Specifically, it appears that female political leaders such as Angela Merkel and Jacinda Ardern were far more successful than many male political leaders such as Boris Johnson and Donald Trump in adapting to the challenges presented by the pandemic. We apply the concept of the paradox mindset to illustrate how female political leaders leaned into COVID-19 paradoxes and improvised solutions where many male political leaders faltered. We consider whether paradoxical leadership and a paradox mindset represents one small step, or one giant leap in understanding what it means to lead and be a leader, especially in times of crisis. We generate several general insights that are useful in the context of major crises and consider the potential for incorporating paradox mindset as instrumental to *not* solving paradox tensions but rather, leaning into paradoxes in order to successfully navigate *through* them.

Keywords: Crisis leadership, leadership, paradox theory, women leaders, Jacinda Ardern, Angela Merkel, Donald Trump, Boris Johnson

Introduction

It is said that in times of crisis the hour of the executive emerges (Kneuer & Wallaschek, 2022) and COVID-19 represented a fine example of crisis so significant that it changed the very nature of human existence (Carmine et al., 2021). Indeed, the COVID-19 pandemic revealed significant limitations and shortcomings in the capabilities of many political actors, as economies faltered, workplaces were shuttered and the reporting of daily mortality rates from infection to the virus defined for many the 'new normal'. COVID-19 was indiscriminate, infecting people from across the socio-economic divide.

Cliodhna MacKenzie, University College Cork, Ireland
Thomas Garavan, University College Cork, Ireland

https://doi.org/10.1515/9783110799101-008

As alluded to by Jacinda Ardern, New Zealand's Prime Minister during the pandemic, COVID-19's emergence was likely to cause upset, anxiety and uncertainty among New Zealanders and would undoubtedly disrupt normal life (Ardern, 2020b). Arguably, the COVID-19 pandemic was just one more crisis in a long series of crises that had created a new sense of normal against a backdrop of the contextual features of 'volatility, uncertainty, complexity and ambiguity' (Li, 2020, p. 503) that had grown in frequency since the global financial crisis of 2008. However, given the reach, impact and human cost of COVID-19, this was a different type of crisis. Put simply, COVID-19 was a game changer.

At a general level, political leadership across the globe was, in many cases, found wanting; lacking both competency and compassion (Simpson et al., 2022), agility and adaptability (Förster, Paparella, Duchek, & Güttel, 2022), and the ability to find a balance between short-term and long-term outcomes (Kneuer & Wallaschek, 2022). What proved especially challenging for many leaders was having to remain accountable as an individual leader whilst sharing when necessary, leadership with the 'collective' such was the complexity, ambiguity and tensions posed by the pandemic (Spyridonidis, Cote, Currie, & Denis, 2022). In this context, it is generally understood that leaders such as Jacinda Ardern and Angela Merkel – who was the Germany's Chancellor – responded much more successfully in coping with the impact posed by COVID-19 due to their more empathetic leadership approach (Dada, Ashworth, Bewa, & Dhatt, 2021, Johnson & Williams, 2020). These leaders demonstrated a willingness to be honest but firm, able to take decisive action, while also conveying a sense of empathy and social togetherness. In addition, they showed a capacity to shift from leading, to being led by the science and the public health professionals, whose knowledge and expertise was critical in ensuring the citizens of their countries remained safe but not isolated during the most challenging stages of the crisis. Both Angela Merkel and Jacinda Ardern demonstrated that COVID-19's rapid emergence necessitated swift action, adaptability while acknowledging known processes, *and* at the same time, improvisation when the rule book did not work out (Simpson et al., 2022).

The numbers associated with the pandemic are staggering. As of January 18, 2023, there had been over 663 million cases of infection across the globe with more than 6.707 million deaths associated with the virus (WHO, 2023). The long-term effects of the pandemic on the global labor force is even more pronounced with geopolitical instability in Eastern Europe, high inflation and more localized economic instability (Brexit) hampering post-pandemic labor force recovery resulting in a deficit of between 40 and 52 million full-time jobs (ILO, 2022). Indeed, the human cost of the pandemic far exceeds the reported fatalities. The long-term effects of exposure to various strains of the virus for example, have impacted significant numbers of individuals with no underlying comorbidities (Huang et al., 2021) and provides startling evidence that the pandemic has been life-changing for many and for whom, the 'new normal' far transcends the changing nature of work.

COVID-19 has also brought into sharp focus the realization that the global economy was every bit as vulnerable to microscopic pathogens as human beings. Although many have argued the pandemic was not a matter of if, but when (Kain & Fowler, 2019), very few could have predicted the degree to which it would impact societies and business enterprises (Li, 2020). However, despite decades of knowledge and experience dealing with pandemics, many political leaders failed to both adequately prepare for, and respond to the effects of COVID-19 when it emerged. Unsurprisingly, very few countries had learned lessons from the SARS outbreak in 2003, with some notable exceptions (e.g., New Zealand and South Korea). Arguing that there was simply nothing in the playbook to which one could refer and respond when it came to COVID-19 demonstrates that lessons are not always learned when crises emerge. The rise of populist political leaders such as Donald J. Trump, Jair Bolsonaro, and Boris Johnson to name but a few, limited the responsiveness of the U.S., Brazil and the U.K. given the predilection of these leaders to minimize or downplay critical public health information from subject matter experts. Instead, they relied on their charisma, guile and perceived intellect to solve a complex public health crisis (McDonnell, 2016). Moreover, these populist leaders were more likely to engage in half-truths, lies, innuendoes and empty verbiage (Foroughi, Gabriel, & Fotaki, 2019) as the lines between the truth-lies, honesty-dishonesty and fiction-nonfiction paradoxes emerged and became blurred. Political leaders such as Donald J. Trump and Boris Johnson for example, laid out aggressive plans to eradicate the virus and in some instances, suggested it would just disappear overnight (Ortega & Orsini, 2020; Paton, 2022; Rutledge, 2020). Somewhat unsurprisingly, their responses to the crisis consisted of poor communication, arrogance, inability to listen and an 'anti-leadership' disposition focused on dividing rather than uniting their citizenry, which ultimately severely limited their ability to effectively manage the crisis (Hu & Liu, 2022).

Not all political leaders' responses to the crisis were, however, flawed. In Norway for example, political leaders worked with both career civil servants and public healthcare professionals to devise a cohesive strategy to protect the citizenry and minimize the impact of the virus (Isaksson & Solvoll, 2022). Interestingly, in the Norwegian case, the acknowledgment and welcoming of division and dissent among various stakeholders were essential elements of the crisis communication, including greater openness and respect for divergent opinions regarding the most appropriate course of action when it came to public health strategies. While some leaders grappled with how much candor, openness, and detail to communicate to citizens, Norwegian leaders accepted that dissent, discord, and debate was necessary to protect their citizens. Norway was an outlier in effective use of government rhetoric that was, on the whole, beneficial for both political leaders and the citizens of the country. Overall however, despite decades of leadership research and associated theory development, many leaders engaged in missteps in their response to dealing with COVID-19 because for many, demonstrating leadership strength and at the same time showing compassion and vulnerability was paradoxical and difficult to achieve concurrently (Simpson & Berti, 2020). Political leaders, and in particular female political leaders appeared to be more comfortable than many male counterparts when faced with these paradoxes.

While there is much debate regarding female leader ability, especially during crisis periods, the evidence is clear: When it came to the recent COVID-19 global pandemic, female leaders succeeded far more than they failed (Wittenberg-Cox, 2020). When political leaders around the globe felt the only response to the pandemic was to exhibit strength, paternalism, and autocracy, female leaders adopted a paradox mindset by embracing empathy and communicating with vulnerability as a strength rather than a weakness. In the case of Angela Merkel, a political leader not known for her leadership charisma, her ability to communicate solidarity and unity during the pandemic, especially in a country facing significant political upheaval surprised many (Kneuer & Wallaschek, 2022). Yet, Merkel's conservatism and perceptions that she was austere, cold and detached told only half the story (Kurbjuweit, 2011). Her academic background (Ph.D. in quantum chemistry) should have limited her ability to improvise; yet she communicated with stark honesty *but* with humanity, and united a divided country during one of the most challenging periods since she became Chancellor in 2005 (Mayer & May, 2021). Arguably, given Merkel's academic credentials, when faced with a pandemic of global proportions, she adapted and improvised.

The COVID-19 pandemic therefore represents an ideal context in which to explore the operation of paradoxical tensions because at the core of the pandemic were paradoxes, tensions, and dilemmas. In an effort to protect people from the COVID-19 virus, political leaders were faced with making decisions that pitted human health protection against economic necessity (Carmine et al., 2021). Insightfully, Simpson et al. (2022) noted, the tensions between "societal health, economic productivity and personal freedom imposed by COVID-19" created an unwieldy environment that challenged even those leaders whose paradoxical thinking might be a natural default, forcing them to make decisions on-the-fly in a "fog of uncertainty" that produced 'chaotic learning' before arriving at a "paradox embracing strategy". Ultimately, the pandemic forced political leaders to embrace uncertainty and approach COVID-19 tensions not from an either/or but a both/and perspective (Smith & Lewis, 2011) where the ability to pivot and improvise trumped cautious calculations as the pandemic raged on. It is this theme that we explore in this chapter and use paradox theory as our theoretical lens to understand how political leaders were effective or not effective in dealing with the COVID-19 pandemic.

Paradox Theory and its Application to the Pandemic

> *The problem is not the problem; the problem is the way we think about the* problem (Watzlawick, Weakland & Fisch, 1974 cited in Miron-Spektor, Ingram, Keller, Smith, & Lewis, 2018, p.4)

COVID-19 manifested the paradox tensions faced by the political elite among other leaders across the globe, creating situations of almost impossible choice (Putnam, Fairhurst, & Banghart, 2016). Paradoxes are defined as the existence of persistent contradictions between interdependent elements that produce tensions that exist over time (Sharma et al., 2021; Smith & Lewis, 2011). Smith & Lewis (2011, p. 397), for example, argued that fundamental to the paradox is the premise that 'tensions are integral to complex systems', and that most decisions are made within a context that demands "attending to contradictory yet *interwoven demands simultaneously*". These observations therefore potentially provide novel insights into why some political leaders responded more effectively or failed to respond at all to the pandemic. The multiple paradoxes facing political leaders during the pandemic were myriad, and in the face of constant volatility, rising mortality rates, and competing demands for action, some political leaders became paralyzed by what Putnam et al. (2016) refer to as the irrationality and absurdity of the situation: restricting movement and economic activity while keeping the economy open and moving – an impossible choice *for some.*

A critical dimension of paradoxes however, is the necessity to engage in *some* form of action (Berti & Simpson, 2021) and push through the tensions and contradictions of the paradox despite the interdependence of competing elements and irrationality of the decision a leader is faced with. Drawing on knowledge and experience, some leaders became paralyzed when faced with pandemic paradoxes, searching for a solution to the source of tension, making 'either/or' trade-offs that limited, rather than enhanced response effectiveness. The real challenge with paradoxes is not the paradox itself as insightfully articulated by Watzlawick et al. (1974) but the ability to recognize that the challenge lies in how we *think* about the problem the paradox presents. In essence, in accepting that paradoxes and associated tensions will always exist, the real challenge is to become comfortable with *not* solving the paradox but instead finding a way to navigate *through* it, or more specifically, *leaning into* it. Therefore, the *most* appropriate response to the pandemic, running counterintuitive to what a leader might *want* to do, was to pursue a "both/and' rather than 'either/or" strategy (Jay, 2013) to deal with paradoxical tensions (problems) and associated paralysis by analysis and ultimately *inaction.*

The importance of considering paradox theory as a lens to explore political leader successes and failures during the COVID-19 pandemic is underscored by the fact that paradoxes and contradictions play a central role in the process-based literature on organizational change and innovation (Putnam et al., 2016), arguably key issues that emerged for every leader during the COVID-19 pandemic. Although, and as previously argued, there was widespread recognition that many nations had anticipated a global pandemic (e.g., U.S. concerns about the spread of Ebola) many countries were unable to predict when exactly it would happen, the degree to which it would spread, and its impact on economic activity. Accordingly, leadership responsiveness was very much a mixed bag ranging from effective to ineffective. Globalization and internationalization have been cited as significant risk factors when it comes to the pandemic and its rapid spread (Li, 2020; Tourish, 2020). However, the inability of many leaders to properly respond to the pandemic crisis was more reflective of a rapidly evolving environment where information was ambiguous and at times misleading, or incorrect (Siebenhaar,

Kother, & Alpers, 2020) rather than the effects of globalization. Critically however, some leaders' pandemic inaction was not predicated on over analyzing impossible choices but based purely on lies, innuendo and conspiracy theories (Kapucu & Moynihan, 2021; Rutledge, 2020). The pandemic was a crisis that required *prompt* rational decision-making whilst also paradoxically, necessitating leaders remain flexible, and improvise when years of experience told them to 'stick to the plan'. For some leaders, these paradoxical tensions resulted in finding resolutions and only temporary reprieves. For other leaders, however, those who embraced and were able to *lean-in* to the paradox tensions, developed a 'comfort in their discomfort' and learned to manage, rather than solve the paradox (Mayer & May, 2021). This was the crisis management equivalent of *steering into the skid.*

In understanding why many leaders may have failed to adequately respond to the pandemic, we draw on Miron-Spektor, Ingram, Keller, Smith, & Lewis' (2018) concept of the paradox mindset. By considering political leaders' responses to the pandemic from a paradox mindset, we gain a greater insight into why some political leaders failed to properly manage the pandemic when it emerged. Arguably, some political leaders responses were predicated on solving an immediate problem (stopping the spread of the virus) which in the short-term, worked; however, without appropriately learning from pandemic successes in the past (evidence from government responses to the SARS outbreak in 2003) – *solving* the "COVID-19 spread problem" would only have been a short-term solution as is now being evidence in China (Ridley, 2022). A paradox mindset requires actors to "accept" and "live with" paradox as living with paradox necessitates actors shift their comfort with rationality and accept paradox as 'persistent unsolved puzzles' (Smith & Lewis, 2011, p. 385). Leaning into and embracing stress *reduces* rather than increases defensiveness, thus making leaders more receptive to lateral thinking and improvisation. Nevertheless, despite the importance of leveraging stress and accepting paradox, some political leaders lacked an appropriate level of emotional and cognitive ability (Luscher & Lewis, 2008) necessary to embrace stress and tension but more importantly, learn from the challenges they were faced with when it came to the pandemic. For actors that exhibited a paradox mindset, embracing and leaning-in to the tensions energizes their emotions as they reflect on the benefits derived from improvising. But for actors that were more challenged by paradox tensions and could only visualize a "either/or" zero-sum outcome, they may have become emotionally drained by feeling compelled to choose one option over the other rather than *both* simultaneously, the paradox mindset shift proving too difficult to adjust to.

The importance of a paradox mindset for any leader facing a crisis situation cannot be overstated because in accepting the tensions inherent in a paradox, leaders can *learn* to accept that the complex interplay between the competing elements doesn't mean trade-offs need to be made because the paradox is not a zero-sum scenario that needs to be played out. By embracing and learning from paradox tensions, leaders can recognize the don't need to eliminate tensions but acknowledge the potential benefits to be accrued by engaging in both (Miron-Spektor et al., 2018). Leveraging paradox tensions and employing a "both/and" strategy increases the likelihood actors will engage in *double-loop* learning as they continually adjust their thinking and learning when faced with competing elements in a synergistically beneficial manner (Andriopoulos & Lewis, 2009). This is the very essence of improvisation.

It is suggested that a paradox mindset can be the difference between success in the face of adversity or abject failure despite the potential for opportunity and growth. Paradoxes and associated tensions provide opportunities for double-loop learning but only as long as actors are willing to embrace uncertainty, accept ambiguity, and welcome the stress of seemingly conflicting and contradictory choices. Ultimately, dealing with paradoxes and the conflicts and tensions they generate require both cognitive and emotional reserves, and unless actors can tap into both in equal measure, it is unlikely that these actors will possess a paradox mindset. Moreover, when faced with a crisis that is paradoxical in nature, it is unlikely these actors will be successful in the medium to long-term as initial "either/or" decision-making is likely to result in only short-term benefits. Learning from previous crises can equip leaders with the appropriate skills to *lean-in* to the paradox tensions and become comfortable with improvisation rather than solving the problem associated with the paradox tensions. As Wendt (1998, p. 361) perceptively noted "the wisdom extracted from organizational paradoxes can change *how* (emphasis in original) we think more than *what* we think" but in order develop that mindset, leaders must be willing to be receptive and consider the potential benefits from engaging in competing tensions *simultaneously*.

Leader Responses to COVID-19: Maligning, Dividing, and Improvising

> *There comes a time when one must take a position that is neither safe, nor politic, nor popular, but he must take it because conscience tells him it is right.* (King, 1968)

The myth of the great leader and the imagery it portrays is one where the leader exudes confidence, charisma and authority and is unassailable in *his* knowledge. Of course, that's the romanticism of leadership. Despite advances in developing theories that reflect the nuance of what it means to be a leader, or excel in a leadership role, no one theory can adequately explain *or* predict how any leader might respond in crisis situations. To paraphrase Heifetz et al. (2009), leaders cannot erect firewalls against crises that emerge from economic, geopolitical and natural causes; all they can do is create stability when crises emerge and adapt, as best they can, when it is known what the root cause of the crisis is. While somewhat reductive, crisis leadership aptly describes the environment in which many leaders found themselves, and subsequent responses, especially among political leaders across the globe. While Heifetz et al. (2009) describe the approach to crises when the cause is known, COVID-19 presented a highly dynamic context in which knowing what the root cause was provided little benefit as many leaders struggled to stabilize and adapt to what was an environment characterized by multiple paradoxes competing against each other for solutions that were unachievable. For political leaders such as Jacinda Ardern and Angela Merkel, the pandemic proved challenging to navigate; however, their handling of the pandemic has been viewed as more successful when compared with male political leaders such as Donald Trump and Boris Johnson (Friedman, 2020; Kneuer & Wallaschek, 2022; Lee, 2020; Mayer & May, 2021; McGuire, Cunningham, Reynolds, & Matthews-Smith, 2020; Rutledge, 2020; Tomkins, 2020). Arguably, leadership approaches may have accounted for the differences in perceived successes and failures in pandemic responsiveness. Nonetheless, it is also possible that both Trump and Johnson may have lacked a paradox mindset that allowed them to innovate and improvise rather than rationalize and prioritize and this lack of a paradox mindset (among other character flaws) was critical in their inability to respond appropriately to the pandemic.

The complexity of leadership as alluded to by Hansen, Ropo, and Sauer (2007) describes the undulating landscape leaders constantly find themselves navigating. Like the death and taxes truism, leaders face constant pressure to choose between competing social and economic demands (Smith, Besharov, Wessels, & Chertok, 2012). In the context of COVID-19, leaders had to navigate the paradoxes of ensuring structure and stability with freedom and flexibility, of necessitating stringent control over free movement in an effort to stop the spread of the virus, with a plea for collaboration and unity in the face of great uncertainty and personal freedom sacrifices (Förster et al., 2022). More crucially, political leaders had to become comfortable with being uncomfortable, especially when it came to discounting trade-offs (pursuit of economic growth and the need to lock down the economy) in their decision-making. COVID-19 illustrated that leadership and leading was about embracing discomfort and that to *lead*, one must also be willing to *follow*. That is something many political leaders struggled with during the pandemic, and it may help illuminate why some leaders were more successful than others when faced with a crisis of global proportions. COVID-19 was a global crisis that starkly illustrated how and why leaders can fail when faced with a crisis.

Paradox theory posits that paradoxes or "persistent contradictions between interdependent elements" (Schad, Lewis, Raisch, & Smith, 2016, p. 10) cannot be avoided in an organizational [or political] context (Smith & Lewis, 2011). Undoubtedly, COVID-19 presented governments and organizations with paradoxes such as how to keep employees safe from the virus while maintaining a focus on economic viability, providing scope to develop new technology skills in a remote work environment with inherent performance management tensions. Political leaders, too, were faced with unprecedented paradoxes that required deft ability to balance the tensions of the common good with individual privacy rights (Carmine et al., 2021). The complexity of political leadership necessitates a mindset that is able to balance economic, political, social, legal and national interest simultaneously, and quite often, in competition with each other, which illustrates that political leaders, above all other leaders, always operate in turbulent contexts (Morrell & Hartley, 2006). Moreover, of any leader, political leaders face significantly more complex social, political, and legal tensions than other leaders working in industry or public sector organizations. Indeed, deft political leaders who are successful in finding balance between competing, simultaneous demands could arguably be considered paradox leaders.

Political leadership as distinct from other types of leadership (public/private sector) is concerned with finding creative approaches to solving complex problems, often against a backdrop of competing demands among diverse multi-stakeholder groups. When faced with crisis situations, political leaders leverage citizens' knowledge, expertise and buy-in to co-create innovative solutions that work, they are effectively constantly improvising (de Clercy & Ferguson, 2016; Torfing & Sorensen, 2019). Therefore, a critical dimension of political leadership is the ability of the leader to utilize their interpersonal skill and collaborate with a wide range of stakeholders when formulating public policy that may have a detrimental and negative impact on government and business interests (Lees-Marshment & Jones, 2018). This co-creative and collaborative approach to leadership necessitates devolving power and ceding authority to subject matter experts outside of the corridors of political power when the situation calls for it, and frequently it does (Hatcher, 2020; Taraktas, Esen, & Uskudarli, 2022). Unfortunately, against the backdrop of COVID-19, political leaders such as Donald J. Trump and Boris Johnson failed to harness active citizen participation in solving what de Clercy & Ferguson (2016) refer to as wicked problems in precarious contexts. Interestingly, as alluded to by Miller (2020), Angela Merkel, the former German Chancellor, managed to navigate the pandemic's murky waters by acting rationally *and* with "uncharacteristic sentimentality" in guiding her country through the pandemic.

The inability (or lack of capability) of some political leaders is in stark contrast to other political leaders who excelled during very trying conditions in achieving much lower mortality rates and at the same time, the support of citizens whose fundamental right to freedom had been suspended. We consider the successes and failures of four political leaders (Jacinda Ardern, Angela Merkel, Donald Trump and Boris Johnson) in the context of the pandemic by applying the features of Miron-Spektor et al.'s (2018) paradox mindset and argue that for any leader to successfully navigate crises and paradoxes, they have to learn to become comfortable with being uncomfortable when it comes to making decisions in a volatile environment (Jay, 2013; Miron-Spektor, Gino, & Argote, 2011).

Of Crises, Pandemics, and Improvisation

Much has been written about Angela Merkel over the years, and most of it has not been particularly flattering (Kurbjuweit, 2011). When the COVID-19 pandemic emerged, Angela Merkel's leadership became noteworthy, not because her scientific background made it easier for her to assess the scientific information related to the pandemic and make decisions in a cool, calm and collected manner (Miller, 2020), but because of her ability to communicate clearly and with compassion and empathy in the face of uncertainty. Smithson (2022), in her critique of senior leaders' handling of the COVID-19 crisis in a tertiary health service in Australia, noted the inherent difficulties leaders had with being comfortable operating in a command and control style of leadership but simultaneously using a more relational approach. In her study, she observed the discomfort leaders felt was less to do with leadership styles and more with the tension associated with enacting behaviors that were not aligned with their values and leadership preferences. Despite Merkel's science background, she was able to navigate through her own discomfort and operate outside of a rational, fact-based approach to problem-solving that had served her well during her political career. In a rare televised speech to the country, Angela Merkel spoke of reduced liberty and freedom as a result of COVID-19 and conceded that the very concept of normalcy, public life and social togetherness was being tested like never before (Miller, 2020). Notably, and given Germany's history, Merkel also alluded to Germany's past when she referred to the country's 'darkest hour' stating:

> *Since German reunification, no, since the Second World War, there has not been a challenge for our country in which action in a spirit of solidarity on our part was so important* (Miller, 2020).

What is interesting about Merkel's response to the pandemic crisis was her willingness to accept that she didn't have all the answers, and in spite of her impressive science credentials, she was relying on others (including German citizens) to work together and show solidarity in what was an unprecedented crisis. Moreover, presented with unfathomable options, and recognizing the German people's hard won freedoms, she found a way to embrace both the necessity to be honest and rational about what was required but with humility, humanity and vulnerability (Mayer & May, 2021).

Like Angela Merkel, Jacinda Ardern epitomized leadership during an unprecedented crisis and similar to Merkel, she communicated with the citizenry of New Zealand with honesty, openness and transparency. Strategically, Ardern's response to the crisis was similar to Merkel's as both leaders were led by the science and uncommon for many leaders, they embraced the benefits of distributed leadership (McGuire et al., 2020), empowering public healthcare and medical professionals to take the driving seat and steer government policy when expertise fell outside political corridors of power. Interestingly, Ardern and Merkel shared a similar approach to communications style using collective pronouns 'we' and 'us' but more importantly, both leaders encoded more humanity than many male counterparts when communicating either incomplete information or difficult news.

In her various addresses to the nation, including many dressed in little more than sweatpants having put her toddler to bed, Ardern demonstrates empathy with fellow New Zealanders as they struggled with the isolation of lockdowns. In these addresses,

Ardern communicated a sense of community, acknowledging regional sensitivity while also displaying a sense of identity as a Pacific island nation (Power & Crosthwaite, 2022). Ardern's ability to comfort the nation and convey a sense of community with fellow New Zealanders even when giving uncomfortable news was evidenced in her many Facebook live broadcasts. In one such broadcast, Ardern apologized for her 'casual attire', noting the 'messy business of putting toddlers to bed' (Ardern, 2020a). A common communication approach shared by both Angela Merkel and Jacinda Ardern was their *precise language* when it came to COVID-19 updates and this in spite of the conflicting and oftentimes ambiguous nature of the information both were dealing with (Johnson & Williams, 2020). When compared to a number of male political leaders, the language precision used by both female leaders (referring to the WHO designation of COVID-19) ensured that despite the highly dynamic environment created by COVID-19, they did not deviate or interchange COVID-19 with pandemic (Power & Crosthwaite, 2022). Moreover, Ardern's comfort with managing the paradoxical tensions (her idealism and pragmatism) while yet appearing vulnerable, relatable, and accessible was notable. However, as noted by Simpson et al. (2022, p. 349), it was Ardern's ability to find balance and synergy when engaging in humanistic ideals, practical needs, inclusivity and rationality strategies simultaneously that marked her out. This is the very essence of what Miron-Spektor et al. (2018) refer to as the paradox mindset.

In contrast to both Merkel and Ardern, some less successful male political leaders appeared to lack the ability to embrace paradox tensions, which was laid bare over the course of COVID-19. Both Donald J. Trump and Boris Johnson engaged in similar strategies when it came to their COVID-19 responses, to exercise a masculine 'strongman' (Johnson & Williams, 2020) approach to beating the invisible enemy (Johnson, 2020; Trump, 2020). Critically, Waylen's (2021, p.1165) depiction of Johnson's political leadership during the pandemic as hypermasculine, characterized as 'top-down, monolithic, and over-confident' epitomized the contrasting leadership approaches taken by unsuccessful male political leaders against successful female political leaders. While political leaders across the globe sought to persuade their citizens that COVID-19 was a crisis, Trump and Johnson (as well as Bolsonaro) saw their economies shutting down as *the* crisis emerged and focused instead on maintaining economic activity despite WHO, NHS and CDC recommendations to limit physical contact in an effort to slow the spread of COVID-19. Tisdall (2020) referred to many of these leader's responses to COVID-19 as 'lethal incompetence' and lacking a grip on the reality of the situation.

Trump's and Johnson's behavior was in stark contrast to Merkle's and Ardern's. In an analysis of Boris Johnson and Angela Merkel's COVID-19 policy narratives, Mintrom, Rublee, Bonotti, and Zech (2021) noted differences in relation to the message that was articulated by both leaders, specifically contrasting the empathetic tone taken by Merkel versus a hypermasculine approach of Johnson. Moreover, Merkel utilized more neutral but precise language to describe COVID-19 in contrast to Johnson's less nuanced but more provocative language, referring to the UK's fight against COVID-19 akin to being on a war footing. Notably, while Merkel emphasized the need to follow the science, Johnson personified COVID-19 as a "devilish illness" and "invisible mugger" (p.1226) with the virus being pitched as something the British people could *win* a fight against. Johnson's inability to articulate a coherent public health message to U.K. citizens regarding COVID-19's virulence also resulted in lower levels of trust in the U.K. Government's handling of the crisis (Paton, 2022). Less than two months before the U.K. Government imposed a lockdown on all but essential workers, Johnson stated that "COVID-19 would trigger a panic and desire for market segregation" that would far transcend "what was medically rational to the point of doing real and unnecessary economic damage", going on to proclaim "the UK would be ready to take off its Clark Kent spectacles to become the Superman of the free global market" (Lilleker & Stoeckle, 2021, p. 5). What is clearly evident in Johnson's ardent support of a free-market ideology is the fact that unlike either Merkel or Ardern, he was unable to approach COVID-19 from a both/and perspective. Instead, he was narrowly focused on the U.K.'s economic activity losing out to COVID-19 in a myopic zero-sum game that damaged both Johnson's political legitimacy, and more crucially, timely public health interventions that could have saved lives (Lilleker & Stoeckle, 2021; Power & Crosthwaite, 2022). Similarly, Donald Trump's inability to effectively lead the U.S. or manage the public health narrative around COVID-19 was hampered by both politicizing the pandemic as a problem caused by the previous administration, while celebrating his leadership in managing the crisis *and* at the same time, dismissing public health experts' capacity to curb the virus' spread (Allen & McAleer, 2022).

While there may have been some willingness on the part of Boris Johnson to at least listen to his public health officials with respect to social distancing and the transmission threat posed by COVID-19, there was far less of a willingness by Donald Trump to acknowledge the significant threat posed by the virus. Trump repeatedly dismissed the importance of acknowledging public health advice, often going off script with 'optimistic proclamations' regarding when might be a realistic timeframe to relax pandemic restrictions, noting in the early stages of the virus that Easter was a possible date to re-open the [U.S.] economy (Kapucu & Moynihan, 2021). Moreover, Trump's unwillingness to cede power to public health experts was evidenced throughout various stages of the pandemic when he frequently undermined the public health messages and instead placed himself at the center of communications. This contrasts starkly with how Jacinda Ardern and Angela Merkel leveraged the expertise of their respective public health experts in co-creating a narrative that relied on scientific evidence rather than optimistic proclamations. In a content analysis of Trump's White House briefings, Peters, Plott, and Haberman (2020) noted that self-congratulations, often based on exaggerations and falsehoods, were used by Trump in an effort to take credit and cast himself as the hero of the pandemic. This is the inverse of approaches taken by both Ardern and Merkel who emphasized the unity of the Government working hand-in-glove with citizens to face the challenges posed by COVID-19 and navigate through a crisis that would have long-lasting impact for many, constantly emphasizing the need to be vigilant, while remaining isolated with a social togetherness. This is clear evidence that both female leaders were able to lean-in to the paradox tensions, learn from what was working and improvise as and when needed.

Boris Johnson and Donald Trump's failure to achieve the successes of Merkel and Ardern when it came to responding to COVID-19, provides stark evidence of what can happen when leaders fail to improvise, adapt and lead with empathy during crises. The success of Ardern and Merkel in implementing restrictive Governmental policies that severely limited social and economic activity was in stark contrast to either Trump or Johnson. While both female leaders communicated a message of unity, social cohesion and collective pain, Trump and Johnson relied on a hypermasculine persona that positioned them as the only people who could lead their countries through the pandemic. Ultimately, however, the absence of a paradox mindset that would have enabled them to lean-in to the crisis rather than attempting to choose from impossible choices was critical to their failed pandemic leadership. Moreover, had Trump and Johnson embraced stress as a tool in pursuing innovative strategies that were paradoxically restrictive but unifying, fast acting but highly flexible, they may have been far more successful. Arguably, had they done so, they might have generated much needed trust among their citizens. That was the key differentiator in how Angela Merkel and Jacinda Ardern were successful, while Trump and Johnson were far less so.

Therefore, how is it that in a context where leaders faced with a similar crisis, female political leaders arguably fared better? Given the characteristics of New Zealand as a small open economy, heavily reliant on tourism and highly susceptible to exogenous shocks, New Zealand's Prime Minister, Jacinda Ardern, could have failed the leadership test when COVID-19 struck but that was not the case. New Zealand did better than most countries during the initial stages of the pandemic, while the U.S. and the U.K. faced significant and costly outcomes largely due to leadership failures. A notable difference between the approaches taken by both Ardern and Merkel and those taken by Trump and Johnson lies in what Vera and Crossan (2022) refer to as learning by doing and learning by responding: *improvising*. More crucially, and central to having a paradox mindset that is capable of improvising when a crisis situation calls for it, the role of character emerges as a critical pillar in those leaders who were successful and those who were less so. Although there is no clear definition of character, there are behaviors associated with character and personality traits such as conscientiousness and accountability, as well as virtuousness. Indeed, a central aspect of character is that it acts in an integrative manner (Crossan et al., 2017). Indeed, whilst one is in a position of leadership, it does not always follow that one can also lead, especially during times of crisis.

When we consider the successes and failures of political leaders in the context of COVID-19, the intersection of a paradox mindset and leader character played a central role. Applying Miron-Spektor et al. (2018) paradox mindset to the analysis of the four political leaders cited previously, we can clearly see that in the case of Angela Merkel and Jacinda Ardern, they accepted the myriad paradoxes that emerged in the context of COVID-19 and they developed a sense of comfort in competing tensions, which led to greater performance, innovation and improvisation as the pandemic demanded swift but cautious action. Importantly, both Merkel and Ardern enlisted the citizens of their countries to help manage and co-create strategies that resulted in a shared drive to overcome the effects of COVID-19. Conversely, Trump and Johnson, when faced with similar paradox tensions, were unable to consider the possibility of leveraging the expertise of others in helping to manage, rather than to solve the issue of COVID-19. A central pillar running through the paradox mindset in the context of these political leaders is character, or the ability to be self-aware, reflective, curious, vulnerable, and to continually learn and exhibit humility (Vera & Crossan, 2022, p. 9).

Were Donald Trump and Boris Johnson able to engage with the paradox tensions and approach them from a 'both/and' perspective, they may have been able to draw on the expertise they had on hand and co-develop strategies that limited the impact and reach of COVID-19 rather than focusing on short-term objectives of keeping economies open, or as Lee (2020) trenchantly observed, focusing on capitalism, profit making and privilege.

The Way Forward: No Easy Way Out & No Obvious Way Through

The emergence of COVID-19 and the varied responses by many leaders could arguably be characterized as leaders who viewed the paradox tensions inherent in the pandemic as trade-offs or opportunities to learn, and as leaders who exhibited a paralyzing anxiety when faced with paradox tensions (Sharma et al., 2021; Simpson et al., 2022; Vera & Crossan, 2022). Miron-Spektor, Gino, and Argote (2011, p. 26) described the paradox mindset as the "extent to which one is accepting of and energized by tensions" and it is within this willingness to "confront, rather than avoid contradictions" that leaders faced with the paradoxes brought on by COVID-19 succeeded or failed. This tells only half the success story because character and the need to be seen as trustworthy, self-aware, reflective, open to improvisation and willing to be vulnerable were critical features of the leadership exhibited by Angela Merkel and Jacinda Ardern during COVID-19. This was largely absent from the type of leadership exhibited by Donald Trump and Boris Johnson who instead of uniting the citizens of their countries and mobilizing social cohesiveness, focused on hostility and misinformation (Muqsith, Kuswanti, Pratomo, & Muzykant, 2021; Rutledge, 2020) when it came to public health experts and appropriate actions necessary to address COVID-19. While a paradox mindset is crucial for any leader when faced with crisis situations, the leader's character is as important as this allows the leader to be more open, novel, innovative and co-created approaches to managing paradox tensions associated with crises.

While Jacinda Ardern and Angela Merkel appear to have been far more successful in managing the COVID-19 crisis than either Donald Trump or Boris Johnson, a paradox mindset only illustrated their willingness to *lean-in* to the tensions, their character ultimately allowed them to be perceived as more human and relatable in their communications with citizens about COVID-19 and it is this sense of common purpose that may have been the most critical aspect of their success during in crisis management. Leadership crises are always going to be a common feature of being a leader; however, how one manages tensions associated with crises, and adapts and innovates in response to those tensions can be the difference between success and failure, especially at times when paradoxes require leaders to consider responding to competing demands simultaneously.

Ultimately, when leaders are faced with paradox tensions associated with crisis situations, the literature would suggest that leaders who can engage in *double-loop* learning stand a greater chance of successfully navigating through the crisis. According to Miron-Spektor et al. (2018), if leaders can develop a paradox mindset, it can fuel innovation and learning and impact direct reports positively. Wilson (2020) also alluded to the novelty of the "novel coronavirus" when it came to political leader responses but also acknowledged that in order to successful in times of crisis, leaders needed to mobilize collective action, which is something that Ardern and Merkel did and Trump and Johnson failed to do adequately. The politicization, polarization and partisan discourse communicated by Trump ultimately impacted on his effectiveness as a leader.

So, what does all of this say for effective political leadership in the context of a crisis such as the COVID-19 pandemic? First of all, effective political leaders made excellent use of scientific advice and ensured that they could make informed decisions based on the next available evidence. They ruled on facts rather than myths and misinformation. Decisions made in the absence of facts had far reaching implications for the economy and society. Second, explicit recognition that crises such as COVID-19 are highly paradoxical and contradictory and therefore, a political leader should act accordingly. Successful leaders such as Merkel and Ardern aligned their behavior with these paradoxical demands by using opposing behaviors. Rather than trying to solve the paradox, they navigated through it, utilizing underlying beliefs and mindsets that enabled them to cognitively hold two opposing forces at the same time and to consciously and collaboratively deal with these paradoxes as the crisis evolved. Finally, successful political leaders like Ardern and Merkel were able to tap into their emotional reserves, leverage the stress induced by the paradox tensions, and embrace a paradox mindset that enabled innovation and improvisation when faced with impossible choices.

References

Allen, D. E., & McAleer, M. (2022). Trump's COVID-19 tweets and Dr. Fauci's emails. *Scientometrics*, *127*(3), 1643–1655. doi:10.1007/s11192-021-04243-z

Andriopoulos, C., & Lewis, M. W. (2009). Exploitation–Exploration Tensions and Organizational Ambidexterity: Managing Paradoxes of Innovation. *Organization Science*, *20*(4), 696–717. doi:10.1287/orsc.1080.0406

Ardern, J. (2020a). *COVID-19 Alert Level Increased.* https://www.youtube.com/watch?v=xMA6Gz82iiQ

Ardern, J. (2020b). *PM Address – COVID-19 Update.* https://www.beehive.govt.nz/speech/pm-address-COVID-19-update

Berti, M., & Simpson, A. V. (2021). The Dark Side of Organizational Paradoxes: The Dynamics of Disempowerment. *Academy of Management Review*, *46*(2), 252–274. doi:10.5465/amr.2017.0208

Carmine, S., Andriopoulos, C., Gotsi, M., Hartel, C. E. J., Krzeminska, A., Mafico, N., . . . Keller, J. (2021). A Paradox Approach to Organizational Tensions During the Pandemic Crisis. *Journal of Management Inquiry*, *30*(2), 138–153. doi:10.1177/1056492620986863

Crossan, M. M., Byrne, A., Seijts, G. H., Reno, M., Monzani, L., & Gandz, J. (2017). Toward a Framework of Leader Character in Organizations. *Journal of Management Studies*, *54*(7), 986–1018. doi:10.1111/joms.12254

Dada, S., Ashworth, H. C., Bewa, M. J., & Dhatt, R. (2021). Words matter: political and gender analysis of speeches made by heads of government during the COVID-19 pandemic. *Bmj Global Health*, *6*(1). doi:10.1136/bmjgh-2020–003910

de Clercy, C., & Ferguson, P. A. (2016). Leadership in Precarious Contexts: Studying Political Leaders after the Global Financial Crisis. *Politics and Governance*, *4*(2), 104–114. doi:10.17645/pag.v4i2.582

Foroughi, H., Gabriel, Y., & Fotaki, M. (2019). Leadership in a post-truth era: A new narrative disorder? *Leadership*, *15*(2), 135–151. doi:10.1177/1742715019835369

Förster, C., Paparella, C., Duchek, S., & Güttel, W. H. (2022). Leading in the Paradoxical World of Crises: How Leaders Navigate Through Crises. *Schmalenbach Journal of Business Research*, *74*(4), 631–657. doi:10.1007/s41471-022-00147-7

Friedman, U. (2020, March 18th). We Were Warned. *The Atlantic.* https://www.theatlantic.com/politics/archive/2020/03/pandemic-coronavirus-united-states-trump–cdc/608215/

Hansen, H., Ropo, A., & Sauer, E. (2007). Aesthetic leadership. *Leadership Quarterly*, *18*(6), 544–560. doi:10.1016/j.leaqua.2007.09.003

Hatcher, W. (2020). A Failure of Political Communication Not a Failure of Bureaucracy: The Danger of Presidential Misinformation During the COVID-19 Pandemic. *The American Review of Public Administration*, *50*(6–7), 614–620. doi:10.1177/0275074020941734

Heifetz, R., Grashow, A., & Linsky, M. (2009). Leadership in a (Permanent) Crisis. *Harvard Business Review*, *87*(7–8), 62.

Hu, Q., & Liu, Y. (2022). Crisis Management and National Responses to COVID-19: Global Perspectives. *Public Performance & Management Review*, *45*(4), 737–750. doi:10.1080/15309576.2022.2079692

Huang, C. L., Huang, L. X., Wang, Y. M., Li, X., Ren, L. L., Gu, X. Y., . . . Cao, B. (2021). 6-month consequences of COVID-19 in patients discharged from hospital: a cohort study. *Lancet*, *397*(10270), 220–232. doi:10.1016/s0140-6736(20)32656-8

ILO. (2022). *ILO Monitor on the world of work. Tenth Edition – Multiple crises threaten the global labour market recover.* online: International Labor Organization https://www.ilo.org/wcmsp5/groups/public/–dgreports/–dcomm/–publ/documents/briefingnote/wcms_859255.pdf

Isaksson, M., & Solvoll, M. (2022). The rhetoric of the Norwegian government and health authorities during the COVID-19 pandemic. *Journal of Communication Management*. doi:10.1108/jcom-08-2022–0100

Jay, J. (2013). Navigating Paradox as a Mechanism of Change and Innovation in Hybrid Organizations. *Academy of Management Journal*, *56*(1), 137–159. doi:10.5465/amj.2010.0772

Johnson. (2020, March 17th, 2020). Prime Minister's Statement on coronavirus (COVID-19) 17 March 2020. https://www.gov.uk/government/speeches/pm-statement-on-coronavirus-17-march–2020

Johnson, C., & Williams, B. (2020). Gender and Political Leadership in a Time of COVID. *Politics & Gender*, *16* (4), 943–950. doi:10.1017/s1743923x2000029x

Kain, T., & Fowler, R. (2019). Preparing intensive care for the next pandemic influenza. *Critical Care*, *23*(1). doi:10.1186/s13054-019-2616-1

Kapucu, N., & Moynihan, D. (2021). Trump's (mis)management of the COVID-19 pandemic in the US. *Policy Studies*, *42*(5–6), 592–610. doi:10.1080/01442872.2021.1931671

King, M. L. (1968). A Proper Sense of Priorities. https://pnhp.org/news/martin-luther-king-jr-a-proper-sense-of-priorities/

Kneuer, M., & Wallaschek, S. (2022). Framing COVID-19: Public Leadership and Crisis Communication By Chancellor Angela Merkel During the Pandemic in 2020. *German Politics*, 1–24. doi:10.1080/09644008.2022.2028140

Kurbjuweit, D. (2011, December 16th, 2011). Iron Angie Is Only Half of the Story. *Der Spiegel International*. https://www.spiegel.de/international/germany/merkel-s-human-side-iron-angie-is-only-half-the-story-a-800715.html

Lee, D. M. M. (2020). COVID-19: agnotology, inequality, and leadership. *Human Resource Development International*, *23*(4), 333–346. doi:10.1080/13678868.2020.1779544

Lees–Marshment, J., & Jones, O. S. (2018). Being more with less: Exploring the flexible political leadership identities of government ministers. *Leadership*, *14*(4), 460–482. doi:10.1177/1742715016687815

Li, P. P. (2020). Organizational Resilience for a New Normal: Balancing the Paradox of Global Interdependence. *Management and Organization Review*, *16*(3), 503–509. doi:10.1017/mor.2020.30

Lilleker, D. G., & Stoeckle, T. (2021). The challenges of providing certainty in the face of wicked problems: Analysing the UK government's handling of the COVID-19 pandemic. *Journal of Public Affairs*, *21*(4). doi:10.1002/pa.2733

Luscher, L. S., & Lewis, M. W. (2008). Organizational change and managerial sensemaking: Working through paradox. *Academy of Management Journal*, *51*(2), 221–240. doi:10.5465/amj.2008.31767217

Mayer, C.-H., & May, M. S. (2021). Women Leaders Transcending the Demands of COVID-19: A Positive Psychology 2.0 Perspective. *Frontiers in Psychology*, *12*. doi:10.3389/fpsyg.2021.647658

McDonnell, D. (2016). Populist Leaders and Coterie Charisma. *Political Studies*, *64*(3), 719–733. doi:10.1111/1467-9248.12195

McGuire, D., Cunningham, J. E. A., Reynolds, K., & Matthews-Smith, G. (2020). Beating the virus: an examination of the crisis communication approach taken by New Zealand Prime Minister Jacinda Ardern during the COVID-19 pandemic. *Human Resource Development International*, *23*(4), 361–379. doi:10.1080/13678868.2020.1779543

Miller, S. (2020). The Secret to Germany's COVID-19 Success: Angela Merkel Is a Scientist. *The Atlantic*. https://www.theatlantic.com/international/archive/2020/04/angela-merkel-germany-coronavirus-pandemic/610225/

Mintrom, M., Rublee, M. R., Bonotti, M., & Zech, S. T. (2021). Policy narratives, localisation, and public justification: responses to COVID-19. *Journal of European Public Policy*, *28*(8), 1219–1237. doi:10.1080/13501763.2021.1942154

Miron–Spektor, E., Gino, F., & Argote, L. (2011). Paradoxical frames and creative sparks: Enhancing individual creativity through conflict and integration. *Organizational Behavior and Human Decision Processes*, *116*(2), 229–240. doi:10.1016/j.obhdp.2011.03.006

Miron–Spektor, E., Ingram, A., Keller, J., Smith, W. K., & Lewis, M. W. (2018). Microfoundations of Organizational Paradox: The Problem is How We Think About the Problem. *Academy of Management Journal*, *61*(1), 26–45. doi:10.5465/amj.2016.0594

Morrell, K., & Hartley, J. (2006). A model of political leadership. *Human Relations*, *59*(4), 483–504. doi:10.1177/0018726706065371

Muqsith, M. A., Kuswanti, A., Pratomo, R. R., & Muzykant, V. L. (2021). Trump's Twitter Propaganda During COVID-19. *Journal the Messenger*, *13*(3), 223–237. doi:10.26623/themessenger.v13i3.3991

Ortega, F., & Orsini, M. (2020). Governing COVID-19 without government in Brazil: Ignorance, neoliberal authoritarianism, and the collapse of public health leadership. *Global Public Health*, *15*(9), 1257–1277. doi:10.1080/17441692.2020.1795223

Paton, C. (2022). World–beating? Testing Britain's COVID response and tracing the explanation. *Health Economics Policy and Law*, *17*(2), 238–245. doi:10.1017/s174413312000033x

Peters, J. W., Plott, E., & Haberman, M. (2020). 260,000 Words, Full of Self-Praise, From Trump on the Virus. *The New York Times*. https://www.nytimes.com/interactive/2020/04/26/us/politics/trump-coronavirus-briefings-analyzed.html

Power, K., & Crosthwaite, P. (2022). Constructing COVID-19: A corpus-informed analysis of prime ministerial crisis response communication by gender. *Discourse & Society*, *33*(3), 411–437. doi:10.1177/09579265221076612

Putnam, L. L., Fairhurst, G. T., & Banghart, S. (2016). Contradictions, Dialectics, and Paradoxes in Organizations: A Constitutive Approach. *Academy of Management Annals*, *10*(1), 65–171. doi:10.1080/19416520.2016.1162421

Ridley, M. (2022, December 28th, 2022). China's COVID nightmare is the final proof: lockdowns were a total failure. *The Telegraph*. https://www.telegraph.co.uk/news/2022/12/28/chinas-COVID-nightmare-final-proof-lockdowns-total-failure/

Rutledge, P. E. (2020). Trump, COVID-19, and the War on Expertise. *The American Review of Public Administration*, *50*(6–7), 505–511. doi:10.1177/0275074020941683

Schad, J., Lewis, M. W., Raisch, S., & Smith, W. K. (2016). Paradox Research in Management Science: Looking Back to Move Forward. *Academy of Management Annals*, *10*(1), 5–64. doi:10.1080/19416520.2016.1162422

Sharma, G., Bartunek, J., Buzzanell, P. M., Carmine, S., Endres, C., Etter, M., . . . Keller, J. (2021). A Paradox Approach to Societal Tensions during the Pandemic Crisis. *Journal of Management Inquiry*, *30*(2), 121–137. doi:10.1177/1056492620986604

Siebenhaar, K. U., Kother, A. K., & Alpers, G. W. (2020). Dealing With the COVID-19 Infodemic: Distress by Information, Information Avoidance, and Compliance With Preventive Measures. *Frontiers in Psychology*, *11*. doi:10.3389/fpsyg.2020.567905

Simpson, A. V., & Berti, M. (2020). Transcending Organizational Compassion Paradoxes by Enacting Wise Compassion Courageously. *Journal of Management Inquiry*, *29*(4), 433–449. doi:10.1177/1056492618821188

Simpson, A. V., Panayiotou, A., Berti, M., Cunha, M. P., Kanji, S., & Clegg, S. (2022). Pandemic, power and paradox: Improvising as the New Normal during the COVID-19 crisis. *Management Learning*. doi:10.1177/13505076221132980

Smith, W. K., Besharov, M. L., Wessels, A. K., & Chertok, M. (2012). A Paradoxical Leadership Model for Social Entrepreneurs: Challenges, Leadership Skills, and Pedagogical Tools for Managing Social and Commercial Demands. *Academy of Management Learning & Education*, *11*(3), 463–478. doi:10.5465/amle.2011.0021

Smith, W. K., & Lewis, M. W. (2011). Toward a Theory of Paradox: A Dynamic Equilibrium Model of Organizing. *Academy of Management Review*, *36*(2), 381–403. doi:10.5465/amr.2011.59330958

Smithson, R. (2022). The compatibility of multiple leadership styles in responding to a complex crisis: leading a health service COVID-19 response. *Journal of Health Organization and Management*, *36*(4), 469–481. doi:10.1108/jhom-07-2021-0263

Spyridonidis, D., Cote, N., Currie, G., & Denis, J. L. (2022). Leadership configuration in crises: Lessons from the English response to COVID-19. *Leadership*, *18*(5), 680–694. doi:10.1177/17427150221126780

Taraktas, B., Esen, B., & Uskudarli, S. (2022). Tweeting through a Public Health Crisis: Communication Strategies of Right-Wing Populist Leaders during the COVID-19 Pandemic. *Government and Opposition*. doi:10.1017/gov.2022.34

Tisdall, S. (2020). Trump, Putin and Bolsonaro have been complacent. Now the pandemic has made them all vulnerable. *The Guardian*. https://www.theguardian.com/commentisfree/2020/may/17/trump-putin-and-bolsonaro-have-been-complacent-now-the-pandemic-has-made-them-all–vulnerable

Tomkins, L. (2020). Where is Boris Johnson? When and why it matters that leaders show up in a crisis. *Leadership*, *16*(3), 331–342. doi:10.1177/1742715020919657

Torfing, J., & Sorensen, E. (2019). Interactive Political Leadership in Theory and Practice: How Elected Politicians May Benefit from Co–Creating Public Value Outcomes. *Administrative Sciences*, *9*(3). doi:10.3390/admsci9030051

Tourish, D. (2020). Introduction to the special issue: Why the coronavirus crisis is also a crisis of leadership. *Leadership*, *16*(3), 261–272. doi:10.1177/1742715020929242

Trump, D. J. (2020). Coronavirus: Trump calls himself 'wartime president' in battle with 'invisible enemy'. Retrieved from Coronavirus: Trump calls himself 'wartime president' in battle with 'invisible enemy'

Vera, D., & Crossan, M. M. (2022). Character-enabled improvisation and the new normal: A paradox perspective. *Management Learning*. doi:10.1177/13505076221118840

Watzlawick, P., Weakland, J. H., & Fisch, R. (1974). *Change: Principles of problem formation and problem resolution*. Norton

Waylen, G. (2021). Gendering political leadership: hypermasculine leadership and COVID-19. *Journal of European Public Policy*, *28*(8), 1153–1173. doi:10.1080/13501763.2021.1942160

Wendt, R. F. (1998). The Sound of One Hand Clapping: Counterintuitive Lessons Extracted from Paradoxes and Double Binds in Participative Organizations. *Management Communication Quarterly*, *11*(3), 323–371. doi:10.1177/0893318998113001

WHO (2023). *WHO Coronavirus (COVID-19) Dashboard*. https://COVID19.who.int

Wilson, S. (2020). Pandemic leadership: Lessons from New Zealand's approach to COVID-19. *Leadership*, *16*(3), 279–293. doi:10.1177/1742715020929151

Wittenberg-Cox, A. (2020, April 13th). What Do Countries With The Best Coronavirus Responses Have In Common? Women Leaders. *Forbes*. https://www.forbes.com/sites/avivahwittenbergcox/2020/04/13/what-do-countries-with-the-best-coronavirus-reponses-have-in-common-women-leaders/?sh=6f4958523dec

Part IV: **Conclusion**

David McGuire and Marie-Line Germain

Chapter 9
Conclusion

Abstract: This chapter summarizes some of the key organizational and sectoral leadership lessons learned from the COVID-19 pandemic and looks at how such lessons will shape leadership actions and activities beyond the pandemic.

Keywords: Employee health, remote work, hybrid work, leadership, resilience, careers, workspaces, workplace design

The COVID-19 pandemic has had a significant impact on leadership at all levels, from global political leaders, higher education leaders, to business owners. Leaders across all sectors played an important role in offering strategic direction and supporting employees through the crisis. The pandemic presented leaders with a set of complex situational demands arising from the global, pervasive and enduring nature of the crisis as well as the increasing interconnectedness and interdependence of markets, supply chains, and work (Riggio & Newstead, 2023). Far from being insulated from the crisis, leaders were thrust forward to deal with complex, time-pressured situations with limited available options, and few obvious solutions. In addition to elevating the importance of contingency planning, the pandemic underlined the need for knowledge, expertise, and experience in emergency planning and crisis response to be shared across all organizational leaders. Galloway (2022, p. 73) maintains that a culture of autonomous problem-solving and distributed leadership helped organizations to produce creative, adaptive, less bureaucratic, and improvised actions to sustain business operations. As we enter a post-pandemic world, it is clear that there has been a discernible shift in the focus of much leadership and human resources research literature. The five most noteworthy trends are presented below.

An Increased Focus on Work and Worker Health

In addition to disrupting public health and medical-care systems, the COVID-19 pandemic forced us to focus our attention on employee health and wellbeing. Le and Nguyen (2023) assert that the pandemic lockdowns generated a significant psychological strain on individuals resulting in mental health issues including anxiety, worry, disin-

David McGuire, Edinburgh Napier University, Scotland
Marie-Line Germain, Western Carolina University, USA

https://doi.org/10.1515/9783110799101-009

terest, and depression. They argue that the financial uncertainty arising from unemployment or reduced incomes, which affected many individuals during the pandemic, had an impact on overall emotional wellbeing. They also maintain that alterations to societal norms and certainties (food security, housing concerns, employment prospects) led to a more pessimistic outlook and psychological distress.

The intensification of economic and social problems brought about by the pandemic has placed a renewed emphasis on personal, work, and family relationships. Daley and Kenke (2022) maintain that COVID-19 has brought about a shift in recognizing the importance of the family system in supporting employee wellbeing. A study by Da et al. (2022) found that family support is vital in preventing burnout and promoting work engagement. It recommended that employers more proactively engage with family-friendly policies as a means of supporting employee health and wellbeing. In contrast, Shirmohammadi et al. (2022) argue that the pandemic revealed a particular vulnerability to work intensity and isolation amongst single workers, who may have been deprived of access to family and emotional support.

A Recognition of the Benefits of Remote and Hybrid Work

Labeled as "The Great COVID-19 Pause" by Bierema (2020), the pandemic forced an acceleration in the adoption of remote work practices, due to enforced social distancing mandates from national governments. This disruption to normal modes of working led many employees to reflect upon their own personal values and priorities (Wiedemann, n.d.). This resulted in calls for organizations to introduce happier, healthier, more human sustainable work practices. The experience of remote working during the pandemic culminated in many employees wanting to continue with this mode of working in a post-pandemic era, in part because of the wellbeing and environmental benefits it affords (including less traffic, shorter commute, ability to undertake exercise, more time with family -and pets!). In reaction to this structural and cultural shift in how and where work is performed, many national governments, including the Welsh and Irish governments, introduced national remote working strategies (Irish Government, 2021; Welsh Government, 2022). Such strategies recognized that, in addition to wellbeing and environmental benefits, remote work resulted in economic well-being benefits through creating job opportunities in rural locations, boosting footfall in villages and smaller towns, and lessening accommodation pressures in towns and cities. They also identified cultural benefits through encouraging a more vibrant local culture and the strengthening of language ties. The Welsh strategy has set a goal for 30% of the workforce to be working remotely on a regular basis (the Irish government established a similar target of 20%) and created a set of regional remote working hubs to provide the right environment for people to work remotely near to their home.

In the United States, a 2023 Stanford University study reveals that much of the remote work comes from hybrid arrangements. Specifically, the researchers found that 12% of U.S. workers work fully remotely, 28% in a hybrid setup, and that 60% work in-person in an office (Goldberg, 2023). The push for remote work is further exacerbated by Gen Z workers who place great value on work flexibility and personal time.

A Re-evaluation of the Importance of Organizational Resilience and Personal Resilience

The experience of the pandemic has emphasized the need to build resilience at all organizational levels. As Lombardi et al. (2021) state, resilience "implies a complex network of variables and it defines the capacity to absorb adversity, trauma, external shocks, or any significant sources of stress, while learning from them, preparing and responding to change" (p. 2). They argue that resilience represents the ability to weather the storm and embrace the learning that results from it, leading to growth and integrity. According to Gamage et al. (2023), organizational resilience centers around two perspectives: the "rebound" perspective, which looks at the capacity of organizations to recover from a crisis and revert to their original state, and the "rebound and overtake" perspective, which examines the ability of organizations to bounce back, but also to learn from the crisis, develop new approaches, and grow from the experience. In light of the pandemic, several commentators are underlining the importance of resilience as a source of competitive advantage (Budd, 2020; Reeves et al., 2022). They argue that resilience helps organizations to anticipate future shocks and build absorptive capacity to deal with unexpected events. They also advocate separation and heterogeneity of business elements (subsidiaries, plants, teams) to help prevent total system collapse and to ensure business continuity.

Alongside organizational resilience, the development of personal resilience is critical in developing problem-solving skills, hardiness and adaptability to cope with difficult and unexpected situations. The provision of organizational support and support from colleagues is viewed as a protective factor against stress and anxiety. It helps employees perform effectively in difficult circumstances (Labrague & De Los Santos, 2020). Many researchers point to the important role played by leaders in promoting resilience. In supporting the mental, psychological, and emotional health of employees, leaders can help employees cope with unexpected events and stressful situations. Through embracing values such as humility, compassion, empowering people and interpersonal acceptance, Cai et al. (2023) maintain that leaders can offer valuable support and reassurance to employees. They argue that leaders can create a positive work environment and can stimulate positive work emotions and psychological resources amongst employees, enabling them to respond to changes more effectively.

A Redesign of Workspaces

The post-COVID-19 era has been marked by organizational efforts to redefine the way in which work is performed and located (de Lucas Ancillo et al., 2021). Prior to the pandemic, the architectural trend towards open-plan seating, internal glass walls and large open central atriums was designed to make employees more visible, offering greater opportunities for management to monitor and evaluate employee performance. Yet, moves were already afoot to reevaluate the thinking and philosophy underpinning workplace design. As Morgan (2018) states, "instead of trying to force people to fit into outdated workplace practices, organizations must redesign their workplace practices to fit with their people" (p. 2). An employee-centered approach to workplace design has now become commonplace with office space being redesigned to support collaboration and digitally co-located work (Kane et al., 2021). Indeed, this forms part of a wider trend of moving work to people (remote working), rather than moving people to work (commuting) (Borland et al., 2020). In other words, there is an increasing emphasis on structuring work to fit optimal settings for its accomplishment. For instance, research suggests that collaborative activities are more suited to face-to-face settings than remote environments (Flores, 2019).

The transition to more nomadic forms of work (Cruz & Pombo, 2022) is not without concerns. Questions have been raised about the design and configuration of home offices when compared to the layout, ventilation, lighting, thermal comfort, and infrastructure typically available in office settings (Mendis, 2016; Prestonjee & Pastakia, 2022). While the return to office working was initially marked by discussions about health and hygiene factors such as cleaning, social distancing and communal spaces (de Lucas Ancillo et al., 2020), consideration is now being given to how office space, including home office space, can be used more effectively to boost productivity across a hybrid workforce.

A Shift in Career Realities

For many employees, the COVID-19 pandemic was a career shock, causing considerable disruption to career plans (Akkermans et al., 2020). In the midst of the pandemic, in the United States alone, fifty percent of workers indicated wanting to make a career change (CNBC, 2021). In response to negative events, Chen et al. (2022) argue that individuals are more likely to engage in improvisation behaviors, seizing opportunities as they arise and thinking "outside the box". Likewise, Seibert et al. (2016) maintain that in difficult circumstances, employees possessing higher resilience levels are likely to develop a growth mindset, reframe career goals, identify training opportunities and strengthen professional networks.

While the pandemic clearly pushed the "fast forward" button on new ways of working (Lund et al., 2020), Hite and McDonald (2020) are clear that some jobs and career structures are likely to disappear post-pandemic, whilst others will undergo significant transformation. With the growth of e-commerce during and post-pandemic, Nikoloski and colleagues (2023) are confident that the gig economy will continue to grow, driven by consumer demand for products and services. However, they also note that gig work is largely low skilled employment with limited job progression, low levels of job protection, and considerable variability in hours worked. Likewise, Spurk and Straub (2020) argue that gig work is associated with increased levels of job insecurity and precariousness. To this end, ACCA (2023) identifies five essential skills needed for work in a post-pandemic environment, namely collaboration, digital proficiency, emotional regulation, career self-management, and flexibility.

Conclusions from the Contributors' Chapters

Having examined the literature on key leadership and Human Resources trends in the post-pandemic environment, this section presents some of the key insights gleaned from each of the chapters contained within this book.

In his chapter, **Zeeshan** identifies the six core competencies that organizational leaders need in difficult situations. He argues that the pandemic has placed a spotlight on the importance of agile and adaptable leadership and recommends that companies should be able to quickly pivot and adapt to changing circumstances. He places significant emphasis on flexibility, strategic thinking, and innovation in leadership as the basis for effective decision-making.

A focus on emergency planning forms the basis of **Wang**'s chapter who points out that past crises have taught us that we should identify the failures in a particular crisis situation, derive important lessons, and make after-action plans. Doing so will help organizations better project and prepare for the next challenge. Outlining four lessons learned from the pandemic, she asserts the need for robust emergency planning, the necessity of real-time learning, the potential of digital technologies, and the value of effective organizational learning.

The pandemic highlighted the importance of empathy and compassion in leadership. As **McGuire** and **Tuite** point out in their chapter, many leaders were guided by an ethic of care which enabled them to demonstrate understanding and support to their employees. One key aspect of an ethics of care that arose during the pandemic was the need to prioritize the wellbeing and safety of vulnerable populations. This included measures such as providing protective equipment and support for healthcare workers, ensuring that marginalized communities had access to testing and healthcare, and taking steps to protect the elderly and immunocompromised individuals. An ethic of care also played a role in shaping the decisions of governments and policy makers. Governments needed to balance the need to protect public health with the need to minimize the economic and social impacts of the pandemic. This often involved making difficult choices, and required leaders to consider the wellbeing of all societal members, not just those who were most immediately affected by the virus.

Strong, decisive leadership offers reassurance and comfort in times of crisis. However, the presence of certain disordered traits can have a destructive impact on both employees and organizational effectiveness. In her chapter, **Germain** defines the characteristics of a narcissistic personality disorder and contrasts the leadership of Donald J. Trump and Jair Bolsonaro with that of Jacinda Ardern. She concludes that effective leadership centers around meeting the needs of followers and stakeholders, rather than prioritizing the leader's interests. She espouses the importance of servant leadership and argues that leaders need to possess greater self-awareness and take a more balanced, healthy and inclusive approach to leadership. She maintains that sound corporate governance structures are the best defense against narcissistic leaders.

Across industry sectors, the COVID-19 pandemic brought about significant and long-lasting change. In their chapter, **Germain** and **McGuire** examine the effects of the pandemic on business in general and the retail industry in particular, technology, hospitality, and healthcare. The COVID-19 pandemic has brought about significant changes in the way businesses operate, requiring leaders to be adaptable, flexible, and able to make quick decisions under uncertainty. It has highlighted the importance of remote work, crisis management, financial management, communication, and collaboration in order for businesses to survive and thrive in this new environment. It has also brought about significant changes in the way technology companies operate and the skills required of their leaders. Technology industry leaders have had to be agile, responsive, and able to quickly adapt to the changing needs of their customers. They have had to be able to lead their teams through the process of digital transformation to ensure the security of their products and services, and to be able to identify new opportunities and generate revenue. The leaders who are able to navigate these challenges and emerge stronger will be the ones who have the right set of leadership skills and mindset. The pandemic has also brought about significant changes in the hospitality industry, requiring new levels of adaptability, creativity, and leadership from hospitality leaders. It has highlighted the importance of health and safety protocols, contactless and digital experiences, flexibility, financial management, and collaboration in order for the industry to survive and thrive. Finally, the pandemic has brought about significant changes in healthcare leadership, including the increased importance of telemedicine, crisis management, collaboration, and forward thinking. It has highlighted the need for healthcare leaders who are adaptable, flexible, and able to effectively communicate and work with others in order to provide the best possible care for patients.

In the education realm, the COVID-19 pandemic had a major worldwide impact on schooling and university structures and how tuition is delivered. In their chapter, **Lekchiri and Eversole** explain that, in response to the spread of the virus, many universities were forced to close their doors and move to online learning platforms. This sudden shift to online learning/distance learning has presented a number of challenges. Many students, particularly those from disadvantaged backgrounds, have struggled to access the internet or had inadequate technology at home. The authors assert that the quality of the education provided was compromised, as it was difficult for educators to effectively engage with students and provide support in an online setting. The pandemic has also had a significant impact on students' mental health. The sudden shift to online learning, the isolation caused by lockdowns, and the social distancing measures have contributed to increased levels of stress and anxiety among students. In addition to the challenges faced by students, the pandemic has also had a significant impact on educators. Many of them had to adapt to teaching in an online setting, which can be challenging for those who are unfamiliar with technology. The sudden shift to online learning has also put additional pressure on teachers, who may be struggling to balance teaching with their own personal and family responsibilities. While the transition to online education was initially met with challenges, a lasting legacy of the pandemic is that it has also helped to legitimize online learning as a viable and effective educational option.

Political leadership was perhaps the most visible manifestation of leadership during the COVID-19 pandemic. **Garavan** and **MacKenzie** make the point that effective political leaders made excellent use of scientific advice and ensured that they could make informed decisions based on evidence. They argue that crises such as COVID-19 are highly paradoxical and contradictory and successful leaders align their behavior with these paradoxical demands by using opposing behaviors, utilizing underlying beliefs and mindsets that enabled them to cognitively hold two opposing forces at the same time. In doing so, the authors maintain that successful leaders are also able to tap into their emotional reserves, leveraging the stress induced by the paradox tensions, and embracing a paradox mindset that enables innovation and improvisation when faced with impossible choices.

Concluding Thoughts

In essence, the COVID-19 pandemic highlighted the importance of leadership as a guiding force affecting the viability of organizations and institutions as well as the health and wellbeing of individuals and communities across the globe. The pandemic has called on us to prioritize the wellbeing and safety of vulnerable populations, to support one another, and to consider the long-term consequences of our actions on the wellbeing of society as a whole. The pandemic highlighted the importance of strong, decisive leadership in times of crisis, the need for adaptability and innovation, and the value of empathy and compassion. These qualities will likely continue to be important for leaders in the post-pandemic world.

References

Akkermans, J., Richardson, J., & Kraimer, M. L. (2020). The COVID-19 Crisis as a Career Shock: Implications for Careers and Vocational Behavior. *Journal of Vocational Behavior, 119*, 103434.

Bierema, L. L. (2020). HRD research and practice after 'The Great COVID-19 Pause': The time is now for bold, critical, research. *Human Resource Development International, 23*(4), 347–360.

Borland, B., DeSmet, A., Palter, R., & Sanghvi, A. (2020). Reimagining the office and work life after COVID. McKinsey Consulting Group. https://www.mckinsey.com/capabilities/people-and-organizational-performance/our-insights/reimagining-the-office-and-work-life-after-COVID-19

Budd, G. (2020). Resilience as a Competitive Advantage. *Forbes* (December 9th 2020). https://www.forbes.com/sites/forbestechcouncil/2020/12/09/resilience-as-a-competitive-advantage/

Cai, Z., Mao, Y., Gong, T., Xin, Y., & Lou, J. (2023). The Effect of Servant Leadership on Work Resilience: Evidence from the Hospitality Industry during the COVID-19 Period. *International Journal of Environmental Research and Public Health, 20*(2), 13–22.

Chen, Y., Liu, D., Tang, G., & Hogan, T. M. (2021). Workplace events and employee creativity: A multi-study field investigation. *Personnel Psychology, 74*(2), 211–236.

CNBC (2021, October 12). *'The Great Reimagination of Work': Why 50% of workers want to make a career change.* https://www.cnbc.com/2021/10/12/why-50percent-of-workers-want-to-make-a-career-change-new-survey.html

Cruz, R., & Pombo, F. (2022, June). Designing Furniture for Versatile Spaces of Collaborative Work. COVID-19 Accelerating the Change. In *Advances in Design, Music and Arts II: 8th International Meeting of Research in Music, Arts and Design, EIMAD 2022, July 7–9, 2022* (pp. 456–471). Springer International Publishing. https://doi.org/10.1007/978-3-031-09659-4_34

Da, S., Fladmark, S. F., Wara, I., Christensen, M., & Innstrand, S. T. (2022). To change or not to change: a study of workplace change during the COVID-19 pandemic. *International journal of environmental research and public health, 19*(4), 1982.

Daley, T. C. & Henke, R. M. (2022). Supporting Workplace Mental Health in the COVID Era: Exemplary Practices from the Business Sector. *American Journal of Health Promotion 36*(7), 1241-1244.

de Lucas Ancillo, A., del Val Nunez, M. T., & Gavrila, S. G. (2021). Workplace Change within the COVID-19 Context: A Grounded Theory Approach. *Economic Research, 34*(1), 2297–2316.

Flores, M. F. (2019). Understanding the Challenges of Remote Working at its Impact to Workers. *International Journal of Business, Marketing and Management, 4*(11), 40–44.

Gamage, A., Pyke, J., & deLacy, T. (2023). Building Resilience and Sustainable HRM in the Visitor Economy: An Uneasy Relationship. *Journal of Hospitality and Tourism Management*, Earlycite. DOI:10.1016/j.jhtm.2023.05.006

Goldberg, E. (2023, March 30). Do we know how many people are working from home? *The New York Times*. https://www.nytimes.com/2023/03/30/business/economy/remote-work-measure-surveys.html#:~:text=Much%20of%20that%20remote%20work,person%20and%2028%20percent%20hybrid.

Hite, L. M., & McDonald, K. S. (2020). Careers after COVID-19: Challenges and changes. *Human Resource Development International, 23*(4), 427–437.

Irish Government (2021). *Making Remote Work: National Remote Work Strategy*. https://www.gov.ie/en/publication/51f84-making-remote-work-national-remote-work-strategy/

Kane, G. C., Nanda, R., Philips, A., & Copulsky, J. (2021). Redesigning the Post-Pandemic Workplace. *MIT Sloan Management Review*. https://sloanreview.mit.edu/article/redesigning-the-post-pandemic-workplace/

Labrague, L. J., & De los Santos, J. A. A. (2020). COVID-10 Anxiety among Front-Line Nurses: Predictive Role of Organizational Support, Personal Resilience and Social Support. *Journal of Nursing Management, 28* (7), 1653-1661.

Le, K., & Nguyen, M. (2023). The Psychological Consequences of COVID Lockdowns. In J. Michie and M. Sheehan (eds.) *The Political Economy of COVID-19: COVID-19, Inequality and Government Responses*. Routledge.

Lund, S., Ellingrud, K., Hancock, B., & Manyika, J. (2020, April). COVID-19 and Jobs: Monitoring the U.S. Impact on People and Places. *McKinsey Global Institute*. https://www.mckinsey.com/industries/public-sector/our-insights/COVID-19-and-jobs-monitoring-the-us-impact-on-people-and-places

Mendis, M. S. (2016). Workplace design and job performance: A study of operational level employees in the apparel industry of Sri Lanka. *International Journal of Scientific and Research Publications*, *6*(12), 148–153.

Morgan, J. (2018). *3 things to know about employee experience*. https://www.shrm.org/hr-today/news/hr-magazine/0317/pages/3-things-to-know-about-eMployee-experience-.aspx

Nikoloski, D., Trajkova Najdovska, N., Petrevska Nechkoska, R., & Pechijareski, L. (2023). The Gig Economy in the Post-COVID Era. In R.P. Nechkoska, G. Manceski & G. Poels (eds.), *Facilitation in Complexity: From Creation to Co-creation, from Dreaming to Co-dreaming, from Evolution to Co-evolution* (pp. 93–117). Springer International Publishing.

Reeves, M., O'Dea, A., & Carlsson-Szlezak, P. (2022, March 25). Make Resilience Your Company's Strategic Advantage. *Harvard Business Review*. https://hbr.org/2022/03/make-resilience-your-companys-strategic-advantage#:~:text=Resilience%20provides%20value%20not%20only,favorable%20talent%20and%20acquisition%20markets

Riggio, R. E., & Newstead, T. (2023). Crisis Leadership. *Annual Review of Organizational Psychology and Organizational Behavior* (January 2023). https://www.annualreviews.org/doi/pdf/10.1146/annurev-orgpsych-120920-044838

Shirmohammadi, M., Chan Au, W., & Beigi, M. (2022). Antecedents and outcomes of work-life balance while working from home: A review of the research conducted during the COVID-19 pandemic. *Human Resource Development Review*, *21*(4), 473–516.

Seibert, S. E., Kraimer, M. L., & Heslin, P. A. (2016). Developing Career Resilience and Adaptability. *Organizational Dynamics*, *45*, 245–257.

Wiedemann, C. (n.d.). *The Great Transformation? The Cultural Implications of COVID-19*. https://www.valuescentre.com/COVID/

Welsh Government (2022). *Smarter Working: A Remote Working Strategy for Wales: How we will encourage remote working across Wales*. https://www.gov.wales/smarter-working-remote-working-strategy-wales-html

List of Figures

https://doi.org/10.1515/9783110799101-010

List of Tables

https://doi.org/10.1515/9783110799101-011

Index

https://doi.org/10.1515/9783110799101-012

www.ingramcontent.com/pod-product-compliance
Lightning Source LLC
Chambersburg PA
CBHW061817210326
41599CB00034B/7028